Pirates

PETER LEHR

PIRATES

A NEW HISTORY, FROM VIKINGS TO SOMALI RAIDERS

YALE UNIVERSITY PRESS
NEW HAVEN AND LONDON

For information about this and other Yale University Press publications, please contact:
U.S. Office: sales.press@yale.edu   yalebooks.com
Europe Office: sales@yaleup.co.uk   yalebooks.co.uk

Set in Fournier MT Regular by IDSUK (DataConnection) Ltd
Printed in Great Britain by Gomer Press Ltd, Llandysul, Ceredigion, Wales

Library of Congress Control Number: 2019934850

ISBN 978-0-300-18074-9

A catalogue record for this book is available from the British Library.

10 9 8 7 6 5 4 3 2 1

Contents

The 'Uniquely Violent Nature' of Nigerian Piracy ⁓ Modern Pirates' Modus Operandi ⁓ Modern Variants of the Merry Life ⁓ Piracy and the Law ⁓ Citadels and Robot Ships ⁓ Hunting Pirates at Sea ⁓ Counter-Measures on Pirate Shores

Maps and Illustrations

MAPS

ILLUSTRATIONS IN THE TEXT

PLATE SECTION

1. A Viking raid on an English Channel coast under Olaf Tryggvason, 900s AD. Hand-coloured woodcut of a nineteenth-century illustration. North Wind Picture Archives / Alamy Stock Photo.

2. A Viking raid on the Kent coast. Illustration from Henry D. M. Spence, *The Church of England: A History for the People*, London: Cassell and Company, *c.* 1897. Classic Vision / agefotostock.

3. Anlaff entering the Humber in spring 937. Illustration from *Cassell's History of England: From the Roman Invasion to the Wars of the Roses*, vol. 1, London: Cassell and Company, *c.* 1903. Classic Image / Alamy Stock Photo.

4. Eudes re-enters Paris. Illustration by French painter Alphonse de Neuville (1835–85). The Picture Art Collection / Alamy Stock Photo.

5. The head of the pirate Eustace the Monk on a spike. Illustration by Frederick Gilbert (1827–1902) from *Cassell's History of England: From the Roman Invasion to the Wars of the Roses*, vol. 1, London: Cassell and Company, *c.* 1903. Historical Images Archive / Alamy Stock Photo.

6. Captain Henry Morgan attacking Panama, 1671. Illustration from Alexandre Exquemelin, *The Buccaneers of America*, 1684.

7. A Dutch merchantman attacked by an English privateer off La Rochelle. Oil painting by Cornelis Claesz van Wieringen (1577–1633).

8. A sea fight with Barbary corsairs. Oil painting by Lorenzo a Castro (active *c.* 1664–*c.* 1700).

9. The bombardment of Algiers, 3 July 1830. Painting by Léon Morel-Fatio (1810–71), *c.* 1836–7.

10. A junk attacked by Malay *prahus*. Illustration from Sherard Osborn, *My Journal in Malayan Waters*, London: Routledge, Warne and Routledge, second edition, 1860.

11. British sailors boarding an Algerian corsair. Hand-coloured print by John Fairburn, *c.* 1825. Lebrecht Music & Arts / Alamy Stock Photo.

12. Chinese pirates attacking a European merchant ship. Hand-coloured woodcut of a nineteenth-century illustration. North Wind Picture Archives / Alamy Stock Photo.

13. A sea battle between pirate junks and the Imperial Chinese Navy during the nineteenth century. Illustration from Walter Hutchinson, *History of the Nations*, 1915. Classic Image / Alamy Stock Photo.

14. An execution at Kowloon in 1891: five pirates waiting to be beheaded. Photographer unknown, 1891. Wellcome Collection. CC BY.

15. A pirate boat captured by the Royal Netherlands Navy off the Horn of Africa on display at the Marinemuseum Den Helder in October 2011. Nick-D / CC-BY-SA-3.0.

16. Ransom money is dropped in the vicinity of the *MV Faina* off the coast of Somalia near Hobyo while under observation by a US Navy ship, 4 February 2009. Mass Communications Specialist 1st Class Michael R. McCormick, USN.

17. Container ship MV *Maersk Alabama* leaves Mombasa, Kenya, after spending time in port after a pirate attack that took her captain hostage, 21 April 2009. Laura A. Moore, US Navy.

18. A team from the amphibious assault ship *USS Boxer* (LHD 4) tows the lifeboat from the *Maersk Alabama* to *Boxer* to be processed for evidence after the successful rescue of Captain Richard Phillips, 13 April 2009. Jon Rasmussen, US Navy.

19. *Maersk Alabama* captain Richard Phillips stands alongside Lt Cmdr David Fowler, executive officer of *USS Bainbridge* (DDG 96), after being rescued by US Naval Forces off the coast of Somalia, 12 April 2009. US Navy photo.

20. Suspected pirates keep their hands in the air as directed by the guided-missile cruiser *USS Vella Gulf* (CG-72) as the visit, board, search and seizure (VBSS) team prepares to apprehend them, 11 February 2009.Mass Communications Specialist 2nd Class Jason R. Zalasky, USN.

INTRODUCTION

The Sudden Return of Piracy

A gloomy November day. A vessel cut through the waves of the South China Sea on its way from Shanghai to Port Klang, Malaysia. The crew of twenty-three sailors went about their business, inattentive to the dozens of smaller fishing vessels in the vicinity. Suddenly, out of nowhere, several heavily armed individuals clambered on board, brandishing long knives and guns. They quickly overpowered the startled crew members before locking them in the hold. Some time later, the captives were frog-marched back on deck. They were lined up along the railing, blindfolded, and then clubbed, stabbed or shot. But their final fate was the same: all twenty-three were thrown, some still alive, into the sea to erase all traces of the horrible crime. It has been said that seldom 'in the so-called Golden Age of Piracy in the seventeenth and eighteenth centuries was there ever a more bestial, cold-blooded act of murder on the high seas than that committed by those who took over this ship'.[1] But this attack did not occur in the distant past – it happened on 16 November 1998, and the target was the bulk carrier MV (motor vessel) *Cheung Son*.

The *Cheung Son* massacre and other similar events during the 1990s had one thing in common: despite their barbarity, they went largely unnoticed. If piracy came to the public's attention at all it was usually by way of fictionalised stories – a novel such as Robert Louis Stevenson's *Treasure Island* (1883), or a Hollywood film such as the *Black Pirate* (1926) with Douglas Fairbanks, *Captain Blood* (1935) with Errol Flynn, or, more recently, the amazingly successful *Pirates of the Caribbean* series (2003–) with Johnny Depp. The pirates featured in these books and films were nothing but romantic stereotypes of dashing individuals, far removed from reality.[2] Outside of a comparatively small circle of academic specialists – as well as, of course, seafarers and maritime law enforcement agencies themselves – the menace of piracy seemed to have faded away, such that the term itself came to be associated more with various forms of intellectual property theft than with the maritime crime from which it originated. It was only in November 2005 that this situation changed, when a new breed of high-seas pirates – the Somali pirates –

brought themselves to international prominence with a brazen attack on a modern cruise liner.

The *Seabourn Spirit*[3] was not one of those run-down vessels which tend to ply the waters around the Horn of Africa. It was a top-of-the-line luxury cruise ship, its crew of 164 catering to up to 208 well-off customers, and it had just been voted the best small ship in the annual Conde Nast Traveler Readers' Poll. In November 2005, it was on a cruise from Alexandria in Egypt to Singapore. Its 200 passengers had already enjoyed the voyage through the Red Sea and into the Gulf of Aden via the Bab el-Mandeb. They were now looking forward to exploring Mombasa, their next port of call.

In the early hours of Saturday, 5 November, at 5:30 a.m. local time and about 100 nautical miles off Somalia's Banaadir coast, most of those on board were still sound asleep. On the bridge, it was business as usual: monitoring the position of other ships on the radar screen, and keeping an eye on the small fishing vessels that would crisscross the ship's bow with utter disregard for right-of-way. Suddenly, two small boats sped towards the cruise liner. The crew on the bridge were at first bemused, then alarmed: those aboard the boats were brandishing assault rifles and rocket-propelled grenade launchers (RPGs). It must have taken the bridge crew a couple of heart beats to realise that they were under attack by pirates; although there had been some incidents in the previous months, they had taken place much nearer to the shore, and only targeted smaller local vessels – not a state-of-the-art western cruise ship. That pirates would attack such a vessel was completely unheard of.

Surprised or not, Captain Sven Erik Pedersen wasted no time in sounding the alarm and increasing the speed of the *Seabourn Spirit*. His plan was to outrun and outmanoeuvre the two tiny 7-metre fibreglass boats, and maybe even to ram and capsize one of them. The ship's security team, alerted by the alarm, immediately jumped into action: Michael Groves, a former police officer, engaged the approaching and wildly firing pirates with a high-pressure hose in the hope of swamping their vessels, while the master-at-arms, the former Gurkha soldier Som Bahadur, manned the ship's 'sonic gun', emitting an ear-piercing high-frequency sound that discouraged the attackers from coming too near. The combination of evasive manoeuvres, high-pressure hose and sonic gun turned out to be enough to shake off the pirates, who vanished into the early morning mist. Except for Som Bahadur, who suffered minor shrapnel injuries, no one else was hurt, even though one of the RPGs actually penetrated the ship's hull, damaging a stateroom; another round had harmlessly bounced off the stern.

All in all, what might have turned into a prolonged hostage crisis ended in a lucky escape for the vessel itself, its crew and its passengers. Mainly for security reasons, the ship proceeded to Port Victoria straight away instead of calling at Mombasa as originally planned. From there, it sailed on to Singapore, arriving right on schedule, where the passengers disembarked with quite a story to tell.[4]

In the following years, the international community would grow used to such brazen acts of Somali piracy. In November 2005, however, this incident was so out of the ordinary that many observers, including Anthony Downer, then Australian foreign minister, hesitated to call it piracy – for them, it was more likely that the attack was intended as an act of maritime terrorism, perhaps carried out by al-Qaeda. How on earth could two teams of four pirates ever hope to hijack a modern 134-metre ship with several hundred people on board? Eight men would never have been able to keep all of them under control, they argued. Only gradually did the reality sink in that, yes, this had been a pirate attack, and that, no, hard-nosed Somali pirates armed with assault rifles and RPGs would not hesitate to try to kidnap dozens, or even hundreds, of easily intimidated and mostly unarmed passengers and crew members. From then on, the fictitious pirates of the Caribbean really had to do battle with the real-life pirates of Somalia in order to capture the headlines and the 'good ship Popular Imagination'.[5] Some of the Somali pirates' audacious operations even made it onto the big screen: the botched hijacking of the US-flagged container ship MV *Maersk Alabama* was turned into the 2013 blockbuster movie *Captain Phillips*, starring Tom Hanks.

In April 2009, the *Maersk Alabama* was carrying food aid destined for famine-blighted Somalia. Due to the dire security situation in most of Somalia's own ports, it was heading for the Kenyan port of Mombasa – which still meant the ship had to sail straight through the pirate-haunted waters around the Somali coastline. And, indeed, on 8 April, about 240 nautical miles off the coast of the semi-autonomous Somalian province of Puntland, a skiff with four armed men approached the slow-sailing vessel. Like the crew of the *Seabourn Spirit*, those on the *Maersk Alabama*'s bridge took evasive measures in an attempt to outmanoeuvre the pirates and to prevent them from boarding. Although they managed to flood the pirates' skiff, the Somalis made it aboard ship. The crew fell back on a second line of defence in the shape of a 'citadel' (something like the panic rooms found in some upmarket apartments) to which they could withdraw and from which help could be summoned and the ship controlled. Once more, however, the *Maersk Alabama*'s men were not in luck: although most of the all-American crew managed to reach this citadel in time, the vessel's master, Captain Richard Phillips, and Assistant Technical Manager Zahid Reza were surprised by the pirates and taken hostage. Amazingly, Captain Phillips's crew also managed to take a hostage: no less than the leader of the pirate gang himself, whom Zahid Reza had been forced to show around the ship, and who was overwhelmed by Chief Engineer Perry outside the engine room. A dramatic stand-off then unfolded: on the one side the remaining three pirates with their hostage Captain Phillips, on the other the nineteen American crew members with the pirates' leader as their captive. After some frantic negotiation, it was decided that both hostages would be exchanged, and that the pirates would be allowed to leave the ship on one of the *Maersk Alabama*'s bright orange life boats – their own skiff having by now sunk. But the pirates did not honour the agreement, and set sail with Captain Phillips still in their clutches.

Alerted by the remaining crew, several US warships quickly arrived on the scene, to find themselves facing a peculiar hostage situation: four well-armed Somali pirates holding one hostage on board an 8.5-metre lifeboat in choppy waters. The crisis soon came to a head. With one of the pirates aboard the USS *Bainbridge* for negotiations, Navy SEAL snipers lying in wait were suddenly presented with three clear targets: one of the pirates was clearly visible – though unnervingly he was also aiming an assault rifle at Captain Phillips's head – while the other two had leant out of the lifeboat's windows to catch some fresh air. A couple of expertly aimed shots later and the three pirates were dead, and Captain Phillips was free. The sole surviving pirate was later sentenced to thirty-three years and nine months in a US high-security prison.

Today, Somalis are not the only ones risking their lives as pirates in the hope of getting rich. Currently, there are also plenty of Nigerians who are willing and able to do likewise in the Gulf of Guinea, while incidents of piracy in the Straits of Malacca and the South China Sea are on the rise again as well.

Piracy is on the up – not only in news headlines and huge entertainment franchises but also in a flurry of documentaries, articles and books published on the subject, and a series of academic conferences held all over the world. Together these have tackled the question of why the number of pirate attacks started to dramatically rise from the 1980s: the onset of globalisation and the liberalisation of trade in the late 1970s resulted in a significant increase in maritime traffic, while the collapse of the Soviet Union and the end of the Cold War a decade or so later resulted in a disappearance of warships from many areas which they had previously patrolled. From a pirate's point of view, this meant that there were now both more targets to prey on and a much reduced risk of being captured. Furthermore, various in-depth studies have been published looking at 'what makes pirates tick', which examine individual decisions to become a pirate in current times. But as interesting and insightful as such studies are, they provide an uneven picture, since they invariably focus on specific regions, without providing comparisons between various regions affected by piracy today and across the centuries. They thus leave some significant questions unaddressed. Is what motivates certain individuals to become pirates today the same as in the past? How do the activities of modern pirates compare to those of earlier epochs? Are there any lessons that could be learned from historical attempts to curb piracy which could help us end it today? And, most importantly, if naval power is greater today than ever before, why have we not yet been able to put an end to piracy once and for all? Why does piracy persist, seemingly against all the odds? This book answers these questions, focusing on the pirate's journey across the ages: *becoming a pirate, being a pirate*, and, finally, *walking away from piracy*.[6]

Piracy has a long history, and has occurred in various maritime regions all over the world: we cannot talk about a 'typical pirate's career'. In order then to tease out continuities and discontinuities of piracy across various cultures and various periods, the pirate's journey will be subdivided geographically: the Mediterranean, Northern and Eastern Seas all witnessed major outbreaks of piracy at one time or another, and these will be the main regions looked at in this book. The book is also subdivided into three historical periods. Section I focuses on the years between AD 700 and 1500, when the three maritime regions were still largely unconnected and formed distinct theatres of pirate activities, with no cross-pollination taking place. Section II focuses on the years between 1500 and 1914, a period in which European sea powers gradually gained the upper hand over the formerly powerful 'gunpowder empires' (the Ottoman Empire, Mughal India, and, somewhat later, Qing China) by gradually monopolising 'four sources of social power: ideological, economic, military, and political (IEMP) relationships'.[7] Europe also gained increasing influence over land mass, from controlling 7 per cent in 1500 to 35 per cent by 1800 and, 'By 1914, when this age came to a sudden end, they . . . controlled 84 per cent of the world's land'.[8] We will see that even though local manifestations of piracy remained, the continuing meddling of European powers in regional affairs aggravated the problem of piracy both by importing Western types of vessels and weapons, and by adding Western pirates and adventurers to an already volatile mix. Finally, Section III focuses on the years from 1914 to the present in order to explore how piracy has evolved, or devolved, in the current period of globalisation.

A Short Note on Definitions

Two main concepts that we will frequently encounter in this book need mention here: *pirates* and *privateers* (known as *corsairs* in the Mediterranean). As we shall see, both of these maritime predators use the same tactics, and carry out very similar operations – the difference is that pirates act on their own accord, while privateers or corsairs (the term comes from the Latin *cursarius*, 'raider') act under lawful authority, equipped with a commission. This crucial difference is nicely reflected in the Oxford English Dictionary's definition of piracy: the 'action of committing robbery, kidnap, or violence at sea or from the sea *without* lawful authority'.[9] By extension, privateering can be defined as the action of committing robbery, kidnap or violence at sea or from the sea *with* lawful authority. Many of the protagonists we will meet occupy a rather grey area, operating somewhere between illegal piracy and legal privateering – which is why it is sensible to include privateers in the following discussion.

PART I

Distinct Regions, AD 700 to 1500

Viking
Invasions in
Western Europe

Viking homeland
Viking raids

Iceland

Atlantic Ocean

Faeroes

Shetland

Orkney

Norwegians

Scandinavia

Lindisfarne

Danes

Ireland

Dublin

Britain

Bremen

London

EAST
FRANKISH
EMPIRE
(Germany)

Paris

Rhine

WEST
FRANKISH
EMPIRE
(France)

Danube

Iberia

Italy

Rome

Lisbon

Balearics

Seville

Mediterranean Sea

0   500 miles

0   500 km

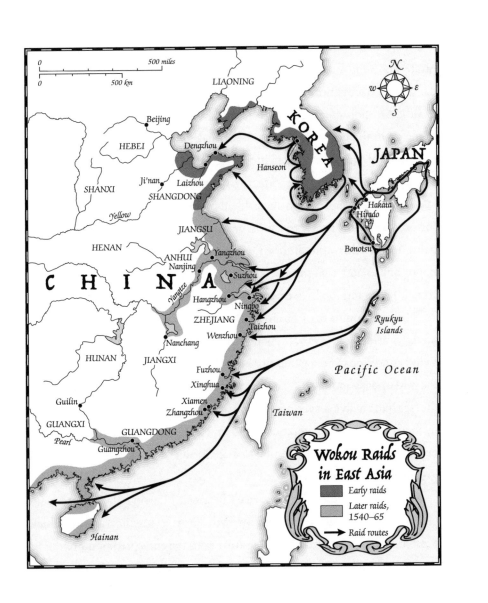

Joining the Wicked Order

Why do people choose to become pirates or privateers, deciding to make a career out of plundering at sea? Most romantic Hollywood franchises and novels about pirates routinely gloss over the ugly truth that being a pirate was, and in many maritime regions of the world still is, a very dangerous occupation, one that may be rather hazardous to the pirate's health. An individual who chose this career in times past was probably doing so in the hopes of getting rich quick. But far more likely were the prospects of drowning, starving to death or dying of scurvy, malaria, plague or any number of exotic, then unnamed diseases; being left mutilated for life either through an accident or a fight; being killed in action or tortured to death in a variety of unpleasant and rather messy ways; or being executed by the authorities, or simply left to rot in jail. So it is important to note that piracy as a career choice is not necessarily born of romanticism and the love of adventure.

The decision to turn pirate was usually driven by one of two forces: on the one hand, grievances such as abject poverty, unemployment, harsh living conditions and a generally bleak future; and, on the other, greed or the lure of easy money. Fleeing from justice was another powerful driver: the 'sea had always served as a refuge for the lawless and criminal elements in society'.[1] The exact mixture of these elements depended not so much on the region but on subregional or even local circumstances which could greatly fluctuate over time.

In the late Middle Ages, the years between 1250 and 1500, there were places that enjoyed economic growth in the Mediterranean which presented many perfectly legal opportunities for enterprising individuals, especially highly skilled artisans. But there were also pockets of stagnation with rising levels of unemployment accelerated by population growth, and spots where endemic poverty was made worse by the incessant raids and counter-raids of various sea powers and their regular navies, who were in turn backed up by privateers – or corsairs – operating with a licence, and pirates operating without one. On the Mediterranean's Christian shores, established sea powers such as Venice, Genoa and Pisa profited from the booming maritime trade with Byzantium, with the main ports of the Muslim empires such as Alexandria, and with the ports along the coasts of the Black Sea such as Kaffa. High-value commodities like silk, spices, porcelain, precious stones, gold, silver, furs and slaves made the merchants of Venice, Genoa and Pisa rich, along with those of Byzantium and Alexandria. If the citizens of these booming port cities went a-pirating, then they did so mainly driven by greed, and as corsairs, licensed pirates. Unsurprisingly, it was largely the occupants of the lower rungs of the social ladder who signed up: they had the least to lose and the most to gain by entering such a high-risk profession. In the case of the ports of Béjaïa (Algeria) and Trapani (Sicily), for example, 'people of modest origin' such as workers, retailers or artisans, fishermen and sailors participated in piratical activities on a part-time basis.[2] As for the islands dotting the sea lanes, many poor fishermen and peasants eking out a living must have watched the heavily laden merchant vessels passing by with covetous eyes. These locations were usually cut off from economic progress, and more often than not regularly ravaged by corsairs hunting for slaves while also carrying away anything that could be turned into profit. Not surprisingly, grievance and greed worked together to turn some of these locations into piracy hot spots – some of which survived into the nineteenth century.

In Northern European waters, harsh living conditions were also at the heart of the rise of loosely organised fleets of pirates and privateers known first as the 'Victual Brothers', later as 'Likedeelers', who operated in the Baltic and North Seas in the last decade of the fourteenth century and the first years of the fifteenth. In this region, incessant maritime wars laid waste to many coastal areas, while an oppressive feudal order on land held peasants under rigid, intrusive control; great numbers of peasants and landless workers moved to the cities during the thirteenth and fourteenth centuries in the hope of a better life there, only to find that their misery deepened in the relative anonymity of city life. This was especially the case in the State of the Teutonic Order, a territory comprising parts of modern-day Estonia, Latvia, Lithuania, Poland, Russia and Sweden, formed by a Catholic military order which was embroiled in crusades against non-Christian tribal kingdoms and principalities until the early fifteenth century.

Acts of piracy were already rather frequent in Baltic waters, and for exactly the same reasons as they occurred elsewhere: there was dense maritime traffic that made for rich pickings, while the ever-shifting political alliances of the coastal states all but guaranteed an absence of effective maritime policing. In 1158, for example, the populations of the Danish coastal regions of Jutland and Zealand had fled inland due to consistent raids, leaving behind uncultivated and unprotected land: 'everywhere else desolation reigned. No reliance could be placed on weapons or on strongholds.'³ Duke John of Mecklenburg's decision to offer privateering commissions to all and sundry in his war against Queen Margaret of Denmark in the last decade of the fourteenth century further opened the floodgates, turning the unorganised pirates into large, organised fleets. The predominantly maritime war of Mecklenburg against Denmark required many new ships to be built – ships that needed to be crewed. And since the war also came with the prospect of large-scale plunder and pillage, a hodgepodge crowd of adventurous or desperate individuals of mostly Northern German origin descended on Mecklenburg's ports, eager to enlist. The *Detmar Chronicle* describes them as follows:

In this year [1392] an unruly mob of courtiers, burghers of many towns, office holders and peasants came together, calling themselves the Victual Brothers. They said that they would march on the Queen of Denmark to free the King of Sweden whom she held prisoner, and that they would capture and plunder nobody but support those [of Mecklenburg] with goods and help against the Queen.

Breaking this promise, the Victual Brothers went on to threaten 'the whole sea and all merchants, whether friend or foe'.[4]

So, like other large-scale organised piracy groups, the Victual Brothers and their successors, the Likedeelers, did not burst onto the scene out of the blue. Whether it was greed or grievance that prompted their bands of men to become sea robbers can only be a matter for speculation, given that none of the mostly illiterate cohort left behind a memoir, but it is likely that both factors played a part in spurring on many of those who joined from the great Hanseatic cities. They would have found the Duke of Mecklenburg's call for privateers irresistible – a chance to escape abject poverty and to get rich, or at least to die trying.[5] For existing sailors to join the Victual Brothers made even more sense: although the terms of Mecklenburg's privateer contracts may have included a 'no plunder, no pay' clause, the chance of enriching themselves by pillaging must nonetheless have been compelling. If the sailors' master decided to join the pirate brotherhood then the crew did not even need to embark on another vessel. The difference between merchantmen on the one hand and privateers or pirates on the other was simply that the vessels belonging to the latter group were better manned and better armed.

Given all this, the names under which these alliances of sea robbers were known are particularly revealing. 'Victual Brothers' is often said to refer to one of the group's missions while they were employed as privateers: in 1390, the Brothers were tasked with supplying – or 'victualising' – the starving population of Stockholm, a city cut off from supplies by the Danish enemy.[6] A more plausible explanation is that the name Victual Brothers simply refers to their practice of self-provisioning.[7] The reference to 'brothers' or 'brotherhood' suggests mutuality if not equality; this element becomes much more prominent in the (Middle Low German) name 'Likedeelers', which appeared in contemporary German sources around 1398 and means 'equal sharers'. At a time when society was strictly hierarchical and all were supposed to know their place, the quasi-socialist concept of sharing equally despite one's origin was itself a challenge to the political elite – the aristocracy, the church and the powerful Hanseatic merchants.

Interestingly, it was not only the downtrodden who decided to go pirating or privateering in the Middle Ages. The career of a pirate or privateer could tempt even the nobility – and often for very similar reasons: escaping a life of poverty and misery, brought upon them by an unkind fate. Of course, their poverty was a relative one, and many a nobleman arguably did take to the sea more from of a sense of adventure than anything else. Yet there were still many individuals of noble birth who became pirates or privateers under duress. For instance, in fourteenth-century Italy, frequent violent clashes between various city-states, and even between factions within them, resulted in numerous leading families having to flee their home towns. They 'sought to maintain their status (or, more likely, to survive) by turning to piracy and brigandage. Around 1325 scores of Ghibelline[8] galleys from Genoa attacked convoys, raided, and robbed'.[9] In 1464, even the duke and archbishop of Genoa, Paolo Fregoso, became a pirate – and a notorious one at that – after being expelled from the city by his political enemies.[10] Nor were Italian exiles the only members of the nobility to fall on hard times in this period – Catalan knights also suffered after an unexpected outbreak of peace in 1302 resulted in wide-spread unemployment. Many of them rallied to the flag of a certain Roger de Flor, a former sergeant of the Knights Templar who, after being expelled from the order due to alleged misconduct, turned pirate – a profession he possessed vast experience of, having been exposed to sea raiding since the age of eight when acting as a page aboard a Knights Templar galley. Under the name of the Catalan Grand Company, these professional mercenaries were mainly active in the Eastern Mediterranean during most of the fourteenth century either as privateers or as pirates, depending on whether they were fighting for an overlord or for themselves.[11]

The situation was only slightly different for the Victual Brothers and the Baltic Sea at the end of the same century. Many of the lower ranks of the nobility in this region languished in a state of *infausta paupertas* or 'unhappy poverty' despite their noble trappings and pretensions.[12] The majority of them depended on income from their land holdings, making them eminently vulnerable to the frequent agrarian crises when prices for produce fell to rock bottom. As typical products of their unsettled, war-prone times, these noblemen possessed at least one marketable skill: a well-tested fighting ability, honed in the frequent wars, large and small, in which they fought. On top of that, and as a result of their dire straits, they usually considered robbing and plundering as 'lesser' or 'venial sins' without much stigma attached. A contemporary saying confirms this: 'ruten, roven, det en is gheyen schande, dat doint die besten von dem lande' ('to roam and to rob brings no disgrace, the best of the land do that').[13] It was thus a rational choice to extend this practice of robbing on land to the sea as well.

Of course, and again unlike the 'ordinary' folk, the majority of those noblemen who decided to join did so as leaders. Drawing on their feeble means, they bought a vessel, equipped it and manned it with their own battle-hardened followers in the not unfounded hope that they could recoup their investment via a successful raid or two. A few other noblemen of the poorer kind were so skilled in the arts of fighting and leading men that they were able to join the leadership ranks of the pirates without having to buy their own vessel first. Such was the case with two monks from a mendicant order who rose to the leadership of the Victual Brothers.[14]

What prompted these two monks to join the freebooters is unknown. But, surprisingly, they were not the first monastics to become pirates.[15] Eustace the Monk, also known as the Black Monk, was born Eustace Bousquet in Boulonnais in France in around 1170, into a noble family: his father Bauduin was one of the senior barons of this coastal area, and Eustace seems to have been well trained both in knighthood and in seamanship; his later exploits as privateer and pirate indicate that he probably cut his teeth in the Mediterranean as a corsair.[16] Why he decided to join a Benedictine monastery as a monk is unclear. Somewhat clearer are the reasons why he left the monkhood: rumours of certain alleged misdeeds aside, he intended to avenge the death of his father who was killed by another nobleman. After a short stint as an outlaw in the vicinity of Boulonnais, he put his skills as a former corsair to good use, probably in 1204, by joining the privateers of King John of England who was embroiled in a protracted war against the French king Philip II. For nearly ten years, Eustace attacked French shipping as well as the French Channel coasts, turning the island of Sark into a semi-independent pirate base, to the chagrin of the nearby English ports of Hastings, New Romney, Hythe, Dover and Sandwich (also known as the Cinque Ports), which also suffered from his depredations. When in 1212–13 the English court turned against him, he swiftly transferred his allegiance back to France, now raiding English shipping and English coasts instead. He finally met his fate on 24 August 1217 during the battle of Sandwich, when English sailors managed to board his vessel after having blinded the French defenders by throwing powdered lime in their eyes: 'They jumped on to Eustace's ship and treated his men very cruelly. All the barons were captured and Eustace the Monk was killed. His head was cut off and at once the battle ended.'[17]

It was not only the occasional Christian monk who broke his solemn vows to go a-pirating: on the other side of the globe, we also find the odd Buddhist monk who did so. Xu Hai (or Hsü Hai) for instance led an uneventful life as a learned and well-respected monk in the famous Tiger Haunt Monastery outside the city of Hangzhou for many years.[18] But in 1556, for reasons unknown, he suddenly decided to leave and join the Wako pirates, who were active between the 1440s and the 1560s in the East and South China Seas.[19] His familiarity with rites, chants and divination served him well, winning him 'the loyalty of his crew, who called him "general commissioned by heaven to pacify the oceans"'.[20] But like the Christian monks of the North and Baltic Seas who turned to piracy, he was the exception rather than the rule: the Wako drew their recruits mainly from Japanese, Chinese and Malay societies who were driven either by greed or grievance or both. The bulk of them were probably seasoned former Chinese sailors previously manning the ships of the regular navy. What helped trigger the surge in recruits was the passing of severe restrictions or outright 'sea bans' (*haijin*) on maritime trade and the disbanding of the powerful Ming high-seas fleets that had roamed the Indian Ocean under the command of Admiral Zheng He between 1405 and 1433.

This sudden change in Chinese maritime policy resulted in thousands of unemployed and destitute sailors desperately trying to find a new life. Many merchants opted to continue their now largely illegal business operations by taking part in piracy – either actively by organising raids or passively by fencing the plunder. The most powerful of these merchant-pirates, Wang Zhi, had been a rich and well-respected salt merchant before he turned pirate. He set up base in Kyushu, under the protection of Japanese feudal lords, from where he controlled his rapidly growing pirate empire without actively involving himself in any raids. In his case, the transformation from respected merchant to feared merchant-pirate was an involuntary one: the Ming sea bans had destroyed his business, which was based on maritime trade.[21] For him there was no choice.

God Wills It

It was much easier to be a pirate if there was no social stigma attached to it. In some maritime cultures, such as that of the Vikings who raided the coasts of the British Isles, Ireland and mainland Europe in the early Middle Ages from the eighth century onwards, or, on the other side of the world at about the same time, that of the Orang Laut ('Sea People') who descended on the coasts of the Straits of Malacca, marauders were seen as noble warriors deserving of admiration and respect.[22] In such cultures, taking part in a pirate raid was one of the accepted ways to gain a reputation for oneself, as well as to acquire some wealth.

For those who belonged to a warrior society and intended to establish themselves as feudal lords in their own right, three elements were of the utmost importance: gaining a reputation as a fierce fighter, acquiring manpower by obtaining slaves, and accumulating wealth. This was particularly important to the Vikings:

> Wealth in the Viking world was not the passive accumulation of gold and silver, hidden away in the ground or in the bottom of a chest, but rather richness in position, alliances, and connections. The Scandinavian societies of the Viking period were open systems in which every member or individual family had continually to defend his or their position against others, theoretically of equal rank.[23]

To keep or to improve one's position in this society, ready access to disposable wealth was required for dispensing lavish gifts befitting one's status, and there is no doubt as to what kind of wealth was preferable: gold and silver.[24] The continuous pressure to offer gifts at least equal to what was received resulted in a penchant for plunder with a 'no holds barred' approach. Unsurprisingly, in the absence of legitimate raiding possibilities during one of the rather infrequent and short times of peace, piracy – the less legitimate, although most certainly not frowned upon, form of maritime raiding – offered a socially acceptable alternative. Hence, 'quick profits in movable wealth and slaves must have tempted many to brigandage'.[25] This practice survived the Christianisation of the Vikings between the tenth and the twelfth centuries.

Against the backdrop of widespread late medieval piety on both sides of the Mediterranean, religion greatly facilitates 'us versus them' thinking, offering a convincing narrative of why 'they' can, nay, must be attacked and destroyed. Mediterranean privateers, be they the Saracen pirates of the eighth to thirteenth centuries, the Barbary corsairs, or those of 'the Religion', the Knights Hospitaller of St John, used this rather crude dichotomy to justify their activities, though the underlying motives were more of an economic and political nature. Long before Pope Urban II used this motto at the Council of Clermont in 1095 to declare the first crusade, *Deus vult* or 'God wills it' proved to be a powerful justification for otherwise rather dubious acts of maritime raiding – which is why we can find many Christian knights participating in such ventures. The 'other', Muslim, side that, in the absence of regular naval forces, depended far more on piratical raids to whittle down the established Christian naval powers, saw it in exactly the same light: Muslim pirates and corsairs envisioned themselves as *ghazis*, knights fighting for Islam. Needless to say, this religiously motivated component in the maritime struggle for political and economic gain could also be found in the Indian Ocean as well as in the South China Sea and the Far East, wherever Muslim and Christian political and economic interests clashed.

Real religious fervour and zeal as expressed by *Deus vult* was a very powerful motivator in these ventures; the Knights Hospitaller, for example, 'neglected to live, but were prepared to die, in the service of Christ', as the great English historian Edward Gibbon eloquently puts it.[26] Pisa and Genoa actively raided Muslim ports along the North African coasts and 'used their profits to glorify God, for they donated part of them to the great cathedral of Santa Maria that the Pisans were beginning to construct'.[27] Such actions strongly point to the fact that religion was used to legitimise piracy: 'These forays generated a sense that they were engaged in a holy struggle against the Muslims. God would reward their efforts with victory, with booty and with what were as yet ill-defined spiritual benefits.'[28] However, framing the above-mentioned conflicts only in religious terms would be far too simplistic: powerful economic and political motives tended to cut across this vaunted religious abyss with consummate ease if required. It is telling that the very pious early fifteenth-century Castilian corsair Don Pero Niño, who had become a privateer on the orders of his king, Henry III of Castile, politely visited the ports of Gibraltar and Malaga, then part of the Muslim Emirate of Córdoba, after having been invited by the local authorities to do so – his biographer notes that 'they brought him cows, sheep, fowls, abundance of baked bread and great flat plates full of kouss-kouss and other spiced meats; not that the Captain would touch any of the things that the Moors gave him'.[29] Nevertheless, since Castile was not at war with Córdoba at that time, the Muslims were safe from him – unlike their brethren along the coast of North Africa with whom Castile was at war. Even for the zealous Knights Hospitaller of St John, not every Muslim was an enemy – there were certain exceptions according to the famous 'the enemy of my enemy is my friend' principle.

On the Muslim side, similar mechanics were at work. Although corsairing was seen as a maritime extension of the land-bound jihad ('holy war'), and those who participated in it were notionally warriors for Islam or *ghazis*, many Greek, Calabrian, Albanian, Genoese or even Jewish renegades joined their ranks – not necessarily due to new-found religious zeal after a conversion to Islam (most of these renegades did not actually convert), but because of economic motivations: greed and the lure of easy money.[30] A particularly telling case is that of the fearsome fourteenth-century 'pirate-emir' Umur Pasha. His credentials as a warrior for Islam were impeccable: he was known to prefer to 'send the souls of captured Franks to hell' rather than to keep them for ransom, and Pope Clement VI declared a crusade against him personally due to the danger he posed. However, this did not stop Umur Pasha from privateering for the Christian Greek-Orthodox Byzantine emperor Andronikos III and his successor John VI; although the authors of the 2,000-verse-long poem celebrating Umur Pasha's life, the *Destan d'Umur Pasha* (literally 'the epic of Umur Pasha'), hastened to add that 'the emperor and his son submitted like slaves', in an obvious attempt to gloss over his blatant betrayal of the 'true cause', presumably also mainly for economic reasons.[31]

Turning a Blind Eye

For piracy to really flourish, something beyond the individual pirate's political and economic motives or religious zeal was required: the connivance of corrupt officials, certain ports or even the political system itself, all of which were required to create an 'enabling environment'. Unfortunately, the available medieval sources are rather vague on the role of individual office holders in this respect. There is, however, sufficient information about certain ports to allow some light to be shed on this particular part of the enabling environment. Major ports, as opposed to comparatively small and remote pirate lairs, played a crucial role in the context of piracy not only as safe havens but also as important locations for the disposal of the pirates' plunder.[32] Furthermore, in these major ports, crews could be recruited, and important up-to-date information about ship movements and possible anti-piracy measures could be found.

'Holy war' in the Mediterranean, whether fought against Muslims as a crusade or against Christians as jihad, helped to offer a veneer of respectability for ports either actively engaged in maritime raiding or passively profiting from it by offering pirates safe havens where they could replenish supplies and trade. Port cities such as Algiers, Bougie, Tunis or Tripoli would not have survived without direct participation in maritime raiding.

Along the coasts of the Northern Seas in the Middle Ages, pre-Christian religions had all but died out by the thirteenth century, while Islam had not made it that far north. The pretext of 'holy war' as a way of legitimising piracy did not exist here. Instead, what greatly helped the emergence of pirate-friendly ports in this region was political fragmentation and comparatively weak state control over remote coastal areas. For example, in the North Sea and Baltic Sea, the main political entities were the Hanseatic League (a loose mercantile federation of port cities), and a number of territorial states: the kingdoms of Denmark, Norway and Sweden, the Duchy of Mecklenburg, and the monastic state of the Teutonic Order. Several of the Hanseatic cities also functioned as the main ports of some of these territorial states: Wismar and Rostock, for instance, fulfilled this role for the Duchy of Mecklenburg. The result of this fragmentation was endemic power struggles between these political entities, and between various factions of the Hanseatic League. This created a near-perfect enabling environment for the Victual Brothers:

there was always a port or two with a 'no questions asked' policy willing to offer a safe haven. After the Victual Brothers had finally been ousted from their Baltic Sea hunting grounds in early 1398 by a combined effort of the Teutonic Order and the Hanseatic City of Lübeck (see below), they found a smattering of smaller ports willing to do business with them on the Frisian coast of the North Sea: the 'coast of eastern Friesland, with its extensive marshes, was not under the domination of any single feudal landlord, but was divided into different rural parishes, over which local *hovetlinge*, or chieftains, exercised power'.[33] Since these chieftains (for example, Widzel tom Brok, Edo Wiemken and Sibet Lubbenson) constantly feuded with one other, the battle-hardened Victual Brothers offered a convenient source of additional soldiers who fought on a 'no plunder, no pay' basis, while also bringing relative wealth in the shape of booty, which would be traded in the local markets.

In eastern waters, comparable piracy-facilitating circumstances were at work. Here, feudal lords, members of the bureaucracy and the gentry frequently colluded with the Wako pirates active along Chinese coasts. The gentry included scholars who had passed the government-controlled examinations and occupied leading roles in local and regional government. Hence, in 1548, Zhu Wan, the grand coordinator for the coastal defences of the provinces of Zhejiang and Fujian, quipped, 'Doing away with foreign pirates . . . is easy, but doing away with Chinese pirates is difficult. Doing away with Chinese pirates along the coast is still easy, but doing away with Chinese pirates in gowns and caps . . . is particularly difficult.'[34] The mutually beneficial relationship between pirates and the elite can also be seen at work in the case of the Japanese pirates of the late fourteenth and fifteenth centuries who operated as part of the Wako. Various coastal lords on the island of Kyushu regularly used these pirates' services to protect their maritime trade while harassing their competitors' ships:

Sponsorship suited both landed elites and pirates alike. The pirates hoped to gain further control of essential strategic maritime locations and additional license to engage in aggrandising activities such as attacking shipping and extorting fees for safe passage. Landed patrons such as warlords hoped to acquire indirect control of remote maritime regions that might otherwise have escaped their grasp.[35]

Commissioning pirates had its risks, however: while in the short run it was a successful strategy, in the long run it resulted in unintended consequences. In the South China Sea, for example, the rulers of Srivijaya (a sea power based on Sumatra, Java and the Malay Peninsula centred on the Straits of Malacca between the eighth and the thirteenth centuries) employed the Orang Laut as their naval mercenaries for the purpose of forcing merchant vessels passing through the Straits of Malacca to sail to the Srivijayan port of Palembang, where they were heavily taxed. However, whenever the grip of the ruling dynasty was perceived to be slipping, or when it was challenged by some other princeling, the Orang Laut promptly turned to piracy, now simply robbing the very same merchant vessels they were supposed to shepherd into port. In the East China Sea and the Sea of Japan, the pirate clans along the coasts of Kyushu also proved to be rather fickle and difficult-to-control allies for the coastal lords.

Despite the different contexts, none of these groups, be they the Victual Brothers roaming the North Sea and the Baltic, the pirates active in the Channel, the Orang Laut in the South China Sea, or Japanese pirates of the East China Sea and the Sea of Japan, hesitated to work either for themselves as 'unsanctioned' pirates or to switch to service more powerful and richer competitors – whichever seemed to be the more lucrative. From the employers' perspective, whether it was the Duke of Mecklenburg, King John, the rulers of Srivijaya or the Japanese coastal lords, the same rationale applied: outfitting and maintaining regular warships was simply too expensive. The practice of sanctioning pirates was far more cost-effective – at least in the short term. Over time, however, the practice was prone to backfire because 'pirates did not necessarily become submissive to the landed power [but] felt free to ignore the dictates of their oaths and accept alternate patronage offers'.[36]

There Was No Choice

Sometimes, Mother Nature herself creates 'trigger events' that force people into piracy. In Imperial China, natural disasters such as floods, droughts and typhoons were among the main drivers of large-scale piracy; usually followed by man-made disasters in the shape of famines and epidemics, they frequently resulted in food riots, rebellions and banditry in the countryside – and in a rapid rise of the latter's maritime equivalent, piracy, along the coasts.[37] In the case of Japan, floods, famines and widespread epidemics that destroyed livelihoods on land and disrupted internal peace and stability also regularly contributed to the outbreak of large-scale piracy. The famine of 1134 led to a hunger-driven wave of piracy whose main targets were the grain ships bound for the imperial court at Kyoto; immediate action was thus taken against them, and two campaigns spearheaded by one of the leading samurai, Taira Tadamori, in 1134 and again in 1135, brought the pirates to heel.[38]

From the third century onwards, Angles, Saxons and Jutes in northern Europe took to the sea as pirates when the steady rise in sea levels gradually flooded the arable land they had previously ploughed as farmers.[39] It is clear that banditry, and piracy, tended to become endemic in times of pauperisation and was basically 'a form of self-help to escape it in particular circumstances'.[40] Sometimes, there was simply no choice. This is further evident in other societies situated in vulnerable locations. The Nordic society from which the Vikings emerged is a case in point. The Nordic states sat on the fringes of a complicated coastal geography featuring countless fjords, rivers and a chain of steep mountain ranges that rendered transport via land difficult, if not impossible. Together with a rising population and possibly a gradual change in climate, geographical factors all but forced this society out to sea as traders or raiders, or both, between the eighth and the eleventh centuries.[41] As warrior cultures that held acts of individual bravery on the battlefield in the highest esteem, Nordic states frequently waged wars against each other: Danes against Swedes, Swedes against Norwegians, Norwegians against Danes. Many of these wars included sea battles and frequent maritime raids that laid waste to coastal settlements. Archaeological excavations on the Swedish island of Gotland, for example, have found many carefully buried hoards containing gold, silver and other valuables dating back to this unsettled period. It was only a matter of time before these coastal raids were extended to the more lucrative shores of Britain, Ireland and mainland Europe.

Mother Nature does not only push whole societies into piracy but often also 'pulls' them into it, by offering an environment that greatly facilitates sea raiding. The many small islands dotting the Caribbean, the South China Sea or the waters between Greece and the Levant are good illustrations of this: many of them straddle major sea lines of communication and are thus perfect locations for an ambush or simply to lie in wait for a suitable unsuspecting vessel. In the Mediterranean, the Aegean islands were ideal for this. The area between Lesbos, Tenedos and the Dardanelles controls the convergence of three major sea lanes that connected Constantinople with the other major ports of the Mediterranean: one from Venice via the Adriatic Sea, a second from the Barbary Coast and Alexandria hugging the Levant and Asia Minor, and a third via the Cyclades and Chios. In the region of the Aegean islands, these routes passed through confined waters, made even more treacherous by unpredictable squalls, strong currents and dangerous reefs. 'During peak periods of the year for navigation, particularly in spring and again in autumn, these sectors must have been crowded with shipping', making them 'the favourite hunting grounds of pirates and corsairs of all persuasions'.[42]

In the north, the coasts of the North Sea and the Baltic also offered numerous hiding places in the form of bights, small rocks and reefs as well as marshes where a pirate or privateer vessel could hide out of sight and wait for prey. The Channel Islands – Jersey, Guernsey, Alderney,

Sark – were particularly pirate-prone: Eustace the Monk had made the latter his base of operations because it was perfectly located to intercept maritime traffic. The practice of staying near to the coast in these early days of navigation during the late medieval period made avoiding such obvious pirate hot spots rather difficult for all but the most experienced seafarers; in any case, it was not always possible since certain destinations necessitated passing points of piratical danger. For example, the two large islands of Sjælland and Fyn formed a 'maritime choke point' in the Kattegat (the narrow sea that leads from the North Sea into the Baltic Sea), permitting only three narrow routes into and out of the Baltic – the Oresund, the Great Belt and the Little Belt, collectively known as the Danish Straits. In the days of the Victual Brothers and the Likedeelers, these waters were so notorious for pirate attacks that merchantmen passing through them usually sailed in convoy for mutual protection.

In the Eastern Seas, dense mangrove forests such as those along the coasts of the Straits of Malacca – yet another formidable maritime choke point – and the Andaman Sea enabled pirates to lie in ambush and seemingly disappear without trace after a swift attack.

The Bab el-Mandeb or 'Gate of Tears' connecting the Red Sea with the Gulf of Aden and the Strait of Hormuz connecting the Persian Gulf with the Western Indian Ocean are maritime choke points that gained notoriety as piracy-prone locations. Atolls, reefs and small islands played a similar role, allowing smaller vessels to escape while preventing larger ones from navigating through the narrow and shallow waterways between them. Much later, in the nineteenth century, Captain Henry Keppel of the Royal Navy quipped that as 'surely as spiders abound where there are nooks and crannies, so have pirates sprung up wherever there is a nest of islands offering creeks and shallows, headlands, rocks and reefs – facilities in short for lurking, for surprise, for attack, for escape'.[43] Although Keppel was speaking of the pirates whom he fought against in the nineteenth century, he could easily be speaking of the late medieval pirates half a millennium earlier.

In spite of the influence environmental factors had over the development of piracy, they cannot be held solely to blame: those who turned pirate still had a choice. The Sards, for example, turned their backs to their coastline and developed into a pastoral society instead of transforming Sardinia into a pirate lair.[44] Even the Vikings, sitting on the fringes of a complicated coastal geography, could have opted to be traders pure and simple without branching out into maritime raiding.

Spotting Ships at Sea

Going a-pirating requires a vessel from which to plunder and pillage in the first place. For a newly formed, 'start-up' pirate gang in the medieval period, this problem was usually solved either by way of a mutiny on board a merchant vessel or warship, or by the theft of a suitable but unguarded vessel lying at anchor. Many pirates began their operations with one of these two approaches. Unfortunately, however, the sources covering the Middle Ages do not provide any detailed accounts on the beginnings of pirate gangs: the information available tends to focus on pirates who had already made a name for themselves, such as Klaus Störtebeker or Godeke Michels from the Victual Brothers and Likedeelers, or on privateers such as Eustace the Monk or Don Pero Niño, who acquired their ships from their respective overlords. We shall see later examples of successful pirates who began their careers either by instigating a mutiny or by stealing an unguarded vessel, but this was certainly going on in this earlier period, too.

Well-established pirate gangs chose a certain type of ship depending on their favourite hunting waters. If these were coastal waters not far from their own bases, light and swift vessels were used since they were perfect for ambushes; the Uskoks – pirates who roamed the Adriatic in the 1500s – had a preference for comparatively small galleys known as *brazzere* for this very reason. On the other hand, when the hunting waters were on the high seas, pirates opted for sea-going vessels – usually the same that were used by honest sea traders. For example, the Victual

Brothers used the same vessels as the Hanseatic League – the ubiquitous 'cogs' – but with larger crew and with fighting castles at bow and stern. These pirate ships hence looked exactly like the League's warships, known as *Friedeschiffe* or 'peace ships'. The Chinese and Japanese pirates in the East China Sea of the same period also preferred converted merchant ships – the vessels of choice were Chinese junks – due to their prevalence and innocent appearance.[45] For swift coastal raids, smaller oared vessels were also used, often converted into warships by adding one or two fighting towers in the bow and stern, and by taking on board a larger-than-usual complement of crew.

Once the pirates had acquired a suitable vessel and made it out to sea, they then needed to find their target. Before the invention of radar, spotting a vessel depended on one's position. According to the usual mathematical formula, the observable horizon for a person of 5 foot 8 inches in height standing at sea level is about 5 kilometres; for somebody of the same height standing on top of a 100-metre cliff, it is about 40 kilometres. Since cliffs tended to be in short supply on the high seas, the alternative was using the crow's nest of the main mast to artificially increase the range of vision to about 15 to 20 kilometres, depending on the height of the mast. This still meant that the chance of missing a target was disturbingly high.

Of course, pirates stacked the cards in their favour by choosing convenient places where they could expect to encounter plenty of ships – either by actively searching for them along the major sea routes, or lying in wait at a suitable hiding place to ambush the unsuspecting vessel. Sometimes, even previously safe ports and their anchorages could become ambush locations. In his travelogue, the fifteenth-century Genoese nobleman Anselme Adorno tells the story of an ambush outside a well-known and previously safe port. In May 1470, he voyaged to the Holy Land on board a huge, 700-ton Genoese vessel 'well provided with cannon, crossbow and javelins and . . . with a complement of 110 armed men to repel pirates or Turks'.[46] En route, the ship was meant to moor in the Sardinian port of Alghero, but, given its size, had to anchor outside, with Adorno and his fellow pilgrims using the vessel's long-boats to visit the port. In the port itself, nothing untoward happened. When they rowed back, however, pirates suddenly pounced, trying to manoeuvre their own boats between the Genoese long-boats and their 'floating fortress'. The master of the Genoese vessel saved the day with his decisive counter-measures: he immediately had his crew open fire on the pirates to discourage them from coming any closer, and dispatched two boats manned with armed sailors to escort the pilgrims safely back to the ship.[47] In other cases, crews and passengers were not so lucky – they were caught, stripped of all their valuables, and kept as prisoners until ransom was paid.[48]

Some pirates were better organised and tried to obtain prior information about when a ship with lucrative cargo would make its appearance at a certain location in order that they could ambush it. The Uskok pirates, for example, were known to have spotters and informers in the ports of the Adriatic, even in Venice itself. On one occasion, in September 1586, the Venetian government 'discovered that a clerical official from Lesina, Francesco da Bruzza, was a spy: he not only informed the Uskoks of the departure of every vessel, but pointed out where goods belonging to Turkish subjects might be found'.[49]

For those pirates who operated in open waters, with their ships staying off the coast and out of sight, a degree of cooperation with each other was required. Late thirteenth-century pirates of the Arabian Sea, off the west coast of India, would attempt to spot, intercept and overwhelm the defences of merchant vessels, most of which still hugged the coast for safety reasons. As the famous traveller Marco Polo recalled:

You must know that from Malabar, and from a neighbouring province called Gujarat, more than 100 ships cruise out every year as corsairs, seizing other ships and robbing the merchants . . . Most of these villainous corsairs scatter here and there, . . . but sometimes . . . they cruise in line, that is to say in distances of about five miles apart . . .

And as soon as they catch sight of a merchant ship, one signals to another by means of beacons, so that not a ship can pass through this sea undetected.[50]

Marco Polo also described the counter-measures taken by these early sea-farers: 'the merchants, who are quite familiar with the habits of these villainous corsairs ... go so well armed and equipped, that they ... defend themselves stoutly and inflict great damage on their attackers'.[51] Nevertheless, many vessels still fell prey to pirates.[52]

For the more proactive pirate or privateer, or one just tired of lying in wait without spotting any sail, cruising up and down coasts well known for dense maritime traffic and weak defences could also be a winning formula. If the pirate or privateer thought himself strong enough, or was in command of a small fleet, raiding coastal villages and towns was also an option – again one not without risk, but with the advantage that the location was known in advance. For Christian and Muslim corsairs in the Mediterranean, raiding coasts was a common strategy: the capture of locals to be sold on in slave markets was part of their particular business model.

Occasionally, if a pirate was unlucky enough to chance upon warships on an anti-piracy mission, the hunter became the hunted. Another risk for the hunting pirate was running out of fresh water and victuals far away from friendly shores. Galleys cruising for lengthy periods were particularly vulnerable due to their huge crews, usually including more than a hundred oarsmen on top of a sizeable number of sailors and soldiers, who needed to be provisioned. For example, a light galley, manned by a crew of two hundred or so oarsmen, sailors, soldiers and officers who consumed about 90 gallons (340 litres) of water per day, usually carried 800 to 1,500 gallons (3,000 to 5,600 litres).[53] This suggests a maximum cruising range of only about two weeks before the drinking water ran out. Since corsair captains were ever dependent on weather conditions, they could not always reach safe harbours for the purpose of replenishing their galleys. In 1404, for instance, the Castilian corsair Don Pero Niño found his fleet of several well-armed and well-manned galleys trapped on a barren island off the Barbary Coast after heavy storms had prevented their return to Spain. Having made his water supplies last an astonishing twenty days, he convinced his now very desperate and very thirsty crew to try and get water from the hostile Barbary Coast despite running the risk of being ambushed and annihilated there. Luck was with Pero Niño and his crew on that day: just when they had finished filling their barrels with fresh water, a Muslim levy bore down on them.[54] The galleys made their escape without any of their crews being captured or harmed, but it was a close call. This incident highlights just how risky the life of a pirate or a corsair was – even before they had managed to find their prey.

Overwhelming the Prey

The heroes of Hollywood pirate films are usually seen swinging onto the deck of the ship under attack to join a lusty battle fought with rapiers, sabres, daggers, pistols and muskets. Most pirates, however, hoped to avoid bloody encounters, and banked on what we would now call 'shock and awe' to cow their targets into submission without a single shot being fired: in the words of historian Peter Earle, it 'was the value of the prize that mattered rather than the glory of getting it'.[55] That said, not all pirates were eager to avoid battle entirely. The Vikings, for example, considered themselves warriors, and perishing in battle was something they looked forward to. As far as we can judge, based on scant sources, a similar case can be made for the Orang Laut or 'Sea People' operating in the waters of Southeast Asia, and the Wako pirates active in the East China Sea. There are even incidents on record where a couple of pirates launched suicidal attacks to draw enemy fire[56] – an act more in line with regular armed forces. But these were exceptions: most 'ordinary' pirates expected to get their way just by hoisting their pirate flag.

They would often approach an unsuspecting vessel while themselves flying the flag of a legitimate merchant vessel, then suddenly haul up

their notorious black flag with its skull and crossbones, or a local equivalent – a failsafe way of getting the other vessel's full attention. Usually,
the terrorised crew surrendered without a fight in the hope of surviving
the encounter, even if it meant losing their possessions and their ship. A
quick comparison of crew sizes illustrates that any attempt to resist would
have been futile. While a standard merchant vessel was rather economically manned and usually had not many more than two dozen hands on
deck, pirate ships nearly always had far more numerous crews of well-
trained and battle-hardened sailors-cum-fighters. Seeing them jostling
about on the bulwarks brandishing a wide-ranging arsenal of deadly
weapons including cutlasses and sabres and hearing their yells and taunts
must have been quite an ordeal for a merchantman's crew. The feeling of
utter terror, and the knowledge that the pirates would only show mercy if
no attempt to resist was made, meant that many crews refused to fight
despite the orders of their masters. In other words, the pirates had won
the psychological battle without having to risk their lives – which was
exactly what they hoped for. The prolonged and systematic plundering
that followed a capture was usually a continuation of this shock-and-awe
element. In the first rush of success, boarding pirates tended to be very
brutal indeed, reinforcing the message that resistance was futile.

Battle, however, could not always be avoided. If the ship under attack
chose to fight to the bitter end, this tended to be a protracted affair with
bloody clashes at close quarters. An instance of this took place in the early
1150s between a small Viking squadron and a huge Muslim vessel in the
Mediterranean. Jarl ('Earl') Rognvald Kali Kolsson, accompanied by a
bishop named William, was on a pilgrimage tour to Rome and the Holy
Land. Despite the pious purpose of the Jarl's voyage, he saw nothing
wrong in looting the Muslim 'heathens' he encountered on his way – and
he assuaged his conscience by vowing to donate half the spoils to the poor.
The Muslim vessel his fleet of nine longships met somewhere off the
Sardinian coast was a truly formidable one: the Vikings, mistaking it first
for a bank of clouds, eventually identified it as a dromond, a large galley.

This was a well-defended, forbidding foe, as the bishop warned: 'I think you'll find it difficult to lay your ship alongside . . . The best you'll be able to do will be to hook a broad-axe onto the gunwale, and then they'll have sulphur and boiling pitch to drench you with, head to foot.'[57] Here, the bishop is most likely referring to a variant of the infamous 'Greek fire', a liquid incendiary device like modern-day napalm fired at an enemy vessel via siphons powered by pressure pumps. In order to overcome the formidable vessel, the Vikings made use of the fact that they had the larger fleet. While some of their vessels fired salvo after salvo of arrows at the dromond to keep its crew busy, others swiftly moved alongside the enemy ship – time was of the essence since the siphons could not be depressed enough to engage targets close-up. The close-quarters battle that unfolded was fierce: 'The people on the dromond being Saracens . . . among them a good many black men . . . put up a strong resistance' – strong enough to earn a Viking warrior named Erling his nickname: 'Erling got a nasty wound on the neck just above the shoulder as he leapt aboard the dromond and it healed so badly that for the rest of his life he carried his head to one side, which is why he got the nickname Wry-Neck.' In the end, the Vikings prevailed, killing everybody on board the dromond with the exception of a tall man they considered to be the Saracen leader and a few others whom they took prisoner. After looting the dromond the Vikings set it on fire, while Earl Rognvald celebrated the successful battle and Erling's bravery with a poem, which included praise for his opponents: 'Erling, honoured aimer of spears, eagerly advanced toward the vessel in victory, with banners of blood: the black warriors, brave lads, we captured or killed, crimsoning our blades.'[58]

Even the courageous Castilian corsair Don Pero Niño could not always avoid battle. In 1404, his galleys had been lying in ambush at an island near Tunis for several days in the hope of capturing an unsuspecting Muslim vessel. However, no vessel passed by. Finally, losing patience, Pero Niño decided to make straight for Tunis itself – quite an audacious move given the defences of the port. Nevertheless, in Tunis his

men managed to surprise a galley and killed or captured all they encountered. They then went on to attack a huge Tunisian merchant vessel.
Here, the rashness of Pero Niño becomes apparent: although the Tunisian
ship retreated into a narrow channel, he did not abandon the chase as he
probably should have, but followed in hot pursuit. When his galley's ram
collided with the enemy vessel's poop, he immediately jumped over,
probably assuming he was the first of a large boarding party. The shock
of the collision with the massive galleass, however, threw his own smaller
vessel back, and prevented his crew making it across as well. His ever
loyal aide-de-camp and biographer Diaz de Gamez asserts that Pero
Niño, marooned on the enemy's poop deck, fought like a lion until his
own vessel was back in position, allowing other crew members to come to
his aid. But rescuing their brave but impetuous captain from his own
rashness was not their only problem: the narrowness of the channel meant
that Tunisian sailors and soldiers had now started to swarm aboard both
vessels from the landside, turning what had initially been seen as an
opportunity for a victorious raid into an ever more desperate battle for
survival: 'so great was the multitude that an arrow could not have been
loosed among them without finding a mark, nor a blow struck that did
not find home'.[59] In the end, a seriously injured Pero Niño managed to
leap back onto his own vessel, which his cousin's galley towed out of the
channel and to safety. Artistic licence notwithstanding, Diaz de Gamez
neatly encapsulates the very personal, bloody, chaotic and messy nature
of boarding an enemy vessel that was well prepared to defend itself – in
this case, with more than a little help from the port's inhabitants.

In northern waters during this period, specialised warships such as
galleys did not yet exist. Rather, both the merchants and pirates used
lumbering cogs which were fitted with fighting platforms and manned by
crews armed with daggers, swords, axes, pikes, bows and crossbows, and,
in some cases, with the then new harquebuses: rather heavy, cumbersome
and inaccurate – and wildly expensive – muzzle-loaded matchlock firearms.[60] In a sense, such firearms often evened the odds in the normally

one-sided encounter between an alert Hanseatic merchant vessel and a pirate ship: the pirates did not always have it their way. In 1391, several Victual Brothers' vessels attacked a huge cog from Stralsund, probably under the assumption that their mere appearance would be enough to make the merchantman 'strike its colours' (surrender). To the surprise of the pirates, however, the numerous and well-equipped crew of the Stralsundian cog put up a fierce fight. They not only courageously repelled the boarding attempts of the pirates, but even carried the fight to the decks of the pirate vessels. Although the enfolding close-quarter battle must have been rather bloody, the Stralsundians came out as the victors, capturing more than a hundred pirates.[61] As they did not have enough chains and foot irons, the triumphant and vengeful Stralsundian crew simply put their captives into large barrels, with only the head protruding from a hole hacked into them. These barrels with their human cargo were then stored in exactly the same way as any ordinary barrels – with utter disregard for the safety of those within.[62] The captured Victual Brothers were released from their barrels once the ship was safely back in Stralsund – only to be beheaded there hours later.[63]

Raiding the Coasts

Pirate attacks did not just take place at sea – there was also high-end piracy in the shape of veritable pirate fleets, big and small, conducting large-scale amphibious operations against targets on land. Saracen pirates in the time of the Abbasid and Fatimid caliphates (750–1258) regularly carried out organised raids on the Mediterranean coasts of Christendom, from the Greek islands all the way to France and Spain. In 838, for example, a fleet of Saracen pirates attacked Marseilles, plundering and pillaging the town before setting it alight. They also ransacked churches and monasteries, taking clergymen, nuns and laypeople captive, either to be ransomed or sold in the slave markets.[64] During another attack four years later, in October 842, Saracen pirates sailed 30 kilometres up the River Rhône to

Arles, wreaking havoc along the way without meeting any organised resistance.[65] This was not their first raid on Arles, or their last: they kept coming back until they were finally engaged and soundly defeated in 973 by the forces of William I, Count of Arles. But the Saracens did not content themselves with ravaging the French coast: on 27 August 846, a powerful pirate fleet attacked Rome. Even though they could not penetrate the sturdy walls of the city itself, they found enough plunder in the rich and undefended villas lying on the city's outskirts as well as in the basilica of St Peter.[66] The Saracen pirates did not live long enough to enjoy their new wealth, though; on their voyage home, their ships were apparently sunk by a 'terrible storm', because they had 'blasphemed with their foul mouths against God and our Lord Jesus Christ and his apostles', as the Annals of Saint Bertin piously recorded.[67] It was even said that some of the treasures stolen from the basilica were later found washed up on the shores of the Tyrrhenian Sea – together with the corpses of the pirates still clutching them – and were brought back to Rome in triumph. But this is probably more pious wishful thinking than a narration of facts.

Just a few years later Saracens and Christians encountered each other again. In September 869, a Saracen fleet raiding the Camargue managed to surprise and capture a veritable archbishop, Rolland of Arles. Ironically, the archbishop was in the process of inspecting the coastal defensive anti-piracy measures when he was captured. As was usually the case for such noble hostages, a ransom was demanded and paid. Unfortunately, the elderly Rolland died before he could be released. The Saracens, true to their word, handed over his corpse, seated on a chair and resplendent in full regalia.

It was not only the Mediterranean coasts of Christendom that suffered from devastating, large-scale raids. In the north, the Vikings were engaged in significant and sustained coastal raiding. These attacks were initially small and largely exploratory expeditions venturing across the North Sea to British, Irish and Frankish shores, targeting coastal areas as well as navigable river systems. Usually, only about ten to twelve vessels – with a combined crew of up to five hundred[68] – were involved in such raids, which were essentially smash-and-grab assaults.[69] The first was reported to have taken place against Portland on the Dorset coast in the year 787:

> This year, King Beorhtric [of Wessex] married Eadburg, Offa's daughter. And in his days there came for the first time three ships of Northmen, from Hordaland [in Norway]. Then the Reeve [chief magistrate] rode to meet them; he intended to have them go to the king's town because he did not know what they were. They killed him. These were the first Danish ships to attack the land of the English people.[70]

Taking them for honest merchants was an understandable mistake for the unsuspecting chief magistrate, Royal Steward Beaduheard, since in this period 'traders and raiders may not have always been distinguishable' – quite often, they were the same people, deciding whether to trade or to raid depending on the local circumstances.[71] But the mistake was a lethal one. This initial puzzlement about the motives of the 'visitors' gave way to utter shock a couple of years later when in 793 the Vikings sacked and looted the famous monastery of Lindisfarne.

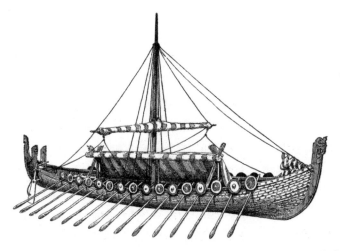

1. A Viking *drakkar* (longship), used for pirate raids like the one on Lindisfarne.

The attack came like a bolt from the blue: none of the monks on the island had any inkling of what was about to happen when they commenced their day. Since no one expected any danger from the sea, there was no lookout on duty and so no warning about what was coming. There may have been some curious glances at the fast-approaching longships, and a feeling of dread – but by then it would have been too late to do anything other than run. As the English chronicler and monk Simeon of Durham reports,

> the church of Lindisfarne was miserably filled with devastation, blood, and rapine, and all but entirely and thoroughly ruined. [They] trod the holy things under their polluted feet, they dug down the altars, and plundered all the treasures of the church. Some of the brethren they slew, some they carried off with them in chains, the greater number they stripped naked, insulted, and cast out of doors, and some drowned in the sea.[72]

The terrifying attack on Lindisfarne was a historic watershed moment, after which the world seemed to be a different place; this was the onset of the 'Viking Age'.

Unsurprisingly, the Vikings were seen to have targeted the church out of religious hatred, 'ravening for Christian blood', as the Icelandic writer Magnus Magnusson colourfully puts it.[73] But from the Vikings' perspective, churches and monasteries were simply places where they were sure to find enough portable loot to make their raids lucrative and worthwhile.[74] Religious centres like Lindisfarne were not only places of worship but also workshops where highly skilled artisans including goldsmiths and silversmiths resided to produce fine pieces of art to adorn altars, reliquaries and missals; in a medieval landscape dotted with farmsteads, tiny villages and a smattering of comparatively small towns, monasteries were among the most logical locations for anything of economic or cultural significance to be stored.[75] Finally, and quite ironically, since monasteries had been purposely built on islands or along coasts as sanctuaries secure from the endemic land wars, they happened to be not only rich but also easy pickings for seaborne marauders. Taken together, it was not creed (that is, religion) but greed (that is, plunder) that turned defenceless monks and priests into lucrative targets.

Incessant dynastic squabbles and accompanying civil wars in France and Germany enabled the Vikings to launch ever more daring raids into the very heart of the continent without having to fear a coordinated defence. The monastic scholar Ermentarius of Noirmoutier, writing in 860, illustrates the sheer scale of the devastation: 'The number of ships grows; the endless stream of Vikings never ceases to increase. Everywhere the Christians are the victims of massacres, burnings, plunderings. The Vikings conquer all in their path and nothing resists them.'[76] In 885, a substantial Viking force of about 30,000 men on 700 ships, under one Sigfred, leader of the Danes, laid siege to Paris itself. This was the third time the Vikings had undertaken such a venture, although on this occasion without their usual success. Ably led by Odo, Count of Paris, the few but determined defenders, two hundred men-at-arms and a levy of citizens, managed to repulse the fearsome warriors against all the odds.

Pirates of the Eastern Seas also engaged in Viking-style smash-and-grab attacks – albeit later in the period. When Japanese raiders descended on the Chinese coast in the fifteenth century, the Ming Chronicles reported: 'The Japanese are cunning by nature. They often transport local Japanese products and weapons on their ships. They appear, then disappear along the coast. Given the opportunity, they take out their weapons and wantonly plunder. Otherwise they present their local products as tribute.'[77] Again, it was difficult to distinguish between traders and raiders because quite often these were the very same people. As in the case of the Vikings, these early and somewhat opportunistic attacks quickly escalated into large-scale coastal raids conducted by fleets of dozens or even hundreds of vessels. The pirates also entered navigable rivers to plunder cities that were far away from shore and thus had no anti-piracy measures in place. If these raids were not stopped by vigorous counter-measures, they quickly morphed into land warfare, even empire-building. The Buddhist monk Xu Hai, for example, had more in common with a Viking warlord than a mere pirate captain: in the spring of 1556, he unleashed two Wako pirate gangs with a combined force of several thousand men on the ports and settlements on either side of the Yangtze River, mercilessly plundering, raping and killing the inhabitants. The resistance they encountered was feeble, amounting only to ineffective local militias. Unfortunately for the victims, the well-trained regular government armies were busy battling the fearsome Mongols in the northern parts of the Chinese empire.[78] After the raids, however, the pirates fell out with each other over the distribution of the booty.[79] This was their undoing. One year after their success, the pirates were annihilated by regular government forces which had returned and were ably led by the generals Hu Tsung-hsien and Yüan O. These generals used clever tactics to reduce the number of the pirate troops before engaging them:

> Hu, considering guile better than force in the circumstances, baited the raiders with a skiff loaded with more than a hundred jugs of poisoned wine and manned by two reliable soldiers disguised as troop victuallers, who fled at first sight of the enemy vanguard. Seizing the poisoned wine, the raiders halted and made merry. Some died.[80]

Nonetheless, when it came to operations and tactics, the Viking and Wako raiders had the upper hand over defenders, because they could choose where to strike. They conducted littoral surveillance operations, carried out amphibious landings to secure beachheads, and then advanced further into the interior, outflanking and outmanoeuvring defending forces. Where possible, the invaders made use of navigable river systems. The Vikings frequently sailed up the Rhine, the Seine, the Loire and the Guadalquivir to target population centres such as Cologne, Trier, Paris,

Chartres and Córdoba. Likewise, Wako fleets ventured deep into the heart of China, using major river systems and channel networks to attack inland cities. Eyewitness Xiu Jie recounted that, at first, 'the pirates only kidnapped people and forced their relatives to go to their lair to pay ransom. Then they occupied our interior, stayed were they were, killed our commanding officers, attacked our cities and almost created an irretrievable situation.'[81] The exploits of the Vikings and the Wako were clearly a far cry from the sea encounters normally associated with piracy. Their operations even beg the question of when pirates stop being pirates and become something else – empire builders, for example. Nevertheless, if piracy is defined as the action of committing robbery, kidnap or violence at sea or from the sea without lawful authority, it is obvious that the Vikings and Wako were very much at the forefront of its operational development during the medieval and early modern periods.

Pirate Violence

Pirates' use of violence was primarily determined by their 'business model': if the intention was to kidnap the crew and passengers for ransom, as was the case for the Mediterranean corsairs, the Orang Laut and the Wako, then the captives would be treated fairly well – they were 'money on legs'. On the other hand, if the main objective was pillage and plunder, the captives' lives were at grave risk, especially if they had not surrendered without a fight and thus incensed the pirates. Women were at additional risk of rape. However, although there were those who relished what they did simply for the sake of it, most pirates used violence instrumentally: torture, for instance, was a tool to extract information about hidden valuables.

Acts of cruelty had an additional objective beyond maximising the loot. They were also intended to send a message to several audiences: first, to the pirates themselves; second, to all those sailing through the pirates' waters or living in regions frequently visited by them; and third,

to the enemy, that is navies, militias and judicial and administrative officers. In the first instance, violent acts were 'team-building' exercises in
which most pirates participated, thus turning them into accomplices to
the crime – which made deserting more difficult. In the second instance,
acts of torture had a psychological 'it could have been me' effect, particularly when often grossly distorted and embellished news of atrocities
reached the harbours and ports. The message here was: do not offer any
kind of resistance, do not hide anything of value, since the consequences
of doing so will be too horrible for you to imagine. Hence, by their sheer
brutality, imagined or real, the pirates created a 'brand name' for themselves as 'bloody, merciless ruffians', never to be resisted.[82] In the third
instance, the sheer brutality of the pirates acted as a formidable disincen-
tive against the inauguration of counter-measures. In particular, government officials in remote locations who could not draw on the support of
regular armies or warships thought twice before they even contemplated
moving against pirates active in their port or province: the risk of losing
their lives in gruesome fashion was simply too high. Likewise, militias
drawn from the local population also tended to be reluctant to engage
battle-hardened pirates. They would probably have subscribed to the
famous idiom 'he who fights and runs away, lives to fight another day'. In
any case, the pirates' message to all those who could oppose them was: if
you are our enemy, watch your step.

Efforts to End Piracy on Land

Many different strategies and tactics were tried and tested to end piracy.
Pirates were hunted down on sea and on land, bribed with money or
amnesties, co-opted as pirate hunters, and occasionally forcibly resettled at
locations far from the sea. One of the most seemingly straightforward
solutions was simply to reduce the maritime trade on which pirates
depended for their livelihood. No maritime trade, no piracy – or at least so
thought two emperors of the Ming dynasty. In 1368, Zhu Yuanzhang, the

first Ming emperor (also known under his era name as the Hongwu Emperor), passed a series of 'maritime prohibitions' (*haijin*). Another series of such prohibitions was passed in the early fifteenth century by Emperor Zhu Gaochi (also known as the Hongxi Emperor) after the death of his father, Emperor Zhu Di (the Yongle Emperor), who had sponsored seven large-scale expeditions into the Indian Ocean. The dynasty even dismantled its formidable high-seas fleet, let the ships rot away in their ports, laid off the sailors who had manned them, and thereafter banned ships above a certain tonnage. The dynasty's decision was strengthened by the Confucian belief that nothing good came from overseas anyway, and that China could find everything it needed within its own extensive borders or within the vast Asian interior. However, the Imperial Court's measures resulted in an increase in maritime crime, not in a reduction: faced with no alternative, Chinese merchants resorted to smuggling and piracy. They were joined by thousands of now-unemployed sailors from the scrapped high-seas fleet and by substantial numbers of coastal government officials and gentry who either turned a blind eye to raids or actively participated in them. The well-intended Ming anti-piracy policy backfired spectacularly, boosting the wave of Wako pirates instead of defeating it. Local militias had to be hastily formed in order to offer at least some semblance of resistance. In was not until 1567 when, due to a combination of large-scale military operations and the repeal of the maritime prohibitions, the Wako were finally defeated.[83]

Banning all seaborne trade to combat piracy proved disastrous enough for Ming China, a fairly self-sufficient empire, but for those societies which depended on this kind of trade to provide daily necessities for the masses, such a drastic measure was simply not an option. Nevertheless, other regions did take land-based anti-piracy measures too, although to a less radical degree. From antiquity onwards, the coastal populations of the Mediterranean, for instance, took defensive measures not only because it had been decreed by Imperial Rome, and then Constantinople, but quite simply to protect their way of life – especially in times of crisis when no major empire's fleets policed the seas. Periodically attacked by waves of piracy, coastal populations would abandon those villages which they deemed to be indefensible and move to somewhat safer settlements further inland – but still near enough to the sea to allow them to go on with their usual fishing and small-scale maritime trading. Those who remained on the shores organised some simple protective measures such as watchtowers and spotters in the hills, backed up by nearby fortifications to which the population could flee when pirate vessels appeared. A case in point is the island of Cyprus which, after the fall of Constantinople in 1453, became very exposed. It protected its coasts by setting up a network of watchtowers in order to detect approaching pirate and privateering fleets as early as possible:

> Every half-mile two villagers, furnished with wood, watched out for ships approaching the island; if they saw any they were to make as much fire as possible. After the going down of the sun, each sentinel was obliged, upon discovery of something, to make a fire that would burn as long as it took to say six paternosters.[84]

There were also the small fortresses known as Martello towers, first built by the Corsicans in the fifteenth century and later by the Genoese at the height of their power between 1530 and 1620 to defend ports and coastal villages against the frequent raids of the Barbary corsairs and pirates. These simple fortresses were heavily fortified towers 12 to 15 metres wide and often equipped with heavy cannon on their roof terraces. They were later adopted by the British and went on to be used all over the world.[85] Similar measures, including fortifying ports, towns and villages, were taken to protect the Chinese and Korean coastal populations against successive waves of Wako pirates.[86] Fortified ports, towns and villages were also used in the North Sea to protect the inhabitants of the Carolingian Empire's coasts against the Vikings, as the following more detailed examination will show.

A furore Normannorum libera nos, Domine – 'From the fury of the Norsemen deliver us, Lord.'[87] This medieval antiphon illustrates how the people affected by Viking raids found succour in prayer in the face of the Vikings' remorseless advance deeper and deeper into the interior of mainland Europe. This is not to say that the Carolingians took no proactive measures or made no attempts to set up strong coastal defences against the Vikings. In fact, the great emperor Charlemagne (r. 800–14) himself recognised the severity of the Viking threat and periodically visited the coast during the second half of his long reign (768–814). The defensive measures taken to counter the threat included the building of a fleet to protect the North Sea and Atlantic coastal estuaries, and the construction of a network of watchtowers supported by coastal fortifications.[88] In 800, the *Royal Frankish Annals* reports that the emperor 'left the palace of Aachen in the middle of March and traversed the shores of the Gallic sea. He built a fleet on this sea, which was then infested with pirates, set guards in different places.'[89] Charlemagne's son Louis the Pious (r. 813–40) also saw to it that both the fleet and the coastal fortifications were kept strong. However, as soon as the emperors turned their attention elsewhere and focused on more pressing problems in their vast and decentralised empire, their elaborate coastal defensive measures rapidly fell apart: local feudal lords found the cost of maintaining them without the support of the empire far too high and burdensome, particularly as they were often embroiled in their own feuds which prevented them from keeping an eye on the sea. Unsurprisingly, then, the Vikings could still come and go as they pleased, plundering, ransacking and torching even major cities far removed from the coast, such as Cologne and Trier. Between 834 and 837 the Vikings regularly raided the important Frisian port and trade emporium of Dorestad in the northern Rhine delta – raids became so predictable that in the fourth year, the *Annals of Saint-Bertin* somewhat sarcastically comments: 'The Northmen at this time fell on Frisia with their usual surprise attack.'[90]

Why were they not stopped? Usually, it is hard to block raids: pirates are free to choose the time and place, thus making their movements hard to predict. But the repeated sacking of this crucial port year after year is less easy to account for. The *Annals* hints at the problem when recounting Emperor Louis's public investigation after the fourth attack:

> Now the Emperor summoned a general assembly and held an inquiry with those magnates to whom he had delegated the task of guarding that coast. It became clear from the discussion that partly through the sheer impossibility of the task, partly through the disobedience of certain men, it had not been possible for them to offer any resistance to the attackers.[91]

In the absence of a firm reign over the coasts, caused in part by the protracted civil wars between Louis the Pious and his sons Pippin of Aquitaine, Louis the German and Lothar I, the Vikings were able to run amok. The repeated sack of Dorestad also indicates that the Carolingian fleet organised in the times of Charlemagne had ceased to be an effective fighting force – if it had ever been one. Emperor Louis ordered a new fleet to be 'made ready to go more speedily in pursuit in whatever direction might be required',[92] but against the backdrop of recurring reports of Danish pirates ravaging Frisia, it is doubtful whether it had better success than his father's fleet.

After Louis's death in 840, the Carolingian Empire broke apart, and potential successors fought over the spoils. The long-drawn out civil war allowed the Vikings to penetrate ever deeper into the interior without encountering much organised resistance. Only the 860s and 870s brought some respite for the beleaguered townspeople and villagers. After establishing firm control over his part of the Carolingian Empire, King Charles the Bald embarked on a 'carrot and stick' policy to deal with the Vikings: he would pay them off where their forces were too strong to be defeated, and would enter into temporary alliances to play them off against each other. Yet he also constructed a network of fortresses and fortified bridges along the Seine and the Loire to block Viking fleets.[93] After his death in

877, however, a new civil war weakened the defences of the empire. In 881, the Viking fleets returned in force, some cruising up the River Rhine to attack cities including Aix-la-Chapelle (Aachen), Cologne and Trier,[94] while others sacked and looted the French interior so thoroughly that by 884 'the scale of destruction resembled scenes familiar from modern warfare'.[95] If we compare these Viking raids with those conducted in Spain, it quickly becomes apparent that a determined and organised resistance made a huge difference: in 844, Viking raiders managed to sack Lisbon and Cadiz, but they were then decisively repulsed at Seville by a well-prepared Muslim army led by the Emirate of Córdoba. The Vikings returned to the Mediterranean in 859–60 and faced little resistance along French and Italian coasts, but were again defeated by Muslim levies along the Spanish seaboard. This series of Viking raids was 'the boldest and most far-reaching Viking foray into the Mediterranean but it was no campaign of conquest. The Vikings were raiders and booty collectors who relied on speed and surprise to achieve their ends. Faced by real resistance, they soon left to look for softer targets.'[96]

It is clear from these examples that purely defensive and land-based measures against pirates were bound to fail. Those faced with the threat of piracy were in something of a bind: if initial exploratory raids remained unchecked, opportunistic smash-and-grab pirate attacks had the potential to evolve into large-scale raids which could culminate in the overthrow of established realms. And yet it was impossible to defend long coastlines against each and every onslaught: the Vikings and Wako pirates could choose where to attack, and when. Like the Vikings, the Wako could easily penetrate feeble coastal defences and sail up main rivers such as the Yangtze, the Yellow River and the Grand Canal. It was hard to take lasting measures against their assaults. After the initial attack, there would be an immediate rush to strengthen defences and an atmosphere of heightened alert and vigilance. But then the 'business as usual' approach would return and gradually undermine previous preparations. After all, watchtowers were only useful if they were manned, and warships only if they were

kept in good condition – both of which came at a cost. Nor did interne-
cine warfare and political squabbles help defenders, as can be seen in the
case of the woefully ineffective response of the divided Franks compared
to the coordinated counter-measures of the Emirate of Córdoba.

Efforts to End Piracy at Sea

Different defensive tactics were adopted against pirates at sea. Seafarers
would often choose a large and well-armed vessel when venturing out
into pirate-prone waters. The dromond captured by Jarl Rognvald's fleet
is a case in point: it was not only large and well manned, but also armed
with Greek fire siphons which were as effective as modern flamethrowers.
Such 'floating fortresses' were not defenceless prey but formidable opponents capable of resisting all but the most determined pirates[97] – which
explains why, before the advent of broadside artillery, seafarers of all
waters employed big vessels to dissuade pirates from attacking. In the
fifteenth century, for example, to protect their perilous but immensely
profitable run to Alexandria and Beirut, the Venetian arsenal built huge
three-decked ships with imposing castles on the prow and on the poop,
manned them with 100 to 150 well-armed soldiers and equipped them
with up to 4 bombards with a range of 600 paces.[98] Similar floating
fortresses were used in the Eastern Seas. In these waters, seafarers
preferred large high-seas junks, some of which were also equipped with
flamethrower-like weapons. In the Northern Seas, the Hanseatic League
used similarly large vessels, cogs, as floating fortresses on their trade
routes, usually with twice as many crew members as were required for
actually operating the vessel.

Another form of defence was safety in numbers and seafarers would
sometimes sail in convoys: the sight of dromonds, galleasses or cogs
sailing together would usually deter pirates from attacking, and this
approach became the norm in the Mediterranean in the time of the great
Italian sea powers of Venice, Pisa and Genoa.[99] Although free and unreg-

ulated merchant shipping – what is now known as tramp trade – did exist, vessels carrying valuable cargo were under the jurisdiction of a regulated convoy or *muda* system. This was particularly the case for vessels on the trans-Mediterranean voyage to the Levant, and for vessels on the Atlantic voyage to Flanders and Antwerp. The convoy would be placed under the command of an admiral or *capitano*, who would also usually have several warships under his command for further protection.[100] In northern waters, the Hanseatic League organised convoys of merchant vessels to protect their shipping against the Victual Brothers and the Likedeelers. In the east, the Ming Chronicles mention pirate attacks on Chinese convoys – which implies that organised convoys, probably also escorted by regular warships, existed there as well. But available sources do not provide a great deal of further information on this.

Another form of defence was going it alone in vessels of superior speed and manoeuvrability. Masters in command of such vessels knew that joining a convoy came at a price. First, there was the obligation to wait for other ships to gather before the convoy finally set sail; many masters 'objected violently to having to await' at the assembly point.[101] Second, a convoy could only sail as fast as its slowest vessels. The temptation to go it alone, rules and regulations notwithstanding, must have been very strong, particularly considering that a convoy of ships laden with valuable cargo would have attracted every pirate in the area, whether it was protected by warships or not. Finally, there was a high likelihood that, in any case, the convoy would be dispersed by adverse winds or currents, and that unprotected stragglers would be found and captured. If masters of fast vessels avoided convoys and sailed alone, successfully making use of their greater agility, then they faced a sea free of pirates and thus a smooth voyage. But it should not be forgotten that pirates posed only one of the risks seafarers had to deal with: sudden squalls, storms, uncharted reefs and submerged sands almost certainly resulted in the loss of more ships over the centuries than pirate attacks.

Hunting Pirates

Using warships as escorts was a rather reactive way of combating pirates. More effective was to deploy such ships either individually or in squadrons to hunt pirates. Whether such a strategy was successful depended on numbers: the number of pirate vessels known to be active, and the number of available warships. Apart from a few exceptions, there were always more pirates than pirate hunters. There are several reasons for this. First of all, not every warship could be used as a pirate hunter – many were built to engage other warships, which meant they were big and slow, with a deep draught which prevented them from entering shallow waters. Vessels such as heavy galleasses in the Mediterranean, for instance, or cogs in northern waters, could only be used to hunt pirates if they were supported by a number of smaller, swifter vessels. Organising mixed pirate-hunting flotillas with both superior firepower and speed was a strategy to which Venice resorted in the Mediterranean, as well as the Hanseatic League in the North Sea and the Baltic. Second, concentrating resources and deploying many vessels to hunt down pirates suspected to be at certain locations meant other locations remained unpatrolled, and piracy could flourish there. Finally, sea powers with vast trade networks patrolled immense expanses of water and needed to protect their coasts against regular warships of enemy states. So even at the best of times there were never enough warships available for pirate hunting.

Pirate hunting also depended on luck, an intimate knowledge of potential hiding places and a close familiarity with local maritime conditions such as reefs and shoals, currents, the weather and wind patterns. It also required a lot of patience, as is evident in the case of Don Pero Niño's first major pirate hunting expedition in 1404, carried out on the orders of his king with the aim of suppressing powerful Castilian pirates who were indiscriminately harassing merchant shipping between Spain and the Levant. Lying at anchor in Cartagena, Pero Niño learned that two notorious Castilian pirates, Don Gonzalez de Moranza and another named

Arnaimar, had just been reported attacking merchant vessels off the coast of Aragon.[102] Stalking them for weeks but failing to catch up with their vessels, he finally found them in the port of Marseilles, where Antipope Benedict XIII was resident. It turned out that these Castilian pirates were in the pay of Benedict XIII, who had given them a commission, making them privateers. There was a tense standoff, and while Pero Niño and his crew were entertained by the antipope, the two Castilian corsairs made their escape, heading for Corsica or Sardinia. Pero Niño followed them to Sardinia, but the trail went cold. Instead, he found three other suspected pirates in the Aragonese port of Alguer. Although the three vessels were well armed and lying heavily protected under the sea walls, Pero Niño brashly demanded their surrender. Again, he found himself talked out of an attack: the authorities of Alguer begged him to leave the pirates in peace, 'saying that they could not live without them, since it was only they who guarded the harbours, and brought them provisions'.[103] Pero Niño's own officers were also none too keen to press on with an attack since they knew they could not possibly win a fight against the combined might of the pirates, the fortress's guns and the town militia. The now rather frustrated Pero Niño wisely decided to cruise along the Barbary Coast: that the vessels he encountered there were enemies of Castile and thus fair game was beyond doubt.

Pirate hunting was also undertaken in northern waters – mainly by the Hanseatic League which was dependent on maritime trade and therefore on the security of their sea routes. The privateering commissions issued by Mecklenburg to all those who requested them had seriously aggravated the pirate threat. The pirates had quickly learned how to operate in large fleets to attack targets previously out of their reach. In the summer of 1394, for instance, a fleet of no less than three hundred Victual Brother vessels raided the waters of the Baltic Sea, capturing an English convoy of five ships, among others.[104] This threat persisted even after the peace treaty of Falsterbo of 1395, and put Hanseatic trade routes via the Baltic Sea to Russia at grave risk. Interestingly, not all Hanseatic cities were keen to get rid of the pirates:

while some cities, such as Danzig and Lübeck, suffered from the depredations of the Victual Brothers, others like Wismar and Rostock profited from them. Hence, pirate hunting operations were initially ventures organised by individual cities – if they deemed themselves strong enough to deal with the pirates and if there was something to be gained by it. The city of Dorpat (modern Tartu, Estonia), for example, wisely kept its few *Friedeschiffe* or 'peace ships' in port since there was no hope that they could wage battle against the vastly superior ranks of pirate vessels on their own.[105] But Stralsund, larger and more powerful than Dorpat, deployed some warships that captured a couple of hundred pirates, most of whom were beheaded. Lübeck made the greatest effort, assembling twenty warships for pirate hunting. But even this small fleet could not achieve much against the larger pirate fleets usually consisting of at least several dozen well-manned and well-armed vessels.[106] Prussian attempts in 1397 to organise a *Seewehr* ('sea defence') also came to naught because many of the intended participants preferred to turn a blind eye to the pirates.

The fact that both the Hanseatic League and the pirates used the same types of vessel occasionally resulted in confusion. In July 1396, a Hanseatic flotilla had just negotiated Cape Hoburg at the southwestern tip of Gotland when their lookouts spotted two huge cogs of unknown origin rapidly approaching from windward. Pirates! Anyone not needed for operating the ships hastily donned armour and took up weapons, got into position and nervously waited for the battle to start, with swords, pikes or grapnels in clenched fists, while crossbows were made ready in the fighting tops. At the last moment, the two unknown cogs took evasive action, as if they were trying to avoid a fight and run. Taunts and curses were yelled across the water at the unknown vessels, which seemed to be getting away, too fast for the Hanse cogs, beating against the wind as quickly as they could. But then, quite surprisingly, both vessels slowed down, allowing the Hanse cogs to catch up and go alongside. Just before the hulls bumped against each other, the men on the unknown ships were hailed once again. They denied being pirates, claiming to be from the city of Kalmar – one of the most important cities in Sweden at that time. The commander of the Hanseatic fleet hesitated: maybe they were indeed innocent traders. But his order to wait came too late: some of his crew, spoiling for a fight, had already started to board the suspect vessels. The Hanse crews quickly won the fight. Those who looked as if they could afford to pay ransom were taken prisoner while everybody else was thrown overboard. The captured cogs, assessed to be old, wormy and useless, were burned. Was this another great victory for the mighty Hanse fleet against the pirates? Unfortunately not: it later emerged that the two cogs had indeed been from Kalmar, and were in fact Swedish pirate hunters.[107]

In eastern waters, the regular navy of various Chinese dynasties also occasionally conducted pirate-hunting operations along their coasts and in adjacent waters. These operations reached their peak in terms of scope and magnitude during the reign of the Ming dynasty's Yongle Emperor (r. 1402–24). A case in point is the capture of the notorious Chinese pirate Chen Zuyi in 1407 by the first Chinese treasure fleet dispatched to explore the Indian Ocean under the command of Admiral Zheng He. Chen Zuyi, a native of the Chinese province of Guangdong, had established a maritime pirate kingdom centred on the port city of Palembang in the Straits of Malacca (formerly the seat of the empire of Srivijaya), first coming to the attention of Ming Chinese officialdom in 1400 when his fleet of around ten ships attacked a Chinese convoy. Since then, his ships had regularly preyed on merchant vessels in the Straits of Malacca and raided settlements along the strait's coasts. Before committing his fleet, Admiral Zheng He cautiously gauged the pirates' strength as well as the tactics they would be most likely to use in a battle; although they did not pose a serious challenge to the Chinese fleet, which numbered more than 300 vessels of different sizes and was manned by 27,000 sailors and soldiers, the 'seamen of Palembang had a reputation as fierce fighters in naval battles. Whereas the Chinese navy favoured ramming in sea fights, the Malays tried to board enemy boats with bands of armed soldiers.'[108] Zheng He's caution paid off: the Chinese chronicle *Taizong Shilu* reports that in early 1407, Zheng He found the pirates lying in the port of Penang, and immediately demanded their surrender. After inconclusive negotiations, the pirate fleet set sail, trying to escape to the open sea. This was a risky strategy in the light of the imperial fleet's superiority, but perhaps they saw no other option, and the chronicle does not reveal whether the admiral offered any pardons. More than five thousand pirates perished in the ensuing battle. Chen Zuyi himself and two other leaders were captured alive, brought back to China in chains and executed in October 1407.[109]

Attacking Pirate Bases

Hunting pirates at sea was quite a challenge: pirates always outnumbered pirate hunters. On the other hand, there was only ever a limited number of major pirate bases – places where the pirates could enjoy the 'merry life' while also selling off their booty, replenishing victuals as well as arms and ammunition, and repairing their ships. Thus, instead of hunting individual ships, the logical choice when it came to supressing piracy was to attack their bases – as long as the pirate hunters were strong enough to do so, and if the threat posed by pirates was serious enough to warrant such costly expeditions. In many instances, such as if the pirate base in question was situated in enemy territory, such attacks would require an alliance with other like-minded states in order to have a chance of success.

The Roman and early Byzantine empires had the cards stacked in their favour: they were able to control all the Mediterranean's coasts. After the emergence of the Muslim empires in the second half of the seventh century, this was no longer the case, and political control was continuously contested. This meant that taking a pirate's lair or, indeed, a major safe haven was difficult to accomplish – the latter necessitating a full-scale military effort, usually involving hundreds of vessels and tens of thousands of troops. In 1249, for example, during the time of the Seventh Crusade, a Christian galley fleet temporarily occupied the Egyptian city of Damietta, the homeport of Saracen pirates. A flotilla dispatched to reconnoitre the strength of the enemy was promptly challenged, and a fierce fight unfolded. The chronicler Matthew Paris recalled:

> We therefore shot against them fiery darts and stones from our sea-mangonels [catapults] . . .; and we threw small bottles full of lime . . . against the enemies. Our darts therefore pierced the bodies of their pirates . . . whilst the stones crushed them, and the lime flying out of the broken bottles blinded them.[110]

Many of the enemy's vessels were sunk and hundreds of Saracens were killed. The city itself was quickly captured, but not for long: one year later it had to be surrendered to the Egyptian Mamluks as part of the ransom for the French king Louis IX who had been defeated and taken prisoner after the battle of Al Mansurah, which saw his whole army wiped out. Needless to say, Damietta was immediately back in business as a major base for pirating and corsairing.

The Ottoman Empire also had to learn the hard way just how difficult it was to capture a major corsair or pirate base. Their problem was Rhodes, an island just off the Anatolian coast and notionally under the control of the Byzantine Empire, but since 15 August 1309 in the hands of the crusading order of the Knights Hospitaller, implacable enemies of Islam who had only been ousted from the Holy Land two decades or so before.[111] Aided by the Rhodians who 'provided their new rulers with fine ships and sailors', the Knights Hospitaller took their crusade to the sea and swiftly became formidable corsairs in their own right.[112] The Hospitallers' naval cruises or 'caravans' were not only bad news for Muslim merchant shipping; their continuous raiding 'was considered a threat to the fragile peace treaties that existed between the Christian powers and the Turks'.[113] After promises made by the order's grand master in 1437 and again in 1454 to oust corsairs and pirates from Rhodian territory proved empty, the Ottoman Empire decided that this 'pestilential thorn in the side' must be removed by force.[114]

The first attempt to capture the island fortress was made between 23 May and 17 August 1480. Even though the Ottoman forces of about 70,000 men and 160 ships vastly outnumbered the 300 knights, 300 sergeants and 3,000–4,000 soldiers of the Hospitallers, the invaders were soundly beaten and had to withdraw. While the well-entrenched defenders lost just a couple of dozen of their own, the Ottomans suffered about 9,000 soldiers killed in action with another 15,000 injured. Four decades later, on 24 June 1522, the Ottomans returned – this time with a much bigger force of 200,000 soldiers. Still, it required a siege of no less than six months before the seriously outnumbered knights and their followers finally surrendered. Because of their gallant conduct during the merciless siege, Sultan Suleiman allowed the surviving Hospitallers and five thousand inhabitants to leave unmolested – a generous gesture: the sultan's forces had again suffered serious casualties.[115] This was not the end of the Hospitallers: in 1530, the Holy Roman Emperor Charles V granted them possession of Malta. Due to its perfect location, Malta developed into an even more formidable pirate base than Rhodes.[116]

2. A wooden model of a galley of the Knights Hospitaller.

In northern waters, the peace treaty of Falsterbo of 1395 ended the war in the Baltic, but not the threat to shipping: the Victual Brothers continued to prey on maritime traffic. Now no longer privateers but pirates pure and simple, they could still draw on support in some parts of the Baltic Sea; political fragmentation and ongoing enmity between various kingdoms, dukedoms or port cities provided a ready supply of safe havens. Even worse, shortly before the end of the war, the Victual Brothers had captured the island of Gotland, including the city of Visby, and had turned it into their stronghold.[117] In early 1398, and after a series of inconclusive talks with the Hanseatic League, Prussia decided to act. Konrad von Jungingen, the grand master of the Teutonic Order, assembled a massive fleet of eighty-four vessels, five thousand soldiers, four hundred horses and fifty Teutonic Knights. This force successfully landed on Gotland on 21 March. Having destroyed three pirate castles, the Prussian force laid siege to Visby, whose defenders quickly capitulated.[118] While the end of the island as a pirate base did not spell the end of the Victual Brothers, they were greatly weakened. Prussian diplomacy, aided by diplomatic missions from Lübeck, gradually turned the tables against them: port after port, state after state, monarch after monarch fell in line with Prussia. The last of the Victual Brothers, formerly so powerful but now reduced to about four hundred men, made a final attempt to find another patron to help them to regroup, but when one potential supporter, Duke Bernim of Stettin (modern Szczecin), showed some interest, the Hanseatic League quickly assembled a fleet and blockaded the city – and that was the end of the story. After the loss of all their bases in the Baltic Sea, the Victual Brothers had to withdraw to the North Sea. They initially found ready support from the Friesian chieftains, but several Hanseatic expeditions during 1400 put an end to that as well, and the Victual Brothers – or Likedeelers as they now called themselves – quickly faded into history.

In eastern waters there existed similar notorious pirate bases as 'pestilential thorns in the side' of coastal realms depending on maritime traffic. The most formidable was the island of Tsushima, situated in the

120-nautical-mile-wide Korean strait that divides the Korean Peninsula from the Japanese islands and links the Sea of Japan with the East China Sea. Whoever controlled Tsushima thus had a virtual stranglehold over maritime traffic passing through the strait and along its coasts. In the fourteenth century, for example, Japanese pirates used Tsushima for their relentless attacks on Korean coastal settlements. In 1389, Taejo, king of Korea, dispatched a large fleet of warships to carry out a retaliatory strike against the island. Three hundred Wako ships and hundreds of houses were set alight, and ten Korean captives rescued.[119] The pirates laid low for a while, but immediately resumed their attacks when the Korean court turned its attention away from the sea. Now under the control of the Japanese Sō clan, pirate activity from Tsushima Island again grew to pose a threat of such magnitude that on 19 June 1419 the Korean king Sejong the Great sent a fleet of 200 warships and 17,000 soldiers to destroy the notorious pirate base on Tsushima once and for all, and to occupy the island.[120]

The operation, known in Korean history as the Gihae Eastern Expedition and in Japanese texts as the Oei Invasion, was initially successful; with most of the pirates' vessels out at sea the Koreans were able easily to occupy the island. In the following days, 135 pirates were killed or captured, 129 ships were burned and about 2,000 houses destroyed. Furthermore, 131 captives and 21 slaves were freed. Nearly four weeks into the campaign, however, just when it looked as if it was over, the Korean forces were ambushed by a Japanese levy led by Tsushima's de-facto ruler and pirate lord Sō Sadamori in an encounter known locally as the battle of Nukadake. Having lost 150 of their own men in this brief but ferocious fight, the Koreans decided to cut their losses. They negotiated a truce with the Sō and evacuated the island on 3 July 1419, probably having believed Sō Sadamori's clever claim that a major typhoon was on its way.[121] Once again, after a brief lull, the pirates resumed their attacks. In the end, the solution to the scourge of piracy turned out to be not military but diplomatic. In 1443, the Korean court granted the Sō clan substantial trading privileges, with 'the understanding that they would endeavour to eliminate piracy and prevent Japanese ships that traded at Korean ports from using forged documents or counterfeit seals'.[122] Allowing the Sō clan to get rich on legitimate trade, while tasking them with policing the waters between Korea and Japan to eradicate both piracy and illicit smuggling, proved to be a durable solution.

It should be clear by now that piracy was not so much about romanticism and adventure as about greed and grievance, with some measure of creed or religion thrown into the mix. In essence, what made individuals become pirates was an exercise into rational choice that included factors such as current living conditions, expected returns from piracy, and the probability of getting away with it. Here, societal approval or enabling environments in the shape of corrupt officials, 'no questions asked' ports and conniving governments certainly played their part. Religion was also a powerful factor behind the decision of individuals or whole groups to become pirates: if God (or Allah) Himself willed it, taking to the sea as a maritime crusader or *ghazi* was not a crime but a sacred duty, and the plunder that could be captured could thus be conceived of as God's reward for the pirate's demonstrated armed piety – the Knights Hospitaller as the implacable enemies of Islam are a telling case in point in this regard. This reasoning kept the corsairing business alive for centuries, even though genuine religious zeal – as opposed to a mostly declaratory one – seems to have waxed and waned over the period.

It also becomes apparent that piracy was not just about ship-to-ship encounters at sea, as it is often depicted in novels and films. As the cases of the Vikings and the Wako demonstrate, large-scale raids could involve dozens of vessels and hundreds or thousands of pirates descending on coastal villages and towns. Such incidents featured among the most violent and brutal of all pirate attacks: in veritable orgies of pillage and rape, 'carnivals of murder and looting',[123] settlements were sacked, plundered and burned, many of their citizens killed in cold blood, and the survivors driven into slavery. Stopping such large-scale raids depended on the resources and resolve of the targeted state – both of which for a variety of reasons were often found to be wanting. Civil war was one; another was the overall fragmentation of power into several smaller principalities that would have been able to offer meaningful resistance had they stood together. Most of the time, defensive measures were passive rather than active due to the absence of a navy. When the targeted state was both able to assemble the naval forces required and had the political will to carry the fight to the pirates' bases, such operations usually culminated in coastal bombardments and amphibious operations against the strongholds, often resulting in the wholesale destruction of coastal villages, whether their inhabitants were guilty of supporting pirates or not, in exactly the same 'carnival of murder and looting' pattern as that typified by the attacks of the pirates themselves.

Finally, it is interesting that, due to common root causes such as harsh living conditions, abject poverty and endemic warfare, piracy manifested itself very similarly in the three maritime regions discussed above – the Mediterranean, the Northern Seas and the Eastern Seas – even though during this period these three piracy hot spots were still fairly isolated from each other. There are some exceptions: some corsairs such as Don Pero Niño occasionally made forays into the North Sea from his main areas of operation in the Mediterranean, while Viking fleets sometimes descended into the Mediterranean from the north. Nevertheless, all possible forms of piracy emerged on their own in these waters, from the ad hoc part-time pirates who normally went about their business as fishermen but sporadically attacked vessels weaker than theirs, to organised pirate fleets – the Saracens in the Mediterranean, the Vikings in the north and the Wako in the east. Thus, although it is fair to say that piracy was already a global phenomenon, it had truly local origins. This is a point that should be borne in mind during our discussion of the next period, the years 1500 to 1914. In this period, we will see piracy – especially Western piracy – going global.

PART II

The Rise of European Sea Power, 1500 to 1914

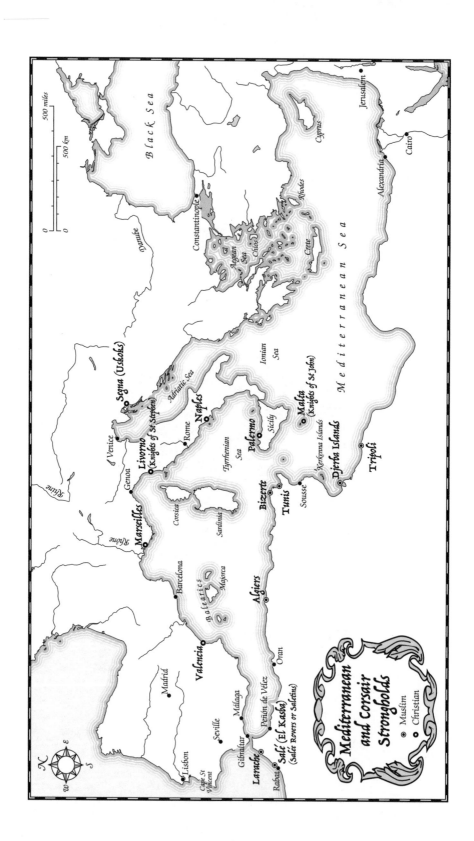

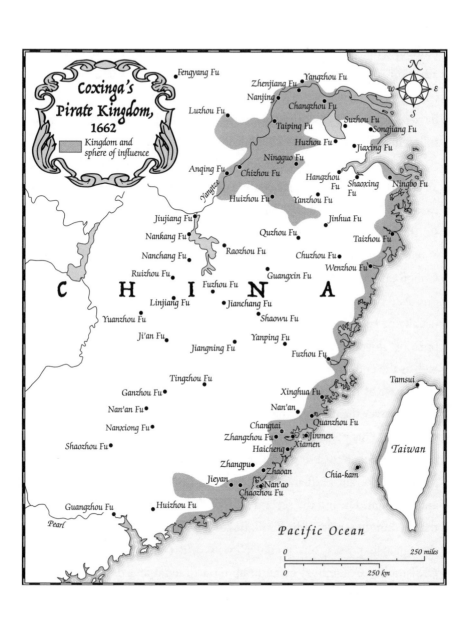

Coxinga's
Pirate Kingdom,
1662

Kingdom and
sphere of influence

Fengyang Fu

Zhenjiang Fu · Yangzhou Fu

Nanjing · Changzhou Fu

Luzhou Fu

Taiping Fu · Suzhou Fu

Huzhou Fu · Songjiang Fu

Ningguo Fu · Jiaxing Fu

Anqing Fu · Chizhou Fu

Hangzhou Fu · Shaoxing Fu · Ningbo Fu

Huizhou Fu · Yanzhou Fu

Jiujiang Fu · Jinhua Fu

Nankang Fu · Quzhou Fu · Taizhou Fu

Nanchang Fu · Raozhou Fu · Chuzhou Fu · Wenzhou Fu

Ruizhou Fu · Guangxin Fu

C H I N A

Fuzhou Fu

Linjiang Fu · Jianchang Fu

Yuanzhou Fu · Shaowu Fu

Ji'an Fu · Yanping Fu

Jiangning Fu · Fuzhou Fu

Tingzhou Fu · Tamsui

Ganzhou Fu · Xinghua Fu

Nan'an Fu · Nan'an

Nanxiong Fu · Changtai · Quanzhou Fu

Zhangzhou Fu · Jinmen

Shaozhou Fu · Haicheng · Xiamen · Taiwan

Zhangpu

Jieyan · Zhaoan

Nan'ao · Chia-kam

Guangzhou Fu · Huizhou Fu · Chaozhou Fu

Pearl

Yangtze

Pacific Ocean

0   250 miles

0   250 km

Seeking a Merry Life and a Short One

It is important to recall that being a pirate or a privateer was a dangerous occupation, with the chance of dying much higher than striking it rich. Although there probably was at least some vague romanticism or love of adventure involved, a far more mundane set of push-and-pull factors was usually at work when individuals decided to become pirates. This, as we have seen, was the case in the years 700–1500, and holds true also for the following four centuries which we will explore in this section.

The 'pull' factor is easy to explain: the hope of striking it rich, despite all attendant risks of an early death. Indeed, most of those who chose this career path would probably have agreed with pirate captain 'Black Bart' Bartholomew Roberts – born in Casnewydd Bach, Wales on 17 May 1682, and who died before his fortieth year in a shipwreck off Cape Lopez, Gabon on 10 February 1722 – who quipped that 'a merry life and a short one shall be my motto'.[1] The 'push' factors are more variegated, but can usually be summarised as 'harsh living conditions': the individual misery born of abject poverty, exploitation, humiliation and unemployment as well as the endemic wars that resulted in the suffering of whole societies. In the case of the Mediterranean, for instance, the entire trade system had boomed over the close of the fifteenth and the first half of the sixteenth centuries. This period of prosperity had led many industries to rapidly expand, which in turn resulted in the emergence of a highly mobile work-force of itinerant craftsmen crisscrossing Europe looking for lucrative employment. During the second half of the sixteenth century, however, the seemingly never-ending inflationary influx of gold and silver from the Spanish possessions in the New World ('discovered' in 1492 by Christopher Columbus) brought about a gradual and disastrous weakening of the economy which went hand in hand with a steep rise in prices. The consequence was once again a rapid increase in the ranks of the desperately poor.[2] Desperate times call for desperate measures – as economic conditions worsened in the Mediterranean, banditry on land, and piracy at sea, were once more on the rise.

A peasant in seventeenth-century England fared no better than one living in the Mediterranean, albeit for slightly different reasons: under a feudal system, peasants were treated like cattle or worse, living at the mercy of the arbitrary justice meted out by their feudal lord – hence, he (and occasionally she) must have mulled over the same question again and again: is there nothing better than this? Why toil away for about £1 per year when a successful pirate could make an astounding £1,500–£4,000?[3] 'As the laws stood, you would hang for stealing a pound out of a man's pocket. So why not steal a fortune?'[4] English peasants – as well as their Dutch, French, Flemish and German peers – were usually well aware of the amazing treasures that were there for the taking with just a little daring and a little luck – which they learned about from itinerant storytellers, and, from the sixteenth century onwards, from pedlars selling pamphlets and ballads to those literate few who were able to read. These rather tall stories told of the fabulous riches obtained by courageous daredevils from Spanish, Portuguese or Indian treasure ships – ships laden with chests full of gold and silver, sacks of diamonds, rubies, emeralds and pearls.[5] And those living in coastal areas could even listen to the seafarers themselves. Again, why toil away for precious little, when fabulous riches could be won somewhere over the horizon with some pluck and a fair wind?

On the other side of the world, the lives of landless peasants in the days of the Qing dynasty (1644–1911) also offer plentiful examples of harsh living conditions. Such peasants, who worked the land of powerful landowners, were permanently haunted by the spectre of unemployment, low wages, rising living costs and, due to rapid population growth, stiff competition for jobs, which resulted in a race to the bottom as far as income was concerned.[6] Unsurprisingly given their daily struggle for survival, there was always the temptation to turn to criminality – which for coastal people often meant becoming a pirate, either on a part-time basis outside the fishing season or full-time in the hope of escaping poverty once and for all. The sight of wealthy merchants strutting along the quayside, and of rich cargoes being loaded on and off sea-going vessels, would have made it abundantly clear that there was ample opportunity for plunder. The life of the Chinese pirate queen Zheng Yi Sao (1775–1844) is one example of the rags-to-riches career many of these working poor dreamt about. She eked out a living as a prostitute in Canton before marrying pirate leader Zheng Yi (1765–1807) in 1801, with whom she set up a powerful pirate confederation of 40,000–60,000 pirates, who sailed in 400 junks.[7] Her contemporary, the pirate lord Wushi Er (1765–1810), was a petty thief before he joined a pirate gang. When he was finally captured in 1810, he was in command of a pirate fleet of more than a hundred ships.[8]

As in the case of Zheng Yi Sao, it was occasionally coincidence, rather than greed or grievance, that set individuals on a pathway to piracy. Another female pirate, Anne Bonny (1698–1782), is one such example. Born Anne Cormac in 1698 in County Cork, Ireland, she moved with her family to the Caribbean and married a certain James Bonny, a sailor who dabbled in piracy – albeit without much success: he has been described as 'a young Fellow, who belong'd to the Sea, and was not worth a Groat; which provoked [Anne's] Father to such a Degree, that he turn'd her out of Doors'.[9] This rather unhappy marriage, however, proved crucial to the path of Anne Bonny's future life. The couple found their way to the port of Nassau in the Bahamas, where Anne met a far more successful pirate in the shape of Captain John Rackham (1682–1720), also known as 'Calico Jack'. They eloped while Rackham was enjoying a general pardon for pirates issued by King George I. When Rackham grew restless once more, Bonny followed him to sea and became a pirate. Her contemporary, Mary Read (c. 1690–1721), had an adventurous career as a sailor on a warship and then as a soldier in Flanders, always disguised as a man, before boarding a ship bound for the West Indies to seek her fortune there. When English pirates captured her vessel, she turned pirate without hesitation. As fate would have it, Mary Read eventually ended up on the very same vessel on which Bonny and Rackham were sailing.[10]

Coincidence was also at work in the case of Martin Wintergerst (c. 1670–?), a baker from southern Germany. Obviously a restless soul, Wintergerst ended up in Venice in 1689 having made his way there as an itinerant craftsman. Although he quickly found work in a German-owned bakery, Wintergerst did not really like the profession, and he left to work in a tavern owned by a fellow German from Nuremberg, where he became fluent in Italian. As chance would have it, here Wintergerst came to the attention of a Dutch privateer captain, who persuaded him to join his vessel of 46 guns and 180 men as a translator. Thus began Wintergerst's colourful career as a sailor on board privateers, pirate ships, warships and merchantmen – a career that lasted no less than twenty years and saw him sail the length and breadth of the Mediterranean under various flags, venturing out into the North Sea and, finally, voyaging to the South China Sea aboard vessels of the Dutch East India Company. Somehow, against all the odds given his dangerous life, he even made it back to his hometown, where he spent his last years writing his memoirs (he was one of the few commoners who did so: normally, memoirs were penned by the high and mighty either personally or at their behest).[11]

The case of the Spanish corsair Alonso de Contreras (1582–1641) is yet another example of the role of coincidence in the adoption of the pirate's life. Had he followed his mother's advice he would have been a silversmith in Madrid. Instead, having stabbed another boy to death to avenge an insult, he fled from prosecution by joining the Spanish infantry at the tender age of fourteen or fifteen, finding himself a little later in Palermo as the page of a Catalan infantry captain. When his company was ordered to participate in an amphibious operation, Contreras got his first taste of battle at sea on board the flagship of the Sicilian squadron: 'It was here that I first felt cannonballs whistling past my ears as I stood in front of my captain carrying a shield and his gilded lance.'[12] The following year, he went on two cruises along the coasts of the Levant as a soldier on board a galley of the Knights Hospitaller, during which he learned the art of navigation by observing and asking the navigators endless questions.[13]

Contreras gradually became a professional seafarer, working his way up from soldier to become one of the most successful corsairs of his time.

Problems at home at a young age were likewise the main reason why French buccaneer captain Louis Le Golif (*c.* 1640–?) ended up as a professional seafarer. Known as 'Borgnefesse' or 'Half-arse' (a bullet had destroyed one of his buttocks), Le Golif, like Contreras, came from a modest background. His parents made him join a seminary but his sexual appetite got him into trouble very quickly and made him realise that an ecclesiastical career was not for him. At an early age, he left both his family (whom he never saw again) and France on a ship bound for Tortuga in the West Indies, there to become an indentured labourer of the French West India Company for three years to pay for his passage. After he was bought by a planter, who turned out to be a 'most cruel and avaricious man',[14] Le Golif spent eight months on Tortuga under slavery-like conditions before escaping and becoming a buccaneer.[15]

Alexandre Exquemelin (*c.* 1645–1707) also stumbled into buccaneering via a stint as an indentured labourer. He vividly describes his eventful 1666 voyage to Tortuga in the West Indies on board the twenty-eight-gun French ship *St Jean*, and his work, akin to slavery, on the plantations there.[16] Luckily for Exquemelin, his cruel first master sold him to a surgeon who treated him well and set him free after just one year. Not mincing his words, he describes his next step, taken sometime during 1669: 'Being now at liberty, though like unto Adam, when he was first Created by the hands of his maker, that is naked, and destitute, of all human necessaries, nor knowing how to get my living, I determined to enter into the wicked Order of the Pirates, or Robbers at Sea.'[17] Put bluntly, he became a buccaneer. He stayed with them until 1672, and later wrote his famous account *The Buccaneers of America* – one of the most authoritative insights into the world of such pirates. What is obvious in all these cases is that chance events presented themselves and were duly seized upon by these men and women – others would perhaps have chosen different paths.

Tars, Gents and Traders

If the idea of becoming a sea robber was sometimes quite an attractive one for landlubbers, then it must have been even more appealing for sailors. In late sixteenth-century England, for three months' work an experienced sailor on board a Royal Navy warship could expect to earn about £1 10s, while a privateer could bring in a whopping £15 or more.[18] Unsurprisingly, experienced sailors, who formed a marginalised underclass of their own on the fringes of 'respectable' land-based society, made up the bulk of recruits to privateers and pirate ships alike. The career of the early seventeenth-century English pirate and corsair John Ward (c. 1552–1622) is a case in point. Born in obscurity, he worked as an inshore fisherman off the coast of Kent before joining a privateer. Ward rose through the ranks, eventually being rewarded with a captaincy. When James I revoked all privateering commissions in 1603, Ward had no choice but to join the Royal Navy as a lowly deckhand. With his best years behind him (he was by then about fifty years old), and unused to the navy's harsh discipline, he turned pirate at the first opportunity, banding together with a small group of like-minded sailors to steal an unmanned but ready-to-sail barge anchored in the harbour of Portsmouth.[19]

Just as in the centuries before 1500, it was not only the 'downtrodden' who decided to become pirates to escape (relative) poverty. Many of Queen Elizabeth I's 'gentlemen adventurers' were lured into piratical ventures as a way to finance their lavish and extremely expensive courtly lives. Some of them, such as Sir Walter Raleigh (c. 1552–29 October 1618), were continuously in the Crown's debt, while others constantly teetered on the brink of bankruptcy and disgrace, depending on the financial success or failure of their expeditions. Raleigh's contemporary Sir Martin Frobisher (c. 1535–94) provides a good example of the latter.[20] One biographer's unflattering portrait destroys the man in a single scathing sentence: 'Although well born he was uncouth and only semi-literate, and his early career as an inept, low-rent pirate . . . should have ended on the gallows.'[21] Nevertheless, Frobisher's powerful friends and protectors at court saw to it that he was put in command of a small squadron tasked with hunting pirates in the Irish Sea – an unsuccessful case of pirate-turned-pirate hunter (on which more below) – and was later tasked with finding the Northwest Passage. Undertaking three voyages between 1576 and 1578, Frobisher failed to find the passage, and the allegedly gold-bearing ore which he brought back in great quantity turned out to be worthless iron pyrite; but he at least explored the coasts of Baffin Island (one of its south-western bays was later named Frobisher Bay in his honour). Somehow, these scientific exploits, plus his gallant action in the fight against the Spanish Armada in 1588 (for which he was knighted), helped to paper over the lack of success – financial and nautical – of his expeditions, as well as his shady dealings connected to the value-less iron ore. Sir Francis Drake (c. 1540–28 January 1596), on the other hand, was a paragon of success. Several successful expeditions made him the second highest-earning pirate of all time, with an estimated personal wealth of about £90 million ($115 million) in today's money.[22] On top of that, his successful expeditions also greatly facilitated his rise from humble beginnings in a feudal society not necessarily characterised by upward social mobility. His motto – Sic parvis magna ('Greatness from small beginnings') – explicitly referred to this meteoric ascent.

It was not only the English nobility who dabbled in piracy, however: merchants did so as well. The boundaries between licit trade and illicit smuggling-cum-piracy were rather blurred: given the opportunity, a merchantman could swiftly turn into a pirate ship. In 1592, a certain Captain Thomas White, for instance, on the homeward leg of an until then perfectly legitimate trading voyage from London to the Barbary Coast, thought nothing of capturing two large Spanish vessels he encountered, even though he met stiff resistance from their crews. The booty of quicksilver, wine, gilded missals and even a number of papal bulls was worth about £20,000, or £2.6 million ($3.4 million) in today's money.[23] Such convenient encounters aside, some of the more enterprising merchants could be tempted to equip their own expeditions. It can even be said of the privateering ventures of the times of Elizabeth I that merchants were the most important social group of those interested in privateering or even pirating – especially when it came to financing such ventures.[24] At roughly the same time, and on the other side of the world, a Ming official sighed that merchants and pirates were basically the same people: 'When trade is permitted, pirates become merchants. When trade is prohibited, merchants convert to pirates.'[25]

A sense of adventure rather than greed or grievance occasionally also enticed some gentlemen to go a-pirating. Stede Bonnet (c. 1688–1718) was one such figure. Well educated and bookish, he was a wealthy landowner on Barbados and a major in the local militia, living a rather peaceful and respectable life until he suddenly decided to become a pirate in 1717, probably out of sheer boredom. He did so in style, buying a suitable vessel that he named *Revenge* and hiring an experienced crew which he paid well. Unfortunately for him, he lacked the one essential quality required for a successful pirate captain: Bonnet was not a natural leader of men, and his crew quickly abandoned him to join the pirate captain Edward Teach, better known as Blackbeard, who, 'after finding that Bonnet knew nothing of a maritime Life, with the Consent of his own Men, put in another Captain, one Richards, to command Bonnet's Sloop, and took the Major on aboard his own Ship'.[26] Now reduced to the status of Blackbeard's more or less graciously tolerated guest, Bonnet had the good sense to accept a pardon and walk away from piracy in early 1718. Then he suddenly changed his mind, going on the account again under the pseudonym 'Captain Thomas'.[27] This turned out to be a very bad decision: in August 1718, the pirate hunter Colonel William Rhett captured his ship after a short but furious battle. Bonnet survived the fighting, but was swiftly tried and hanged.

Other adventurers fared better, including some individuals nowadays more renowned for their contributions to science than to piracy, such as William Dampier (1651–1715). Today better known as an explorer (he was the first person to circumnavigate the globe three times) and a naturalist who visited the Galapagos Islands around 150 years before Charles

Darwin, Dampier began life as a supervisor on a Jamaican sugar planta-
tion, then turned buccaneer, participating in many piratical ventures along
the coasts of the Spanish Main (that is, the Spanish colonial empire in
Central and South America). Although he later declared that he was
'with them but not one of them',[28] his claim to have been what in social
science is called a 'non-participant observer' is hardly convincing. Rather,
Dampier's career as an explorer, hydrographer and naturalist was always
intertwined with piracy; like his contemporaries of a less scientific incli-
nation, he was not averse to taking part in plunder and pillage when the
occasion arose. In December 1709, at the end of his seafaring career, when
he was navigator and pilot of Captain Woodes Roger's South Seas expedition, he even discovered the treasure ship of his dreams in the shape of
a richly laden Spanish galleon on the way from Manila to Acapulco: the
Nuestra Señora de la Encarnación y Disengaño, which turned out to be
worth a whopping £150,000 – or about £20 million ($26 million) in today's
money. *Sic parvis magna* could have been Dampier's motto too, though he
had much less in common with Drake than he had with Darwin or Cook:
his own two commands, first of HMS *Roebuck* in 1699–1701, then of HMS
St George in 1703–4, can be considered 'abject failures' due to his poor
leadership;[29] like Stede Bonnet, a natural leader of men he was not.

Piracy Brings No Disgrace

Just as no stigma was attached to the piratical raids of the Vikings, so too
were the Malay pirates of the eighteenth and nineteenth centuries far
from stigmatised; on the contrary, they were seen as highly respected
members of their society, and the most successful of them were even
praised as local heroes for their daring exploits, as befitted their status as
warriors. This sentiment is nicely encapsulated in the opinion of an
early-nineteenth century ruler of Johore and Singapore, Sultan Hussein
Shah (r. 1819–24), who asserted that 'piracy brings no disgrace'.[30] A very
similar view was expressed by Captain Charles Hunter of the Royal

Navy, who commented on Datu Laut ('Sea Lord'), a highly respected Iranun[31] lord of the mid-nineteenth century, as follows:

> In his own view he was no criminal; his ancestors from generation to generation had followed the same profession. In fact, the [Iranuns] considered cruising as the most honourable of professions, the only one which a gentleman and a chief could pursue, and would be deeply offended if told they were but robbers on a larger scale ... Notwithstanding his profession, Laut was a gentleman.[32]

Whether these indigenous raiders were 'bloodthirsty pirates' or indeed 'honourable local heroes' conducting warfare on behalf of a legitimate ruler pretty much depends on the perspective one adopts. Seen from a Western point of view, they were clearly pirates: they infested waters which now belonged to various European colonial empires – those of Britain, the Netherlands and Spain. From a regional point of view, however, it was the Europeans who were the pirates: true, they first came as explorers and traders, but they quickly morphed into invaders who plundered and robbed wherever they went, mercilessly destroying local cultures and supplanting them with their own in the process.[33]

When it comes to 'doing the right thing', religion was a strong motivator. In the medieval period the Christian–Muslim us-versus-them dichotomy was a powerful argument justifying the business of corsairing, or any other acts of sea raiding wherever Muslim and Christian zones of influence met. Later, with European ascendancy and hegemony, this dichotomy still existed; what was new was a sense of us-versus-them emerging within Christianity itself after the onset of the Reformation. For instance, in Elizabethan times, sea raiding quickly became associated with 'patriotic' Protestantism,[34] simply because the enemy – Spain – was Catholic and 'Papist'. Francis Drake's hatred for the Spanish (in whose eyes he was a pirate and the English 'Lutheran heretics') was certainly genuine.[35] Drake's undoubted prowess as a sea raider combined with his inveterate hatred for all things Spanish and Catholic made it particularly easy to portray him as the quintessential Protestant hero fighting for plucky little England, a sea-going David against the Goliath of Spain;[36] he was certainly presented as such as early as 1681 by Samuel Johnson, his first biographer. Obviously, becoming a pirate could even end up enhancing one's reputation as a pious and devout member of society.

The reverse, however, was also true: in a pious society such as seventeenth-century England, to abandon one's religion and, by extension, one's own country to become a pirate for the 'other' was most emphatically not the right thing to do, as in the case of the English corsairs who preyed on merchant ships (including English ones) in the Mediterranean in the service of the Muslim rulers of Algiers, Tripoli and Tunis. It was not so much what they did that put them beyond the pale, but for whom they did it – after all, and according to contemporary opinion, they fought for Muslim powers who were the avowed enemy of Christendom (no matter whether Protestant or Catholic), and frequently also the bitter enemies of England. For these 'apostate pirates', there were no mitigating circumstances, and often not even a pardon if they ever dared to think of returning to their countries of birth.[37] In the case of corsair and renegade John Ward, his conversion to Islam in 1608 in effect cemented his reputation as an 'arch pirate', and was also the reason why he was denied a royal pardon by King James I, even though he was prepared to pay quite a princely sum for the honour.

Despite the existence of genuine religious fervour, framing the conflicts mentioned above in religious terms alone would again be far too simplistic: powerful economic motives played a major role here as well; and with regard to political alliances, it is fair to say that they tended to cut across this supposed religious abyss with consummate ease as and when required. This flexible approach towards religion as well as nationality is evident in the practice of the Muslim Barbary Coast principalities of Algiers, Tripoli and Tunis. As well as Christian and Jewish renegades from every corner of the far-flung Ottoman Empire, these countries also routinely employed outsiders as captains of their corsairs, whether they converted to Islam or not. Since Barbary Coast corsairing was usually expressed in terms of a maritime equivalent of jihad, which was meant to be waged by the Muslim faithful against the Christian infidels, the practice of subcontracting it to exactly those infidels is even more astounding. And John Ward was far from exceptional: of the twenty-two corsairs who operated out of Algiers in 1660, sixteen were Christian apostates.[38] Piracy in the Mediterranean 'reveals some of the most extraordinary cases of mixed identity: corsairs from as far away as Scotland and England who, outwardly at least, accepted Islam and preyed on the shipping of the nation from which they came'.[39] All expressed piety notwithstanding, even the corsairs in the Mediterranean were driven mainly by greed. Nevertheless, framing these corsairing ventures in religious terms, and thus elevating political and economic interest to a transcendental clash between 'good' and 'evil', greatly helped rulers to take the moral high ground, from which it was easy to defend their actions while vilifying those of the enemy.

With the onset of colonialism and imperialism, another factor was added: the Christian colonisers' feeling of cultural superiority, being 'modern' and 'civilised' as opposed to the 'backward' and 'uncivilised' soon-to-be-conquered natives. Care is thus necessary when examining contemporary Western sources: they frequently utilise and even overemphasise religion as a factor in the process of 'othering' and as a justification of the Western colonisers' right to conquer and rule – a narrative that fed into the theme of 'us' (honest European traders) versus 'them' (bloodthirsty, savage Malay pirates). Joseph Conrad's novel *The Rescue*[40] provides an illustration of this: 'Conrad, through his not so subtle process of negation, which unduly stresses Muslim religious zeal and fanaticism, makes the "Illanun" seem even more dangerous – as militant Islam served to prolong and nurture mutual hostility in the face of western progress.'[41] By depicting the Iranun in such a way, it also became easier to frame them as pirates, thus denying them the legitimacy they might have had when acting on behalf of a ruler – as many Malay so-called pirates actually did. A piracy definition that until the 1970s appeared in the *Oxford English Dictionary* makes this 'us/civilised-versus-them/uncivilised' bias crystal clear: here, piracy was defined as '[robbery] and depredation on the sea or navigable rivers, or by descent from the sea upon the coast, by persons not holding a commission *from a civilised state*'.[42] This qualification explains why Western maritime actors in the pay of non-Western states, such as the English-born Tunisian corsair John Ward, and non-Western maritime actors such as the Indian admiral Kanhoji Angre (see below, pp. 128–30) were considered pirates and criminals, whereas from a local point of view they were the equivalents of either privateers or naval officers.

The Lure of Easy Money

For piracy really to thrive, to grow into a lucrative business attracting even merchants and members of the nobility, more than the approval of society at large was required. What was crucial for a flourishing pirate business was at the very least 'a nod and a wink' from corrupt officials, if not the state, as had been the case for the pirates of the Middle Ages. What was different now was the rapid expansion of the various Spanish, Portuguese, English, Dutch and French colonial empires, which made this (semi-)official connivance even easier than before. This was mainly due to two factors: first, the now truly enormous booty that could be gained by capturing Spanish or Portuguese treasure ships laden to their gunwales with gold, silver, jewels, silk and spices, or similar treasure ships from India on Hajj (pilgrimage) to the Red Sea and back, or Chinese junks in the East and South China Seas; and, second, the vast distances between imperial centre and colonial periphery. The riches that could be gained in distant waters were worlds apart from the far more mundane booty typical of northern waters: everyday commodities such as fish, salted pork, wine, sugar and the like. Even Elizabeth I succumbed to this 'lure of easy money', as we shall see – no wonder, then, that lower ranks of officialdom did likewise. Nor was this only the case for English officialdom: Dutch and French officials also knew how to feather their nests, while many Spanish and Portuguese officials returned home immensely wealthy. For lower-level officials, this was a high-stakes game, depending on the protection they enjoyed, which might for various reasons be suddenly withdrawn when, for instance, a previously powerful backer lost favour with the Crown. For officials of higher rank, especially for governors, getting rich by taking a slice of the pirates' booty was child's play. For them, the vast distances and the poor communications between the centre of power and the peripheral colonies worked in their favour: what the governments in faraway capitals such as London, Paris, Madrid, Lisbon or The Hague decreed was one thing, and what the local officials actually did was another.

The individual choices and attitudes of local government officials were of paramount interest to maritime raiders: if local powers were favourably inclined towards piracy, a pirate's business was greatly facilitated. The reasons for which appointed governors chose to play their own shady roles with regard to piracy vary, and cannot be reduced to personal greed. While the lazier ones simply did not care about what was going on in their areas of responsibility, many actually feared the very real danger posed by pirates much more than the wrath of a distant government. The military resources at their disposal – regular soldiers, militia and warships – were usually scant (if they existed at all), and not always a match for local pirates. For these officials, it was pretty much a matter of *plata o plomo*: either you take our silver (*plata*), or you will get our lead (*plomo*, in the form of bullets). Furthermore, many of the governors of remote colonies were themselves former pirates. Sir Henry Morgan, for example, ended his illustrious and colourful buccaneering career as lieutenant governor of Jamaica in the second half of the seventeenth century.[43] These pirates-turned-pirate hunters were usually happy to issue commissions to their former comrades without asking questions – as long as a fee was paid; the governor of the French possession Petit-Goâve, Hispaniola, had a habit of providing his captains with blank commissions 'to hand out to anyone they pleased',[44] while the governor of a West Indian island then belonging to Denmark allegedly issued impressive-looking 'privateering commissions', which were in fact only licences for hunting goats and pigs on Hispaniola.[45]

Even in the North Sea, much nearer to European seats of power, governors or feudal lords of small coastal principalities made quick money out of issuing commissions of dubious value. For example, according to Lunsford-Poe, a 'Grave' (Duke) of Ormond in Ireland issued such a document to the Dutch privateer Jan Corneliszoon Knole in the year 1649. Knole's legitimate Dutch commission only permitted him to attack and seize the vessels of Dutch enemies; the Duke of Ormond's commission, however, entitled him to prey on ships along the coast of Dutch Zeeland,[46] which was exactly what he did, promptly attacking and seizing a vessel from Rotterdam. Knole was far from the only privateer who stacked the cards in his favour by accepting another commission from a conveniently uninquisitive party: the more commissions one held, the broader the range of vessels one could legitimately attack. Even had they been inclined to care about legal trifles, most pirates and privateers were illiterate and could not possibly read the conditions and limitations mentioned in their commissions – which helps to explain why the Danish governor of Petit-Goâve could do such a brisk trade selling worthless hunting licences for an island not even under his control: his illiterate customers mistook these impressive-looking documents for privateering commissions.[47]

Against the backdrop of endemic corruption, it is unsurprising that some officials who could not simply hand out fraudulent commissions chose to cross the line in a more obvious way in order to profit from pirates. Usually, they did so by directly aiding and abetting them, as it would nowadays be called in criminal law. In the seventeenth century the aptly named Thomas Crook, justice of the peace and chief officer of the Irish port of Baltimore, openly supplied pirate ships with victuals and other necessities, even entertaining their crews in his house – with the foreseeable effect that other inhabitants of the port also saw it as their right to wheel and deal with the pirates to their hearts' content.[48] It is obvious that in this case, as in many others, the pirates and their supporters on land hailed from a society that saw piracy as a perfectly normal, honest occupation – and probably one far superior to serving a monarch or a government seen as an alien intruder into local affairs. Sir Henry Mainwaring, having himself been a successful pirate before turning pirate hunter for James I, even called Ireland 'the Nursery and Storehouse of Pirates',[49] while his contemporary Lord Falkland, lord deputy of Ireland between 1622 and 1629, opined that Ireland's coasts were favoured by the pirates because there they were 'much more cheaply victualled, much more easily out and in, at and from sea, which lies opener with less impediments of tides and channels'.[50]

Pirate Ports

Many ports in other regions played similar roles. In the Mediterranean, the citizens of the Barbary Coast principalities of Algiers, Tripoli and Tunis depended on piracy and privateering not only for their prosperity but also for their survival as independent entities. For the English pirates harassing Spanish and Portuguese shipping in the Atlantic, the semi-independent Moroccan ports of La Mamora (modern Mehdya) and Salé served as perfect bases where pirates could not only sell their booty but also repair and replenish their ships. On the other side of the Atlantic, the US ports of Charleston, Philadelphia and New York were where some of the real pirates of the Caribbean, for example Captain Kidd, found safe havens, both as bases for their operations and as locations to sell off their loot.

The most famous pirate port of all time, and the backdrop to many pirate stories, films and computer games, was Port Royal, Jamaica. From its founding in 1655 until its destruction in a devastating earthquake less than four decades later in 1692, the port enjoyed a well-earned reputation as a real-life Sodom and Gomorrah, the 'wickedest city in the world'[51] (pious contemporaries would claim its destruction was God's punishment for all the sins committed there). Its close proximity to Spanish settlements in the Caribbean and Central America, as well as to the sea routes used by the Spanish treasure fleets, made Port Royal ideal for piracy and privateering ventures. Its governors' willingness to issue commissions to anybody who could pay the fee, with no questions asked, furthered the port's appeal to all sorts of freebooters, licensed or not.[52] Unsurprisingly, many privateers made Port Royal their home base: in 1670, for example, twenty privateers operated from there, with a combined crew of about twenty thousand men,[53] while many uncommissioned pirate vessels slipped in and out of the port to conduct their own even shadier dealings. Given this brisk and lucrative trade in pillage and plunder, most of the port's inhabitants made their living mainly by catering to pirates' needs. There were arms dealers and armourers ready to replenish pirates' arsenals, victuallers to restock ships' stores, and experienced shipwrights and other specialist marine craftsmen that could quickly return a battered vessel to seaworthiness for another voyage. Furthermore, since all these businesses tended to be exorbitantly expensive, the port also featured a multitude of merchants specialising in turning the pirates' loot and plunder into cash – most of which immediately found its way into the coffers of the port's many inns, taverns, gambling dens and brothels.

Pirate-friendly ports were also to be found in all other piracy-plagued maritime regions. Along the Chinese and Japanese coasts between the sixteenth and nineteenth centuries, many settlements depended solely on doing business with pirates in order to survive, especially in times when maritime trade was officially forbidden. The coastal villages of Fujian and Zhejiang, for example, supported local pirates by providing them with every necessity, and even actively assisted them by producing shot, gunpowder, guns, swords and armour.[54] Many towns and villages in Guangdong, especially those situated in the Pearl River estuary, likewise offered a safe haven to pirates – even though this area, the gateway to the important port city of Canton, was heavily fortified, with a strong imperial army presence.[55] Many of the villagers at least occasionally worked as pirates themselves when the opportunity arose, or when fishing alone did not put enough food on the table. In Japan, a similar situation could be found on the island of Kyushu, whose feudal lords not only actively welcomed pirates[56] but also used them as security guards to protect their own trade. The ports of the Seto Inland Sea between Kyushu and Honshu hosted Japanese as well as Chinese pirate communities, profiting immensely from the trade in contraband goods, mainly sulphur for export and salt-petre for import – the latter an important commodity for the feudal lords and their armies since it was needed to produce high-quality gunpowder.[57]

In the South China Sea, Jolo (part of the Sulu Archipelago) had a reputation as a notorious pirate lair: as the main port and seat of govern-ment of the Sultanate of Sulu, it acted as a clearing house for the selling and buying of illicit goods as well as weapons and ammunition. Port offi-cials also provided invaluable intelligence on maritime traffic in general and on the occasional counter-piracy patrols conducted by the Spanish, Dutch and British colonial powers who had established themselves in the region from the second half of the sixteenth century onwards. Furthermore, Jolo hosted by far the biggest slave market in the area, where captives seized from various locations along the coast of the South China Sea, from the Philippines to Siam (modern Thailand), were either sold or ransomed. Further to the west, Singapore and the nearby Riau Archipelago fulfilled a similar function. Eyewitness reports from British observers and from at least one Malay trader who had been held captive on Pulau Galang[58] in the Riau Archipelago in 1836 leave no doubt as to the nature of the 'goods' exchanged on the island: mostly arms and ammunition, slaves and stolen merchandise. Any signs of cultivation and agriculture were notably absent, which led British observers to believe that all the male inhabitants of the 4,000-strong island population were full-time pirates.[59] It greatly helped the pirates based in Singapore and the

Riau Archipelago that they operated in an ill-defined and contested space between British and Dutch spheres of influence – just as those based in Jolo operated in an equally ill-defined zone between the Spanish, Dutch and British colonial empires. In a sense, the pirates were falling through the cracks of the international colonial system, cracks created by mutual distrust and the difficulty of arranging multinational patrols.

Of all these eastern pirate lairs there was, however, only one comparable in size and ill-repute to Port Royal, and that was the port of Macao. Macao, a peninsula in the Pearl River estuary near Hong Kong, had been occupied by the Portuguese in 1557 and served as an important base for their trade with both China and Japan. What allowed this port to become such an important pirate lair was the peculiar jurisdictional arrangement to which it was subject: although the territory itself was under Portuguese administration, Macao and its Chinese inhabitants were still subject to Chinese law, as the Portuguese had not conquered Macao but only leased it, first from the Ming and then from the Qing dynasties. Furthermore, the Portuguese were very much in the minority: in 1640, for example, they numbered just 1,200 souls out of a population of 26,000.[60] Even better for the criminal elements attracted by this port, the Portuguese port officials were mainly interested in their own private trade, and made only token efforts to suppress the port's endemic crime. This unique combination of a divided jurisdiction, a lacklustre judicial approach by the Portuguese and the fact that criminals could evade the Portuguese criminal justice system simply by crossing over to the mainland or to adjacent islands such as Lantau in effect guaranteed Macao's position as the Port Royal of the east. Like its Caribbean equivalent, Macao also teemed with inns, taverns, brothels and gambling houses, but also opium dens – the latter not to be found in Port Royal, whose pirates preferred rum and grog[61] – and of course with no-questions-asked markets where pirates could sell illicit goods, buy weapons and ammunition, acquire intelligence about ship movements and recruit new crews.[62] Moreover, Macao was one of the places where the large pirate federations, for example that of Zheng

Yi Sao, openly operated their own 'tax bureaus'[63] for the collection of protection money from shippers who had to sail through 'their' waters, and to extract ransoms from the relatives of those wealthy individuals unfortunate enough to have been kidnapped by them.[64]

The Pirate Queen and her Courtiers

However, it would be over-simplistic to blame the comparatively low-level officials in the service of various empires, or those empires' far-flung ports, for enabling piracy by ignoring or profiting from it. Just as in the period covered in Part I, the state itself often turned a blind eye when it suited it – which is why even high nobility felt invited to participate in piracy and privateering. Queen Elizabeth I of England's treatment of Sir Francis Drake after his circumnavigation of the globe (1577–80), during which he had captured several Spanish treasure ships, is a case in point. Having taken note of the enormous amount of booty she would get – 'as great or greater than her entire annual revenue from tax and crown lands combined'[65] – she happily declared Drake to be 'her pirate', thus retroactively sanctioning activities for which he had not had a valid commission. Commenting on this (mal)practice, a Venetian ambassador of the times scathingly stated that

> nothing is thought to have enriched the English or done so much to allow many individuals to amass the wealth they are known to possess as the wars with the Spaniards in the times of Queen Elizabeth. All were permitted to go privateering and they plundered not only Spaniards but all others indifferently, so that they enriched themselves by a constant stream of booty.[66]

His sentiment is shared by some historians, who argue that during Elizabeth's reign, England turned from a nation of pirates into a pirate nation, or even a 'piratocracy', led by Elizabeth as the 'pirate queen'.[67]

Not that the queen had much choice in siding with successful pirates: when she acceded to the throne on 17 November 1558, she found the state coffers empty due to the profligacy of her illustrious predecessors Henry VIII, Edward VI and Mary I. It should be emphasised, however, that for her 'gentlemen adventurers', sheer luck and being in the right place at the right time also played a major role in determining their fate. While a 'state-sanctioned' pirate was at sea, the political constellation at home could change to his detriment, which meant that returning with a prize – even a very rich one – seized in legally murky circumstances was a high-stakes gamble: for some, the favour of the monarch beckoned; for others, the gallows awaited. Drake always got it right, judiciously appearing at court only after having established in which direction the political wind was blowing. Drake's contemporary Sir Walter Raleigh, on the other hand, is an example of those who, getting their timing wrong, were made scapegoats after political changes or crises at court, and were eventually hanged or beheaded as pirates. Unlike Drake, Raleigh was neither quite a political animal nor a successful businessman (he constantly teetered on the brink of bankruptcy) nor a charming entertainer, and was thus nobody's favourite at court.[68] No wonder then that he was thrown into the Tower both by Elizabeth I (albeit only for two months between June and August 1592 for marrying one of her ladies-in-waiting without her permission) and by her successor James I, who had him imprisoned there for no less than thirteen years between 1603 and 1616 for plotting against him – a crime that usually warranted a sentence of death. Rather ironically, Raleigh was finally beheaded on 29 October 1618 on the demand of Count Gondomar, the Spanish ambassador to London, for attacking Spanish settlements, chief among them the town of Santo Tomé de Guyana, in 1617–18 during his second expedition in search of the gold of the fabled El Dorado – the expected vast profits of the venture being the reason he was released from the Tower in the first place.[69] Unfortunately for Raleigh, he found neither El Dorado nor gold, and so – unlike Drake, who had also attacked Spanish settlements and Spanish treasure ships without proper sanction but at least returned with a massive amount of plunder – there were no mitigating circumstances.

The constant stream of valuable booty explains the widespread practice of turning a blind eye to the exact circumstances under which a rich prize had been acquired – a practice starting at the level of harbour masters and town officials, and going all the way up to the monarch, with only a few laudable exceptions. Bending the law in order to render legal a dubious but rich prize further contributed to the blurring of the lines between privateering and piracy, adding yet another shade of grey in the shape of 'retroactively sanctioned' piracy. The need for a continuous influx of booty was also the reason why the government of the Dutch Republic was willing, when advantageous, to overlook the legal differences between privateering and piracy, and why it usually considered them 'points along a continuum'[70] and not polar opposites. In a similar vein, and with essentially the same rationale, Elizabethan England had no moral qualms about using 'that raffish instrument of foreign policy, the privateer'[71] when it suited the national interest – however defined in the context of ever-shifting alliances. One could always wash one's hands of the privateers if needs be, or simply deny that they were in any way connected to official policy – a principle still used in international politics and known as 'plausible deniability'.

Raffish Instruments of Foreign Policy

The costs inflicted on the enemy by privateers and pirates used as plausibly deniable instruments of foreign policy could be quite staggering. For example, from 1568 to 1648, during the Dutch Revolt and the wider Eighty Years' War, the Dutch Republic suffered immensely from the depredations of Spanish, Portuguese and, especially, Dunkirk-based pirates and privateers. Dunkirk until 1646 still belonged to the Spanish Netherlands, serving as a forward operating base from which the Spanish could harass Dutch merchant shipping and fishing – so much so that the hard-pressed Dutch nicknamed Dunkirk the 'Algiers and Tunis of the North', a threat to Dutch maritime interests akin to that posed by the Barbary corsairs. Between 1629 and 1638, regular warships and privateers operating out of Dunkirk seized about 1,880 mainly Dutch vessels with a combined tonnage of 209,448 tons, and between 1625 and 1637 sunk 533 Dutch fishing vessels.[72] Privateers from Dunkirk were not the only problem for the Dutch, however: during the three Anglo-Dutch Wars of 1652–4, 1665–7 and 1781–4, they also suffered crippling ship losses through the activities of English privateers. The numbers speak for themselves: between 1,000 and 1,700 English privateering vessels preyed upon Dutch shipping during the first war, 522 during the second, and about 500 during the third.[73] During the Second Anglo-Dutch War, English privateers even temporarily seized the Dutch-held Caribbean islands of Saba, Sint Eustatius and Tobago. Privateers posed a very real threat, and were far more than just a nuisance.

Economic wars of attrition at sea were a straightforward exercise during wartime, conducted by well-established regular navies as well as by privateers and pirates. In times of peace, however, navies were officially out of the picture. The practice of issuing commissions against a former enemy, however, was rarely seen as a sufficient cause for a resumption of hostilities; thus, ongoing privateering was frequently ignored, with the effect that the regular wars continued as 'guerrilla wars at sea' even during peacetime.[74] The relentless waves of privateers and pirates unleashed against a former enemy was basically – in Clausewitzian terms – a 'continuation of war by other means'. When Elizabeth I dispatched the likes of Drake or Raleigh on missions against the Spanish Main (missions which from the outset were only very thinly disguised pirate raids), she could be confident that the Spanish response would fall short of open war and be limited to local armed resistance in the targeted regions, usually accompanied by diplomatic demarches in London:

Soldiers of fortune like Drake or Raleigh were ideal weapons. For a start they were flexible. If they brought home treasure it filled

Elizabeth's coffers and diminished the [Spanish] imperial war chest. If they failed or provoked hostility they could be written off as common criminals who acted without any kind of authority. And their hostility could be turned on and off like a tap, depending on England's relationship with Spain.[75]

Similar guerrilla wars at sea could also be found in the waters of the South and East China Seas. Here, the continuous squabbles between European colonial powers accompanied by their equally continuous meddling in regional affairs was one of the main causes leading to the emergence of large-scale piracy in response to European interference. The greed of the European colonial powers trading in the South China Sea turned the Iranun into some of the most fearsome pirates in history:

From time immemorial outside commerce with the Archipelago had been in the hands of the Chinese . . . Then came the Portuguese, and after them the Dutch, who, bent on securing the trade for themselves alone, created a system of monopolies, and by treaties with the Malay rulers were able to command the produce at their own rates and so to undersell the Chinese [so] that in time the junks could compete no longer and came no more.[76]

The meddling of outsiders in the affairs of regional political systems was definitely a major factor in the emergence of large-scale piracy. In the South China Sea and its microcosm of sultanates and chiefdoms, for example, all that was needed to tip the local balance of power and to trigger a new wave of maritime raiding was the arrival of an enterprising and adventurous Western skipper with a consignment of modern Western weapons to be sold to the highest bidder.[77]

This meddling in regional affairs was made even worse by the habit of some of the regional powers of the day of employing European adventurers mostly as soldiers, and especially as gunners, but also as ministers, governors and port officials. In Siam (modern Thailand), for example, King Narai (r. 1656–88) made Constantine Phaulkon, a Greek adventurer and former employee of the East India Company (EIC), his prime counsellor in around 1675. Phaulkon, always looking for (European) allies, elevated some of his old EIC friends to high positions – including the Englishmen Samuel White, who was appointed harbourmaster of the port of Mergui (modern Myeik, Burma, at that time Siam's most important hub for the trade with India), Samuel's younger brother George White, who became an admiral of the Siamese fleet, and Richard Burnaby, who was made governor of Mergui.[78] Apart from milking their lucrative positions for all they were worth, Samuel White and Richard Burnaby also went on pirate raids, ostensibly as privateers on behalf of the king – not that Narai knew about that. The king also had no idea that their activities nearly triggered a war between Siam and the powerful EIC (whose fortified headquarters, Fort St George, lay across the Bay of Bengal in Madras), the *casus belli* being the fact that most of the cargo seized by Samuel White's well-armed frigate *Resolution* actually belonged to the company. In June 1687, the president of the EIC in Madras, Elihu Yale, dispatched a frigate and a corvette to Mergui with a summons and an ultimatum: Samuel White was ordered to explain himself in Madras, while Narai (who was unaware of the enfolding crisis in this far corner of his kingdom, and never saw the ultimatum) was given sixty days to pay for the stolen cargoes. Instead of doing as asked, White stalled, wining and dining the commander of the EIC flotilla, Captain Anthony Weltden, for several weeks. Before the ultimatum passed, however, the local Siamese nobility, fearing that the English would try to seize the port for the East India Company, carried out a pre-emptive strike against them. In this surprise attack on 24 July, later known as the Mergui massacre, more than sixty English crew members along with Richard Burnaby were killed, and Weltden was seriously injured. The survivors of the attack fled to their ships and left in a hurry. White himself managed to escape unharmed on board his *Resolution*, taking most of his wealth back to England where he died two years later in January 1689.[79]

In this case, war could be avoided – but meddling in regional affairs both by colonial officers and by Western adventurers continued unabated, for example in the Malayan Archipelago, as we shall see.

Acquiring a Suitable Vessel

Most pirates started their careers simply by signing up to an already existing crew. All this usually required was talking with the right people in the right place – usually a harbourside tavern. But what about those 'start-up' pirates who decided to form their own gang, and thus needed to acquire their first boat one way or another? Simply stealing it was one possibility. Among English and Irish pirates of the seventeenth century, this seemed to have been common practice: many ships lay in harbour either completely unattended but otherwise ready to sail, or manned only by a rump crew who were not always as alert as they should have been. Stealing a vessel was thus a surprisingly easy way to get started:[80] Sir Henry Mainwaring, a pirate turned pirate hunter, noted in 1618 the 'negligence of the Owners of such small Ships, that having no force to defend them keep ill watch, and leave their Sails aboard'.[81] If stealing a vessel was not possible, then guise and guile, or deception and cunning, might work to get aboard a suitable ship, before taking it over by force. John Ward kick-started his career as a pirate by using both tactics. He and some like-minded colleagues captured their first vessel simply by climbing on board a fully laden but unguarded barque lying at anchor in Portsmouth harbour, and sailing it out to sea. The theft was not noticed until the next day. Just off the coast of Cornwall, Ward and his companions found themselves in the company of a French-flagged ship, a flyboat of around 70 tons, equipped with six cannon to keep potential pirates at bay. For Ward and his comrades, this was a much better ship for piracy purposes, and thus a tempting target, though not an easy one: they were outnumbered – and outgunned – by the French crew. But they also had prior experience as privateers (and knew that they would be summarily hanged if caught). Ward developed a cunning plan, making the best of the unassuming appearance of his small vessel and his few companions, most of whom kept themselves out of view: all that the French captain could see was Ward himself and four men in the rigging.[82] Ward also made the French think that he was a lousy navigator, by erratically zigzagging as if he were unable to steer a clear course – all the while keeping the French entertained with a shouted conversation on any topic that came to mind. Thus put at ease, it escaped the French crew's attention that Ward's tiny barque was drawing ever closer to their vessel. 'Ward, halfway through his recitation of a ballad of the recent arrest of the great English seaman Sir Walter Raleigh, gave a powerful shout of "Now, my masters, for us!"' On this command, Ward's men rushed from below deck to board the French ship, whose crew were taken by complete surprise: 'The man who minutes earlier had seemed but an incompetent fool promoted beyond his merits had revealed his true identity: Captain John Ward, soon to be notorious.'[83]

As a new pirate, Ward initially did not have much choice regarding suitable ships, and neither the barque nor the flyboat was a vessel he probably would have picked given a free choice – he simply made the best of the opportunities that presented themselves. However, he quickly developed a predilection for sturdy and utilitarian flyboat-type merchantmen, vessels that with their shallow draught, single deck and three masts were 'as warlike as a coal scuttle', as one naval historian has quipped.[84] But this is exactly what attracted Ward and other pirates to these vessels, since, as will be explored further below, they preferred surprise attacks to open combat:

> If a man-of-war is cutting through the sea with cannon extended and fighting nets at the ready, it was not very difficult to discern its intentions. If a flyboat merchantman comes bobbing through the waves, apparently seeking a companion with whom to sail in convoy, far fewer suspicions were raised.[85]

In addition, the very sturdiness of the flyboats allowed pirates to equip them with an astonishing amount of ordnance – in Ward's case, and after some successful operations, his flyboat carried thirty-two cast-iron guns and a crew of one hundred men.[86] And there was still plenty of room for plunder.

In other cases, pirates acquired their first vessel through an act of mutiny, like Henry 'Long Ben' Avery (20 August 1659–c. 1714), one of the most successful pirates in history. Hailing from Devonshire, he went to sea at a young age and gradually worked his way up through the ranks. Early 1694 saw him as first mate on board one of two heavily armed vessels from Bristol, each with a complement of around 30 guns and 120 crew,[87] employed by the Spanish as privateers to pounce on French pirates harassing Spanish shipping in the Caribbean. Avery's vessel, the *Charles II*,[88] was under the command of a certain Captain Gibson, less known for his leadership skills than for his habit of being continually drunk.[89] His crew detested him, and making a bad situation worse was the fact that they had yet to receive any of the payment promised to them. Hence, when Avery suggested to the disgruntled men that, instead of hunting well-armed French privateers for little money and the glory of Spain, they go a-pirating, he found them to be attentive listeners. Their chance came while lying in La Coruña, waiting for Spanish officers to join them. After ten o'clock at night, with the captain dead-drunk in his cabin and all the crew members not part of the conspiracy sleeping in their hammocks, Avery weighed anchor and set sail. Captain Gibson, woken by the ship's movements, was coolly given the choice of staying aboard and joining the crew, or leaving in a boat with all those who did not intend to turn pirate. Knowing very well how hated he was, Gibson wisely chose the second option. Avery, now in command of a formidable vessel much more in line with usual assumptions of how a 'typical' pirate ship should look, also soon became notorious.

'Sanctioned' pirates, in the shape of privateers and corsairs, had different obstacles to surmount, the most formidable being the financial implications of an expedition or voyage. To begin with, purpose-built privateering vessels such as galleys or galleons were not cheap. Furthermore, a prospective privateer captain had to acquire a commission, which was not free either. Hiring suitable crew members could also be a substantial cost factor: while many sailors and soldiers were willing to join on a 'no plunder no pay' basis, this was not necessarily the case for the crew of French or Maltese corsairs, who expected to get paid as well. If the plan was to outfit not just one vessel but a whole privateering fleet, the costs were immense. In most cases they were thus spread over many investors – both public, such as the state itself, and private, such as interested merchants – all of whom expected their fair share after the successful conclusion of the privateering venture. This of course heightened the pressure on a privateer captain to ensure that the voyage was a successful and profitable one, even if that meant taking a rather generous approach when it came to interpreting the terms of the commission as to what constituted a permitted prize and what did not – yet another explanation of why some of our protagonists moved along the privateer–pirate continuum with consummate ease, often encouraged by their crew as well as (tacitly, at least) their investors.

Stalking and Capturing the Prey

Once out of port, the next steps were the same for pirates and privateers alike: prey had to be spotted, intercepted and boarded. When it comes to stalking vessels, laying in ambush at suitable locations along busy sea routes was still the usual choice. The risks that this tactic entailed were also the same as in previous centuries – for example, being surprised by a more powerful enemy. The corsair Alonso de Contreras reports just such an incident: while his frigate was lying in the creek of a small island somewhere in the Aegean Sea, he was taken by surprise by two swiftly approaching Turkish galleys. What saved Contreras's day was that the captains of the two galleys were as surprised as he was, and rushed into action without proper preparation or coordination. Contreras, an experienced corsair, scoffs at this 'ill-discipline', 'bad seamanship' and 'wild disorder', but admits that this gave him the chance to escape 'by the skin of our teeth'.[90] The two Turkish galleys took a while to catch up with his frigate; when they did so, luck was on their side, and some well-aimed shots shredded the frigate's rigging and sent the main yard tumbling down. Again, Contreras's quick wits saved the day. Making for the island of Samos, whose small harbour was frequently used by Maltese galleys, the wily corsair ordered a sailor up to the main mast with some gunpowder to make smoke signals. Wrongly assuming that other Maltese corsairs were lying in ambush ready to pounce, the two Turkish galleys immediately fled.[91]

Ambushing vessels was but one of many tactics used by Contreras. Like most other corsairs, he preferred actively going after prey. Such an approach came with its own risks, however. In the year 1720, for example, Welsh pirate captain Bartholomew Roberts and his crew cruised up and down the Brazilian coast for nine weeks without spotting any vessel at all until their luck turned and they stumbled across a Portuguese treasure fleet of no less than forty-two sails.[92] Similarly, in 1693, the French corsair René Duguay-Trouin cruised for three months without

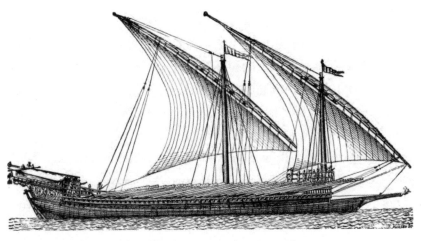

3. A galley running before the wind.

taking any booty at all, and then was almost sunk by a forty-gun Swedish warship that mistook him for a pirate.[93] Even Contreras reports a number of fruitless cruises along the Levantine and North African coasts:

> I found nothing on the coast, so I decided to go to Damietta, which was on the Nile Delta. I went up the Nile to see what I could find but met nothing. I turned back and crossed over in the direction of Syria, a distance of 130 miles. I sighted the shores of the Holy Land, which were only some thirty-five miles from Jerusalem. I passed on and entered the harbour of Jaffa. There were a few barks there, whose crews fled all ashore at my approach.[94]

His opposite numbers, the Barbary Coast corsairs, did not fare any better. In July 1684, the English consul general at Tripoli, Thomas Baker, mentions one particularly unlucky fellow, *Rais* (captain) Mustafa Qadi, who had not made a single prize in twelve voyages. As Baker dryly notes, this corsair captain even managed to return from a thirteenth trip 'without a rag of purchase'.[95] These examples of futile cruises illustrate again why pirates and privateers throughout the ages also routinely conducted sorties against coastal settlements when they were strong enough to do so: unlike the average ship at sea, such settlements were easy to find.

When it came to capturing ships, and especially the perilous act of boarding them, most pirates and privateers active in this period also preferred to do so without having to fight, just like their predecessors (see above, p. 33). Most of the time, simply raising the black flag (or the local equivalent) was enough to cow the crew of the targeted ship into submission. For example, in 1721, the sight of the flag of the much feared pirate captain Bartholomew Roberts was enough to cause the surrender of no less than eleven English, French and Portuguese vessels in the harbour of Ouidah in Benin without a shot being fired, even though 'the French were three stout ships of 30 guns, and upwards of 100 men each'.[96] Once on board a vessel that had just surrendered, Roberts's pirates usually continued to deploy this shock-and-awe element to keep the crew and passengers under tight control and to maximise the loot – as did most other pirates of this period for the very same reason. The case of the *Samuel* of London, captured by Roberts in 1720, demonstrates this:

> The *Samuel* was a rich Ship, and had several Passengers on board, who were used very roughly, in order to make them discover their Money, threatening them every Moment with Death, if they did not resign every Thing up to them. They tore up the Hatches and entered the Hold like a Parcel of Furies, and with Axes and Cutlashes, cut and broke open all the Bales, Cases and Boxes, they could lay their hands on; and when any Goods came upon Deck, that they did not like to carry aboard, instead of tossing them into the Hold again, threw them over-board into the Sea; all this was done with incessant Cursing and Swearing, more like Fiends than Men.[97]

The psychological effect on the crew must have been devastating, again driving home the point that resistance was futile.

If the target was much bigger than the pirates' vessel and well manned, deception frequently led to success where more overt measures might not, and where the hoisting of the pirate flag would be greeted with howls of derisive laughter and some broadsides. Most of the time, this 'guise and guile' approach involved pretending to be a harmless trader, thus gaining the future victim's trust. John Ward's 'acquisition' of the French flyboat is a case in point (see above, pp. 91–2). Similar acts of guise and guile, or treachery from the other side's perspective, were reported in numerous hostile encounters between Spanish, Portuguese, English, French and Dutch vessels in Caribbean waters. On at least one occasion the intended victim turned the tactic to their own advantage. In May 1589, a Spanish treasure-carrying warship in the Gulf of Mexico found itself pursued by a much smaller English galleon, the 70-ton privateer *Dog*. After having been harassed for no less than three days by this obnoxious marauder, and obviously not willing to risk a fight (the *Dog* had already taken three other Spanish vessels in that area), the Spanish called for a truce and a parley, and the English accepted. First, the Spanish officers went over to the *Dog* for an amicable meeting, and then their English counterparts came over to the Spanish vessel to return the honour. Once aboard, they suddenly found themselves set upon by their Spanish hosts, who managed to stab the English pilot, Roger Kingsnod, to death; 'others were served with the like sauce; only William Mace the Master & others, notwithstanding all the prepared traps of the enemy, leaped overboard into the sea, and so came safe to their own ship'.[98] Having narrowly escaped the trap set for them, the survivors decided to abandon the chase and return to Plymouth.[99]

If the conditions were right, a pirate or privateer could also try to sneak aboard a ship unnoticed. The German baker turned privateer Martin Wintergerst describes such an attempt made in 1689. Having just joined the crew of a Dutch privateer of 46 guns and 180 men, he had his first hostile encounter in the Adriatic Sea when a French vessel was spotted on the way to the Venetian port of Zara (modern Zadar, Croatia). Hoisting the flag of neutral Livorno as a ruse, Wintergerst's ship also approached the port. As per custom, they fired a greeting shot, and put a dinghy (an open rowing boat) to water to have a friendly chat with the port authorities. With the help of Wintergerst's language skills, they learned that the French vessel was brand new and carried rich cargo. Unfortunately, it had anchored under the guns of the fortress, putting an open attack out of the question. The remaining option was to try to board the ship under the cover of darkness and overwhelm the hopefully sleeping crew before they could offer resistance. As Wintergerst recounts, in the dead of night two boats quietly approached the French ship, one commanded by the captain himself, the other by his lieutenant. Unfortunately, the French sentries noticed the privateers before they could clamber on board. The French crew rushed to battle stations and a bitter fight ensued. After losing fourteen men, including their captain, the remaining thirteen French sailors finally asked for quarter. The noise of the battle had not gone unnoticed in the fortress, where the guns were now being made ready while the militia were assembled. To avoid the imminent counter-attack, the Dutch towed the captured French ship to a safe distance before they inspected the booty: 5,000 ducats in treasure, and a cargo consisting of 1,500 hundredweight of sulphur, 4,000 pieces of fur, bales of camel hair and other textiles, and about 200 pairs of Turkish boots. Wintergerst and his fellow crew members were pleased, though they had suffered three casualties in the fight as well.[100]

In other cases, this sneaky stratagem worked better. The buccaneer captain Pierre Le Grand, for instance, achieved his greatest triumph this way. In 1665, having set out in a large boat (a piragua) of about 10 metres in length, Le Grand had sailed up and down the Bahama Channel without sighting any vessel, and now was down on his luck: his provisions were running low, and so was the mood of his crew of twenty-eight men. Then their luck turned: they spotted a huge Spanish galleon sailing alone. Attacking this mighty ship, which dwarfed Le Grand's boat, must have seemed preposterous – but this was Le Grand's 'do or die' moment. His crew concurred: this was their chance, and they were determined to seize it. To further encourage them, Le Grand had the surgeon drill holes into the hull of the piragua, causing it slowly to sink. Now there was no way back, 'and without any other arms than a pistol in one of their hands, and a sword in the other, they immediately climbed up the sides of the ship, and ran altogether into the great cabin, where they found the captain, with several of his companions, playing at cards'.[101] Suddenly finding themselves surrounded by tough-looking pirates hardly visible in the dim light of the lantern, and staring into the business ends of their pistols, the shocked Spaniards cried out, 'Jesus bless us! Are these devils or what are they?'[102] In the meantime, the rest of the boarding party had secured the gunroom and the weapons, killing anybody who dared to offer resistance. The puny size of the piragua had been the Spanish vessel's undoing: it turned out that Le Grand and his men had been spotted by crew members of the Spanish ship, and correctly identified as pirates, but the captain had dismissed them as a valid threat: 'What then? Must I be afraid of such a pitiful thing, as this is?'[103] Here, the (mostly incorrect) cliché of the haughty Spaniard outfoxed and outfought by a courageous few who find themselves immensely rich in reward for their bravery can be supported by a real-life story. And, indeed, the booty was so huge that Le Grand sailed straight back to France to enjoy his newfound riches without ever returning to the sea again. What worked in Le Grand's favour was the small size of his vessel, enabling him to make an inconspicuous and seem-ingly innocuous approach. Had he been in command of a larger vessel, the Spanish captain would have been more cautious.

This was exactly the problem Sir Francis Drake had to overcome when he set out to capture the Spanish galleon *Nuestra Señora de la Concepción* on 1 March 1579: how to approach this vessel aboard his equally formidable *Golden Hind* without raising suspicion? Cruising along the Pacific coast of South America, and acting on intelligence he had garnered in various ports which he had raided, he patiently stalked the Spanish treasure ship, which was on its way from Manila to Panama. Not anticipating any trouble – until this incident, the Pacific had been an exclusively 'Spanish Lake' – the Spanish vessel was unarmed, either in the literal sense that no guns were aboard, or in the more likely interpre-tation that its guns were safely stowed away below deck as ballast, making more room for its precious cargo. But since the *Nuestra Señora* was a very fast ship, its captain, San Juan de Antón,[104] might well have expected to outsail any vessel big enough to pose a threat. To prevent the galleon simply hoisting all sails and running for the safety of a port, Drake employed a ruse: he camouflaged the real speed of his own ship by having a drogue made out of cables and mattresses which he used to artificially slow down the *Golden Hind*. This made his ship appear to be a harmless Spanish merchant vessel, unable to build up speed even under full sail due to its heavy cargo. Furthermore, to prepare for the attack, Drake had his pinnace tied alongside the *Golden Hind*, out of view of the treasure ship when he gradually caught up with it. When night fell, Drake attacked, at once cutting loose the drogue and deploying his pinnace. The Spanish captain initially refused to surrender, but did so after a salvo from the *Golden Hind* had felled the mizzen mast, and after he himself had been injured by musket fire. The 'ship's cargo "made" Drake's venture several times over. There was so much silver bullion that it was used to replace ballast on the *Golden Hind,* and in addition there were fourteen chests of silver and gold coins.'[105] No wonder the delighted Queen Elizabeth I later declared him 'her' pirate.

In East Asian waters, pirates also took to guise and guile in order to overcome the well-armed and well-defended high-seas junks which made up their prey. But they went beyond mimicking the behaviour of harmless merchant vessels at sea: they also attacked ships in port or sailed along the major Chinese river systems, and frequently even raided unsuspecting riverine towns, in these cases dressed and behaving like state officials, militia troops, ferrymen or itinerant merchants. Often, this brazen stratagem

4. Sir Francis Drake's *Golden Hind.*

worked perfectly, and river traffic or towns, taken by surprise, were looted by the pirates in no time at all without any resistance being offered.[106] In the South China Sea, Iranun pirates from Mindanao were known as the undisputed masters of guise and guile and the art of hiding in plain sight. They did so by mimicking the behaviour and appearance of local fishing vessels, with their guns hidden under mats and most of their fighters concealed until the last moment.[107] The eyewitness report of Lieutenant Colonel Ibanez y Garcia, a Spanish colonial officer, vividly describes such an encounter in 1857:

> The sea was calm, except for the silvery ripples created by the boat's keel as it knifed effortlessly through the dark-blue waters of Bohol. The vast expanse that lay ahead was peppered with seagulls performing their daily aerial acrobatics, now and then diving into the brine for a delicious catch . . . Suddenly, it happened. As if from nowhere two boats appeared, approaching fast. 'Fishermen to hawk their catch,' so [we] thought. But such complacency was shattered. In lightning fashion, two big wooden planks went over the boat's parapets, as nimble . . . sword-brandishing dark-skinned men climbed over. I and my companions were held at bay. At the same time some set fire to the boat's hull.[108]

And with that, the lieutenant colonel and his entourage were taken captive and held to ransom. He was not the first, and would not be the last: as we shall see, hiding in plain sight by mimicking the behaviour of a fishing vessel before suddenly pouncing is a tactic still used by modern pirates in these waters.

Desperate Battles at Sea

Guise and guile was not always an option; if the targeted ship was well prepared and alert, battle could not be avoided. And as in the period

discussed in Part I, battles tended to be prolonged and bloody affairs –
now more than ever due to the advent of ship-borne artillery. Pirates used
artillery not to sink the ships they targeted but to immobilise them, and to
decimate the crew in preparation for boarding. Hence, instead of
heavy-calibre cannon firing shots of up to 60 pounds meant to shatter the
wooden hulls of ships, lighter guns such as culverins, semi-culverins or
sakers were preferred – guns with a longer range and a higher velocity
compared to cannon, whose 5- to 15-pound shot penetrated ships' hulls,
smashing through anything and anyone in their way, but without causing
the targeted vessel to sink.[109] Due to the usually rather uncoordinated
broadsides fired by pirates – who were far less disciplined than gunners
on board regular warships – this did not always work out as planned.
Pirate captain Robert Culliford, for example, learned the hard way just
how ineffective and inconclusive such gun battles could be: in 1697, his
vessel the *Mocha Frigate* chased the East Indiaman *Dorrill* for several days,
engaging it in a series of gun battles lasting many hours without ever seriously damaging the other vessel or coming near enough to board it.

Generally speaking, though, when well-directed salvoes of canister
shot and musket fire did achieve the aim of immobilising the targeted
vessel and reducing the number of defenders, the ship would be boarded
and a desperate close-quarters battle would unfold. For that, the boarders
usually preferred shorter weapons such as pistols, cutlasses, daggers, axes
and the like: these were ideal for hand-to-hand fighting in confined
spaces. The defenders, on the other hand, also made good use (or tried to
do so, at least initially) of pole weapons such as lances, pikes or halberds.
After all, an 'enemy waiting to swing over the side, or even clamber up it,
was best dealt with at longer than an arm's length'.[110] In support of the
modern weapons of the day – that is, pistols (from the sixteenth century
onwards), harquebuses (until the end of the seventeenth century) and
muskets (the seventeenth century onwards) – older weapons such as
bows and arrows were still widely used due to their accuracy and their
reliability: contrary to the more modern firearms, they did not require

(dry) gunpowder and a spark to function – two items that often were in short supply on the high seas.[111]

That battles could be protracted and bloody affairs was borne out time and again on the oceans. John Ward, this time in command of two Tunisian corsairs cruising along the Turkish coast in April 1607 looking for prey, found it in the form of the Venetian *Reniera e Soderina*, a huge argosy-type sailing vessel of about 1,500 tons.[112] At a time when 500-ton vessels were thought large, argosies were truly massive floating fortresses. Since the argosy was much bigger than Ward's own two vessels, a galley and a flyboat, his small flotilla raked it with cannon fire for three hours in the hope it would surrender.[113] But the battered Venetian vessel did not strike its colours – instead, the crew prepared to repel any boarders by mustering on the fore and stern castles. Just as they had done so, Ward's two vessels fired a final salvo of chain shot.[114] The Venetian official incident report describes the outcome:

> Their plans, designed to terrify, succeeded excellently, because two of those who were defending the quarterdeck were hit by one of their shots, and when they were wounded, indeed torn to pieces, all the rest fled, leaving all their weapons lying on the quarterdeck and all of them running to their own property, even while the two vessels were coming alongside.[115]

The Venetian captain, unable to quell the panic and restore order, had no choice but to surrender. The Venetian ship was taken as a prize, and its surviving crew and passengers were soon on their way to Tunis and its slave markets. As regards Ward himself, the event further contributed to his notoriety as an 'arch pirate' in the eyes of his adversaries.

A few decades later Henry 'Long Ben' Avery was also in action. Having taken over the *Charles II* (now rechristened *Fancy*), Avery had made straight for the Arabian Sea, his intention being to capture Indian vessels sailing along the Hajj pilgrimage route running from Surat on the west coast of India to Jeddah on the Red Sea via the Gulf of Aden and back. Carrying not only hundreds of pilgrims but also merchants trading in silk and spices, such ships were rumoured to be veritable treasure stores:

> It is known that the Eastern People travel with the utmost Magnificence, so that they had with them all their Slaves and Attendants, their rich Habits and Jewels, with Vessels of Gold and Silver, and great Sums of Money to defray the Charges of their Journey by Land; wherefore the Plunder got by this Prize, is not easily computed.[116]

When Avery arrived on the scene, he found five other pirate ships already cruising the area with exactly the same intention (one of them, the *Amity*, under the command of yet another famous pirate, Thomas Tew). In July 1695, the pirate squadron made contact with a pilgrim convoy of twenty-five sails. The huge vessel which the pirate fleet chose as their first target turned out to be the *Fateh Mohammed*, a ship owned by Abdul Ghaffar, one of Surat's richest merchants. Avery kept the *Fancy* at a safe distance and fired at wide range to force the Mughal crew to keep their heads down, allowing two other pirate vessels to sweep in. Suddenly finding himself surrounded by scores of fearsome pirates, the master of the Mughal ship elected to strike its colours. The gold and silver taken from the ship was worth some £50,000, or around £6.5 million (US $8.5 million) in today's values – not bad for a day's work, even though the loot had to be shared with the crews of the other vessels (though not with Thomas Tew, who was killed in the action). And much better was to come: early the next morning, Avery, now operating alone (the other pirates could not keep up with the speed of the *Fancy*), managed to intercept the convoy's flagship: the mighty *Ganj i-Sawai* ('Exceeding Treasure' – a most appropriate name for a ship that belonged to the Mughal emperor Aurangzeb himself).

The *Ganj i-Sawai* was not an easy target: with around 50 guns and 400 musket-armed soldiers on board to protect both the treasure and the high-ranking passengers it carried, it did not surrender without a fight. The battle with the ship raged for two or three hours until Avery got lucky: one of his broadsides felled *the Ganj i-Sawai*'s mainmast, which came down with sails and ropes and tacks, crushing many crew and soldiers. A gun that exploded, maiming and killing bystanders, added to the confusion. But it was only when the master of the vessel, Ibrahim Khan, lost his nerve and fled below deck that the courage of the defenders finally collapsed and the pirates could board.[117] Avery's pirates then systematically worked their way through the decks of the mighty vessel, mercilessly torturing passengers and crew alike either for fun or to make them surrender hidden valuables, and gang-raping the female passengers. The booty was enough to entitle every pirate crew member with claim to a full share to a whopping £1,000 – in today's money at least £130,000 ($175,000).[118]

It should be pointed out that there were variations to this sequence of events, which might be characterised as 'blast away first, then board and butcher, if necessary withdraw and repeat'. One such variation is illustrated by the English privateer Captain Thomas Cavendish's attack on the Spanish galleon *Santa Ana* on 4 November 1587 in the South Sea. The 700-ton *Santa Ana* was no ordinary vessel, but a 'Manila galleon' – a huge galleon purpose-built to transport the profits made in the trade with China via the Philippines to Acapulco in Mexico. Such Manila galleons usually sailed only once a year, full to the gunwales with gold and silver.[119] Cavendish's two-vessel squadron, comprising the 120-ton, 18-gun galleon *Desire* and the 60-ton, 10-gun *Content*, caught this floating fortress unawares, despite the surprise attack by Sir Francis Drake's *Golden Hind* on the *Nuestra Señora de la Concepcion* having occurred just ten years before. Seemingly, nothing had been learned from this episode: exactly as before, the Spanish ship's guns were stowed away below deck to make more room for the cargo, and the crew were unprepared for serious fighting. Since there was no risk of gunfire, Cavendish decided to board the *Santa Ana* without softening it up first. This, however, turned out to be a costly mistake: the Spanish crew barricaded themselves in the fore and stern castles, hacking and stabbing at the boarding party with lances, halberds and rapiers as they tried to force their way in, while at the same time bombarding the low-lying English galleons with heavy ballast stones from their well-protected retreats. Two members of Cavendish's crew were killed and four or five injured in this action, which forced Cavendish to abandon the attempt to board and to stand off. Only then did he decide to give the *Santa Ana* what he called 'a fresh encounter with our great ordnance and also with our small shot, raking them through and through, to the killing and maiming of many of their men'.[120] The Manila galleon finally struck its colours, but only after having endured a bombardment of some six hours, which blasted many of its crew to pieces and reduced the once proud floating fortress to a wreck.

5. A Spanish galleon.

Thomas Cavendish was full of praise for the gallant defenders of the Spanish treasure ship – and he was by no means alone in this regard: many English eyewitnesses of such encounters have much good to say about the bravery of their opponents, Portuguese or Spanish, who fought nobly and courageously. English buccaneer (and author) Basil Ringrose, for example, describes in all its gory detail a battle between two buccaneer piraguas with a crew of sixty and three small Spanish warships in April 1680, before concluding: 'And indeed, to give our enemies their due, no men in the world did ever act more bravely than these Spaniards.'[121] All these eyewitness reports help to debunk the cliché of haughty and cowardly Portuguese or Spaniards on board warships either striking their colours immediately or after some desultory, half-hearted and mainly face-saving counterfire. As historian Benerson Little states, 'these are Spanish men-of-war, but they are not crewed by the buffoonish Spaniards in corset and morion of modern fairy-tale pirate fiction and film. The buccaneers have already fought desperate bloody battles against valiant Spanish commanders and their multiracial crew, and they know well what may lie ahead.'[122] However, every rule has an exception, as we have seen above in the case of Pierre Le Grand's surprise attack on some unwary and, admittedly, haughty Spaniards.

High-End Piracy

Swarming a bigger and better-armed vessel in wolfpack style with several boats acting together was another frequently used tactic. The early (and still mainly French) buccaneers active in Caribbean waters in the seventeenth century employed this approach, either in conjunction with guise and guile or via lightning-strike attacks from well-chosen ambush positions. Using simple dug-out canoes or larger piraguas as their vessels of choice, they made good use of their renowned marksmanship, surrounding the targeted vessel and picking off crew members one by one, aiming especially at the officers on deck and at the helmsman to destroy the chain of command and to render the vessel unsteerable.[123] Similar swarming attacks were the preferred tactic in eastern waters as well: local pirate crafts were inferior in size and firepower to the Chinese and Western vessels they encountered. Sea-going Malay tribes such as the Iranun from Mindanao, the Balangingi from the Sulu Archipelago and the Sea Dayak from Borneo had a reputation, if guise and guile did not work, for ruthlessly attacking nearly all the vessels they encountered in such a fashion, and for never giving quarter to the Europeans they found on these ships, whether they had offered resistance or not. 'Nearly all' means that they usually avoided large junks and the well-armed East Indiamen of the late eighteenth and nineteenth centuries transporting opium to China[124] – which is probably why English navigator and author George Windsor Earl, who encountered Malay pirates in the vicinity of Singapore during his voyage to Southeast Asia in 1832–4, was able to opine – with the typical imperialist bias of his time – that they were 'as cowardly as they [were] cruel'.[125] All other vessels sailing through these waters needed to take precautions against these pirates, who operated in fleets of thirty to forty swift oared vessels known as *prahus*, each with a crew of 100–150 well-armed warriors supported by some cannon and swivel guns.[126]

If Malay pirates chose to attack, they usually began by bearing down on their prey from all sides with dozens of their own boats while firing their guns in order to disable their target, for example by damaging the rudder or bringing down the rigging.[127] In some cases, when the wind was favourable, a particularly lucky ship managed to outrun its pursuers and escape. In a few others, warships that happened to be in the vicinity came to the rescue; in May 1838, for instance, a Chinese junk pursued by six large Iranun *prahus* that rapidly closed in despite the junk's defensive gunfire was saved by the chance appearance of the British sloop HMS *Wolf*, and even more importantly, of the East India Company's paddle steamer *Diana* (one of the harbingers of the dawning Age of Steam). The *Diana*, operating independently of the wind, was able to out-manoeuvre the *prahus* at will, and swiftly sent the whole pirate squadron and many of its crew to the bottom of the sea.[128] But such lucky escapes were rare, and most of the time the *prahus* overtook the fleeing vessel. The Iranun pirates then began to rake the doomed vessel's deck and rigging with well-directed musket fire while throwing grappling hooks to draw it alongside and to prevent escape. Boarding, they cut down the defenders with their lances and *kampilans* (single-edged long swords), all the while raising

a tremendous din, shouting and screaming on top of their lungs in a terrifying trance-like state . . . The high-pitched wailing sound in the midst of the engagement often filled ill-disciplined, poorly-trained and paid merchant crews with such terror that they were unable to either defend themselves or their vessel.[129]

Sometimes, the crews of vessels about to be boarded, all too aware of their fate if they were to fall into the hands of the pirates alive, resorted

6. A typical Chinese junk.

to desperate measures. The Dutch owners of a merchant vessel which was attacked by a swarm of forty *prahus* in the Straits of Banca in 1806, realising that resistance was futile and death a certainty, cold-bloodedly waited until scores of pirates had clambered aboard their ship before blowing it up – presumably by a shot into the powder magazine.[130] Such drastic suicidal action seems to have been neither rare nor new. The authors of the seventeenth-century Persian manuscript *The Ship of Sulaimān* explicitly praised Westerners, or 'Franks' in their parlance, for preferring to burn to death on their ships rather than surrender to pirates – although they mistakenly believed that the Franks had a standing order from their king to do so.[131]

When it came to coastal raids, smash-and-grab attacks such as those carried out by the Vikings and the Wako were still part and parcel of high-end piracy. In the Mediterranean, Christian and Muslim corsairs still raided each other's coasts as they had done in previous centuries. While, with a few exceptions, Christian corsairs usually remained in Mediterranean waters, some of the more adventurous Barbary Coast corsairs ventured out of the Mediterranean, harassing the coasts of England, Ireland and even faraway Iceland. One such corsair was Murat Reis the Younger. Born Jan Janszoon in Haarlem in the Netherlands around 1570, he began his seafaring career on a Dutch privateer in 1600. When he was captured by Algerian corsairs off Lanzarote in 1618, he converted to Islam (or 'turned Turk', as it was usually called in the Christian West) and continued his career under his new name Murat Reis. Knowing the waters of the North Sea very well, he made them his favourite hunting ground, even using the island of Lundy in the Bristol Channel as his forward operating base for no less than five years between 1627 and 1632. His most famous raid was the sack of Baltimore on 20 June 1631. Formerly a pirate lair of ill repute (see above, p. 80–1), Baltimore was by this time just another fishing village populated by English settlers. Around 107 of the unfortunate villagers were dragged away to be sold into slavery before Reis's vessels made off – unmolested by the Royal Navy's purpose-built pirate hunter the *Fifth Whelp*, which seems not to have been seaworthy at the crucial moment.[132]

The amphibious operations of the early French privateers active in the Caribbean from the 1550s onwards, or those of the seventeenth-century buccaneers, belong to the same category of smash-and-grab attacks. They also had the same limited impact: although painful for coastal settlements, and deadly for quite a few of their inhabitants, life went on as normal just a couple of miles away. The horror was largely a vicarious one, as in the case of Lindisfarne (see above, pp. 39–40). Alexandre Exquemelin describes several such small-scale buccaneer operations – including one carried out in the mid-seventeenth century by about seven or eight piraguas under the command of a Captain John Davies. After fruitlessly sailing up and down the northern coast of Cuba hoping to encounter an elusive silver-carrying Spanish fleet, Davies's small flotilla finally descended on the little town of San Agustin on the Atlantic coast of north-eastern Florida. Its inhabitants managed to flee to the castle, from which they and the meagre garrison helplessly watched as their houses were sacked and burned.[133] Exquemelin does not specify the amount of booty captured, but it cannot have been that great: small coastal towns were typically rather poor. Furthermore, many of the inhabitants had enough time to escape to the hills or into the jungle with their belongings as the buccaneers approached. Which is why Sir Henry Morgan, seen as the 'epitome of the buccaneer',[134] did not fare as well as he hoped in his famous sack of Panama in 1671. Forced to repulse several spirited counter-attacks made by the Spanish defenders in the pitched battle that followed his offensive, and having come under sustained fire from well-placed gun batteries and sharpshooters which saw him lose 'men at every step' before the 'last Spanish gunners were cut to pieces' by his men's guns,[135] he learned to his chagrin that most of the gold and silver he was after had been hurriedly carried away while he was approaching the city. On the other hand, the very similar raid on Veracruz on the Gulf of Mexico by the buccaneers Laurens de Graaf, Nicholas van

Hoorn and Michel de Grammont in May 1683 proved to be more lucrative. Since the 1,200 or so pirates who disembarked from five large and eight smaller vessels swiftly overcame the town's defences and defeated the hastily summoned militia, the inhabitants did not have enough time to hide or carry away their possessions; the loot was so substantial that every pirate got a share of 800 pieces of eight (about £21,000, or $28,000, in today's money). Not bad for a time when the average pirate in the Caribbean made between £10 and £20 (the equivalent of 30 to 60 pieces of eight) per successful voyage.[136]

The pirate federation of Zheng Yi Sao, active about a century later in eastern waters, also regularly descended on towns and villages as well. One such attack in autumn 1809 was breathlessly described in great detail by eyewitness Richard Glasspoole, an English sailor of the ship *Marquis of Ely* who had been kidnapped by Chinese pirates in the Pearl River estuary. Glasspoole describes how the pirate fleet anchored in the vicinity of the targeted town one night and launched its attack early the following morning. The pirates

> gave a shout, and rushed into the town, swords in hand. The inhabitants fled to the adjacent hills ... The old and the sick, who were unable to fly, or to make resistance, were either made prisoners or most inhumanely butchered! The boats continued passing and repassing from junks to the shore, in quick succession, laden with booty, and the men besmeared with blood! Two hundred and fifty women, and several children, were made prisoners ... The town being plundered of everything valuable, it was set on fire, and reduced to ashes by the morning.[137]

Similar raids on coastal settlements were conducted by the various warrior pirates of the South China Sea, such as the already mentioned Iranun, Balangingi and Sea Dayak (see p. 109), and the Bugis. Sir James Brooke (1803–68), the rajah of Sarawak in Borneo, their contemporary (and bitter enemy), noted that the pirates' area of operation covered the whole of the South China Sea from the Philippines in the north to Papua in the southeast and the Straits of Malacca and Gulf of Thailand in the west.[138] Commenting on the human toll that these raids took on Borneo alone, Brooke wrote that the 'number of Borneons yearly taken into slavery is very considerable, as a fleet of six or eight boats usually hangs about the island of Labuan, to cut off the trade, and to catch the inhabitants of the city'.[139] The inhabitants of these coasts had a telling name for the easterly monsoon that brought the pirates to their shores: the 'pirate wind'.

Whoring, Drinking and Gambling

There are many credible reports of pirates' penchant for violence, and even for cold-blooded murder long after the heat of the battle had cooled. But simply to tell more bloodcurdling stories would do nothing to contribute to furthering our understanding of what pirates did – or why they did it: often for the lure of booty and the 'merry life' they all craved.

What exactly counted as booty depended on the pirates' business model. Mediterranean corsairs and the Southeast Asian Iranun and Balangingi, for example, were not only after ships' cargo but also their passengers and crews, either for ransom or to be sold into slavery. Other pirates such as the buccaneers cared mainly about a ship's cargo, taking prisoners only if there were well-born officers and passengers who looked as if their families could afford to pay handsomely for their release. Typical cargoes most frequently included sugar, salt, spices, wine, rum, bales of silk, bales of calico, teak, pork, cheese, fish, tobacco and other goods, depending on the location of the ship when it was attacked and the nature of its business. In Asian waters, the bulk of plunder consisted of shipments of rice, while along the coasts of Africa cargoes might also include consignments of slaves. Slaves captured by pirates were simply treated as any other cargo, and sold at a suitable port. Very few, if any, were invited to join the crew; pirates, after all, held the same prejudiced views as everybody else at the time, and were certainly no

'Robin Hoods at sea', as some of the more romantically inclined or revisionist writers would have it. Furthermore, pirates routinely stripped their captures of any nautical instruments, guns, arms, ammunition and powder, tackle and ropes, spare sails and wooden planks, and whatever else they could lay their hands on and carry away; some pirate ships operated far from any friendly shore or port for long periods of time, which means they had to replenish their stocks as well as carry out running repairs as best they could, especially if they happened to suffer extensive damage after battling against a target that did not go down without a fight.

The rather mundane nature of many cargoes also implies that despite their hopes and expectations, most pirates did not exactly strike it rich during their career. As we have seen, the average pirate active in the Caribbean in the seventeenth century would make between around £10 and £20 per cruise,[140] whereas an experienced mariner in the Royal Navy could earn about £2 every three months. Hence, and depending on the length of the cruise, the average pirate made at least five times more than an honest mariner. Not bad, but hardly enough to live the coveted 'merry life' when in pirate ports like Port Royal, Tortuga or Macao prices were sky-high. This style of life was thus only affordable for pirates who had been lucky enough to strike the proverbial jackpot, to capture a – comparatively rare – treasure ship transporting chests full of gold and silver, diamonds, emeralds, rubies and other jewels. Avery's capture of the *Ganj i-Sawai* (see pp. 105–6) was such an incident. Another occurred on 18 August 1720 when English pirate Christopher Condent (born in the 1690s, died in 1770), captain of the *Fiery Dragon*, overwhelmed another Jeddah-bound treasure ship carrying a superb hoard of gold coins, precious stones, spices, drugs, and exquisite commodities such as fine porcelain, glass and silk worth £150,000 (£295 million, or $375 million, in today's money).[141] For Condent and his lucky crew, the 'merry life' was finally theirs. The merriment didn't last long for the buccaneer captain Roche Brasiliano's crew after they struck gold by capturing a Spanish treasure ship, though. '[A]ccording to their custom,' Exquemelin recounts, the crew wasted in a few days, in Taverns and Stews [brothels], all they had gotten, by giving themselves to all manner of debauchery, with Strumpets, and Wine. [They] will spend two or three thousand pieces of eight, in one night, not leaving themselves peradventure a good shirt to wear, on their backs, in the morning . . . I saw one of them give unto a common Strumpet, five hundred pieces of eight, only that he might see her naked.[142]

Three thousand pieces of eight roughly equates to £80,000 today ($104,000) – an incredible sum to blow in just one night. The same might be said about spending the equivalent of £18,000 ($23,500) just to see a prostitute naked. Exquemelin continues: 'My own Master would buy, in like occasions, a whole pipe of wine, and placing it in the street, would force every one, that passed by to drink with him, threatening also to Pistol them, in case they would not do it. At other times he would do the same, with Barrels of Ale, or Beer.'[143]

It was not only Port Royal or the other Caribbean pirate ports such as Tortuga or Nassau in the Bahamas that served as locales for rest and recreation. Ports catering for the needs of pirates and privateers could be found everywhere, the minimum conditions for their existence being lucrative passing maritime traffic and local authorities unconcerned about the origins of goods being brought in by people of questionable repute. Such a 'no questions asked' approach applied in various Mediterranean ports frequented by pirates and corsairs alike, who were spending just as recklessly as the Jamaican pirates and privateers in their pursuit of a merry life; the corsair Alonso de Contreras commented wistfully of the destination of his share of the booty, 'my quiraca [mistress] had the lot'.[144] Pirates visiting Chinese ports in the eighteenth century, especially Macao (the Chinese equivalent of Port Royal or Tortuga), 'would often dawdle away their time visiting opium dens, gambling parlours, and brothels. [Addicted] to fighting, whoring, gambling, drinking and opium smoking, they spent their money as fast as they made it.'[145] For the fortunate pirates who struck it rich, the stereotypical merry life could be had there as well – with the added local bonus of opium smoking.

There was, however, a downside to life in these ports. Teeming with hard-nosed criminals spending days or even weeks in taverns, brothels and gambling parlours, a pirate port could be a dangerous place. Louis Le Golif reports witnessing (and being directly involved in) a number of duels in Tortuga, the preferred base for buccaneers and freebooters, as well as lethal drink-fuelled knife fights that broke out at the drop of a hat. He felt he had to arm himself:

At that time [1678/1679] it was most inadvisable to go for a walk except with a whole arsenal. Besides the sword which never left me, I always carried a sabre, several knifes and four loaded pistols. It will be admitted that a stay in such a country was not calculated to please the man of goodwill I have always tried to be.[146]

He blames a gradual change within the buccaneers and freebooters themselves for that:

It can be seen from all this that the filibusters were no longer what they once were. Many rogues, male and female, had come to mix with us from all corners of the globe, while a number of brave and honest men had left Tortuga to dwell on the mainland . . . while the people who remained on the island were not the best.[147]

The fact that such 'safe havens' held a certain attraction for undesirable members of society should come as no great surprise, however – it also was the case in Macao, for example, where the plethora of gambling houses and opium dens also helped to increase the criminal element to the detriment of the law-abiding citizens.

Typical Ends of Pirate Careers

How long did pirate careers last, and how did they end? After all, not every pirate met a violent death; some simply walked away from piracy and returned to the life of a more or less honest citizen. During the centuries under discussion here, a typical pirate career could be rather short. Capturer of the *Ganj i-Sawai* Henry Avery was a pirate for about two years between 1694 and 1696 – a span that was by no means exceptional: the 'arch pirate' Edward Teach, better known as Blackbeard, was also active for about two years (1716–18) before he met his fate, while the Welsh pirate Bartholomew Roberts operated for three years (1719–22), just like the English pirates Thomas Tew (1692–5), Edward Low (1721–4), John 'Calico Jack' Rackham, Anne Bonny and Mary Read (1717–20), and the Portuguese pirate Bartolomeu Português (1666–9). 'Black Sam' Bellamy, captain of the *Whydah*, only went a-pirating for one-and-a-half years (early 1716–April 1717). Of course, there also were plenty of pirates who roamed the seas for a decade or more. Chinese pirate queen Zheng Yi Sao, for example, was active for about a decade (1801–10), while the pirate lord Wushi Er also operated for about ten years before he was captured in 1810. Other long-time pirates were the Cuban known as Diabolito ('Little Devil'), who was active for about a decade until 1823, and the African pirate Black Caesar (1700s to 1710s). But by and large, the comparatively short careers of at least the Western, buccaneer-style pirates explains why their motto used to be 'a merry life, and a short one' – a phrase that goes back to Bartholomew Roberts.

The reasons why the career of the average Western pirate was relatively short are manifold. Some, like Avery, struck it rich early on and then wisely walked away from piracy while they were ahead. Others accepted individual pardons and turned pirate hunter, like Sir Henry Mainwaring or Sir Henry Morgan. Scores of pirates also made good use of general amnesties. Although the rate of recidivism was high, and many a pirate – such as John Rackham, Woodes Rogers or Stede Bonnet

1. This woodcut vividly illustrates the sudden violence of a Viking raid descending on an unsuspecting English Channel coast in the times of Olaf Tryggvason, King of Norway, at the end of the tenth century. These raids usually came completely out of the blue and did not leave much time to organise a defence, or even to escape.

2. This nineteenth-century illustration shows a Viking raiding party in a surprise attack on an English coastal town – a scene that would have been all too familiar for those living along the exposed shores of Britain, and later on the European continent as well.

3. Viking king Anlaff (aka Olaf Guthfrithson) entering the Humber with a large fleet in spring 937, shortly before the battle of Brunanburh. In this battle, the Vikings and their Scottish allies were defeated by the forces of Aethelstan, king of England. Both sides suffered heavy losses.

4. In November 885, a Viking army descended on Paris. The vastly outnumbered citizens, led by Count Odo (Eudes), vigorously defended their city despite the Vikings' use of heavy siege engines. It was not until October 886 that the Vikings finally lifted the siege. Neuville's illustration shows Count Odo fighting his way back into Paris after having slipped out to petition Emperor Charles the Fat to come to the city's rescue.

5. Eustace the Monk, a notorious privateer and pirate, first fought for King John of England between 1204 and 1213, and then for King Philip II of France. He finally met his fate on 24 August 1217 in the battle of Sandwich when English sailors managed to board his vessel and kill him. His head was later put on a spike and paraded through the streets of Sandwich.

6. In 1671, a large host of buccaneers under the command of Henry Morgan sacked the city of Panama. Due to the spirited defence of the Spanish militia, most of the inhabitants fled the city before the privateers could enter it. They also managed to take most of the potential loot in the shape of gold and silver with them, much to the buccaneers' chagrin.

7. Cornelis Claesz van Wieringen's allegoric painting centres on a Dutch flyboat (fluyt) attacked by a well-armed English privateer. In the background, a French warship is coming to the fluyt's rescue. Flyboats, albeit much better armed ones, were the vessels of choice for corsair John Ward due to their sturdiness and innocent appearance.

8. Sea battles with Barbary corsairs were frequent occurrences until their defeat in the nineteenth century. Here, a British warship, probably the forty-six-gun *HMS Kingfisher*, fights off seven Algerian corsairs in an encounter on 22 May 1681. The *Kingfisher*'s captain, twenty-one-year-old Morgan Kempthorne, was one of eight British sailors killed in the battle.

9. As with all other Barbary corsairs, the threat posed by the Algerian pirates was only ended when France occupied the Barbary Coast principalities. This painting by Léon Morel-Fatio shows the French seventy-four-gun warship *La Provence*, flagship of Vice-Admiral Guy-Victor Dupperé, firing a broadside at the port of Algiers at the beginning of the invasion on 3 July 1830.

10. Malay pirates, including Sea Dayaks, Iranun and Balangingi, used a swarming tactic against larger ships, bearing down on their prey with dozens of vessels. After some well-aimed gunfire which disabled the target vessel, hundreds of pirates would board it, mercilessly cutting down everyone offering resistance. The few survivors were either ransomed or sold in regional slave markets.

11. Following exchanges of broadsides, sea battles usually culminated in bitter hand-to-hand combat – here, an Algerian corsair is boarded and captured by British sailors despite the Algerian crew's desperate resistance.

12. Just like the Malays, Chinese pirates operated in large fleets allowing them to also attack larger vessels, in particular well-armed European ones, again using a wolfpack-style swarming tactic.

13. For the Imperial Chinese Navy of the nineteenth century, fighting fleets of Chinese pirates was a difficult task: often, the battle-hardened pirates who had nothing to lose proved to be formidable opponents – especially since they were equipped with the same types of ships and weapons. Success or failure often depended on determined leadership, the right weather conditions and sheer luck.

14. The usual punishment meted out by Chinese authorities to captured pirates was public execution by beheading. These five pirates belonged to a group captured in a joint Anglo-Chinese pirate hunt in 1891. They are surrounded by Chinese dignitaries, soldiers and a small crowd waiting for the execution to commence.

15. Small skiffs – either wooden, fibreglass or rigid-hull inflatable (RHIB) – are the attack vessels of choice for Somali pirate action groups due to their manoeuvrability and speed. For near-coast operations these skiffs are launched from any suitable stretch of coast, while for high-seas operations they are usually deployed from 'motherships' such as captured freighters or trawlers.

16. A prolonged hostage crisis played out on the cargo ship *MV Faina*: about fifty Somali pirates held the vessel's twenty-one crew members hostage for five months between 25 September 2008 and 5 February 2009, when a ransom of more than $3 million was paid. The crisis was closely watched by several navies due to the sensitive nature of the vessel's cargo, consisting of thirty-three T-72 main battle tanks, anti-aircraft guns and rocket-propelled grenade launchers.

17. The attempted hijack of the containership MV *Maersk Alabama* (*Tygra* since 2016) on 8 April 2009 triggered a hostage crisis that lasted for four days and ended with the rescue of Captain Richard Phillips and the death of three of the four pirates – the surviving pirate was arrested and sentenced to thirty-three years and nine months in prison.

18. After Captain Phillips's rescue, the *Maersk Alabama* lifeboat on which he was held was inspected for evidence, brought to the USA and later put on display at the National SEAL Museum, Fort Pierce, Florida.

19. Captain Phillips (right) is pictured here with Lieutenant Commander David Fowler. Phillips's ordeal was later turned into the Hollywood blockbuster *Captain Phillips* (2013) starring Tom Hanks. Together with Stephan Talty, Phillips also wrote a book about the incident, titled *A Captain's Duty: Somali Pirates, Navy SEALs, and Dangerous Days at Sea*.

20. Telling dangerous Somali pirates from harmless Somali fishermen is not always an easy task for naval forces: if not caught in the act of attacking a vessel, all the Somali pirates need to do to appear innocent is throw any evidence of their ill intent overboard – for instance ladders, grapnels and assault rifles.

– returned to sea as soon as their money was spent, a substantial number of pirates took this golden opportunity to return to the fold, many of them having realised that the brutal reality of being a pirate was worlds apart from the 'merry life' they had dreamt of. Pirates making use of such amnesties were usually allowed to keep the booty they had garnered, and could openly live their lives without having to fear the long arm of the law. A non-Western example of such an amnesty is the negotiated surrender in 1810 of the Chinese pirate queen Zheng Yi Sao and her lover, Zhang Bao, together with hundreds of their followers, to officials of the Qing dynasty. Zheng Yi Sao finally passed away in 1844 aged sixty, having enjoyed since her surrender 'a peaceful life so far as [was] consistent with the keeping of an infamous gambling house'.[148] Her pirate career had lasted nearly a decade, and had seen her rise from prostitute to wife of the pirate leader Zheng Yi, successfully establishing herself after his death in 1807 as his successor and undisputed leader of a federation of 40,000–60,000 pirates, sailing in 400 junks.[149]

The buccaneer Captain Louis Le Golif, as a 'sanctioned' pirate with a proper commission, used the declarations of peace signed by King Louis XIV of France and King Charles II of Spain at Nijmegen between 1678 and 1679 to call it a day. Although many of his fellow buccaneers and freebooters ignored the sudden outbreak of peace, becoming 'real' pirates now that they no longer held valid commissions, Le Golif chose not to follow their example. Yet the frequent quarrels over the distribution of the prizes he took left their mark – not only in the form of duels, which he unsurprisingly won, but also in attempts to poison him, which made him ill. As usual in these unsettled times, peace was fleeting, and Le Golif was invited to return to the sea to attack Spanish possessions in the South Seas as a properly commissioned privateer again under the command of General Laurent de Graff. However, he demurred:

First, because [de Graff] wanted to remain the leader, and I saw no reason why this should not be me; second, because the enterprise rested on an argument which seemed to me in some respects ill-advised and there seemed a risk of slipping into piracy; third, because I was extremely rich, and I felt reluctant to risk those riches, to say nothing of my life, in the hope of acquiring others.[150]

No longer feeling safe on Tortuga, though, he returned to France, and disappeared from history: the last pages of his autobiography were destroyed in a fire.

Many pirates shared the fate of countless merchant mariners and perished in shipwrecks. This was the case for 'Black Sam' Bellamy and his 145-man crew, all but two of whom were drowned off Cape Cod on 26 April 1717 in a 'nor'easter', a cyclone driven by winds coming from the northeast. Aged just twenty-eight at the time of his death, Bellamy would have the posthumous honour of being the most successful and highest-earning pirate of all time, having captured more than fifty ships in the fifteen months he was active and making about £92 million ($120 million) in today's money.[151] Other pirates survived shipwreck only to be captured and killed, as were the French pirate François l'Olonnais's crew around 1662, early in l'Olonnais's pirate career. Having survived running aground near Campeche in the Gulf of Mexico, the crew waded ashore and were immediately set upon by a company of Spanish soldiers. All but l'Olonnais were killed – he survived by playing dead.[152] And then there were those who ended their lives on the gallows, like Captain Kidd (1701) and Calico Jack Rackham (1720); who were beheaded, like Wushi Er (1810); or who died in battle, like Thomas Tew (1695) and Blackbeard (1718). Ironically, Tew, the third highest-earning pirate ever with an estimated fortune of £78 million ($102 million) in today's money at the time of his death,[153] was killed in exactly the same encounter that made Avery and his crew rich beyond their wildest dreams (see p. 105). Tew's stomach was ripped open by a gunshot from the *Fateh Mohammed*, and despite desperately trying to keep his entrails from spilling out, he quickly succumbed to this gruesome injury. L'Olonnais also suffered a violent death in 1669, but not in battle: having survived yet another shipwreck on the coast of Darién, Panama, he was captured by a local tribe who considered both Spanish colonists and buccaneers their enemies. Exquemelin describes the end of this fearsome buccaneer: the tribespeople 'tore him in pieces alive, throwing his Body limb by limb into the fire, and his Ashes into the air; to the intent that no trace nor memory might remain of such an infamous inhumane creature'.[154]

Compared to pirates, their licensed equivalents – privateers and corsairs – had a somewhat better chance of surviving their careers. Of course, they shared with pirates the same risk of perishing either in a battle or a shipwreck, but since they were protected by a commission, they were usually not executed when captured by the enemy; they were more likely to be treated as prisoners of war, and to find themselves imprisoned or, in the Mediterranean, condemned to work the oars on the galleys and, after a while (in some cases, many years), ransomed or exchanged in prisoner swaps. If they survived their hazardous careers, they could honourably retire and live out their lives as leading and well-respected members of their societies. The Spanish corsair Alonso de Contreras (1582–1641) passed away peacefully in his bed, as did the French corsairs René Duguay-Trouin (1637–1736) and Robert Surcouf (1773–1823). Sir Francis Drake, Queen Elizabeth I's most successful privateer, died of dysentery at the age of fifty-five while lying at anchor off Portobello, Panama, his career having spanned thirty-three years from 1563 to that day, 28 January 1596. The corsair and 'arch pirate' John Ward managed to survive his adventurous life at sea and deep love of life on the waves – an English sailor who visited him in 1608 described how he spoke little and was 'almost always swearing. Drunk from morn till night . . . The habits of a thorough salt. A fool and an idiot out of his trade'[155] – to retire around 1612 in his adopted home of Tunis, where he lived in some splendour until his death of the plague in 1622 in the company of several other old captains who, like him, had 'turned Turk'.

The Pitfalls of Co-opting Former Pirates

Since not only privateers but also, under certain circumstances, pirates were seen as 'raffish instruments of foreign policy' with which to conduct undeclared guerrilla wars at sea (see pp. 88–9), states profiting from them were not always keen to curb their activities, lofty declarations on that matter notwithstanding. At times, however, vigorous efforts were made – whether because a new monarch wanted it thus, as in the case of James I of England, or because the pirates, hitherto a minor nuisance, became a major threat to a state that had thus far profited from their piracy – as after the Treaty of Madrid was signed in July 1670 by England and Spain, which stipulated that all English privateering commissions be revoked in exchange for Spanish recognition of all English possessions in the Caribbean. To combat piracy during such times, a 'carrot and stick' approach was usually used, on the one hand encouraging pirates, by means of generous amnesties and individual pardons, to mend their ways and return to the fold, while on the other using the full power of the law against them once captured. Regarding the latter 'stick', authorities always made a public spectacle of the execution of a notorious pirate – as they were prone to do for any execution in that period – in order to instil fear in the population in general, and seafarers in particular, to deter them from going a-pirating. In a sense, the criminal terror inflicted by the pirates on their victims was repaid via state terror.[156] However, unleashing the state's counter-terror on pirates was only possible when pirates had been caught, which was difficult to accomplish.

This brings us to another 'carrot', usually available only to a select few pirate captains of sufficient notoriety and fame: offering them the chance to become pirate hunters to protect the coasts and the waters of the realm, as in the case of Sir Henry Mainwaring under James I. Before he acceded the throne, the English Crown had been sluggish to actually do anything about piracy. As we have seen, officialdom charged with crushing piracy quite often turned a blind eye for the sake of private enrichment (see pp. 22–6), while the Crown itself had other reasons for tolerating piracy – especially so if the acts of piracy happened in distant waters and targeted England's competitors.[157] James's reign brought a gradual end to this turning a blind eye to pirates. Knowing all too well that his own admirals and governors were not keen to fight pirates, James looked for a pirate willing to turn pirate hunter. He soon found him, somewhat coincidentally, in Sir Henry Mainwaring. The well-educated Mainwaring had attended Oxford's illustrious Brasenose College and studied law at the Inner Temple in London before embarking on a career as a pirate in 1612, aged twenty-five.[158] Two notable differences set him apart from his Elizabethan predecessors: first, unlike Drake and Raleigh, he did not work for his monarch as a 'state-sanctioned' pirate, but only for himself; and, second, he did not operate out of English ports but from La Mamora, a Moroccan base just outside the Strait of Gibraltar, where he preyed upon Dutch, French, Portuguese and Spanish shipping. Mainwaring studiously avoided attacking English vessels, claiming in a letter to James I seeking a pardon that he could have been more than £100,000 better off had he done so.[159] Sparing English vessels certainly made granting a pardon easier for James, who did so on 9 June 1616.

Although the royal pardon did not stipulate that Mainwaring had to serve as pirate hunter, the grateful ex-pirate voluntarily did just that, expressing his gratitude immediately after the pardon was issued by proceeding 'to suppress any pirate that chanced to cross his path' – including a 'Turkish pirate' whose vessel Mainwaring found anchoring in the Thames 'as high up the river as Leigh'.[160] However, the main contribution to pirate hunting of his 'Majesty's new Creature' (thus the sign-off of his pardon-seeking letter) lay elsewhere: in early 1618, he presented the king with a treatise entitled 'On the Beginnings, Practices, and Suppression of Pirates'. Of more lasting importance than his occupation as an active pirate hunter during 1616, the text opened the door to a knighthood, a promotion to the rank of vice admiral and, finally, a career as a member of parliament.

The five-chapter treatise first describes how the average English pirate started his career (by stealing a suitable vessel, as we have seen – pp. 29, 91), how he learned his new trade, and what role an enabling environment played in this regard. Although Ireland is mentioned specifically, Mainwaring points out that England played an even bigger role in piracy because 'there is more plenty of Ports and Shipping, as also more abundance of Seamen'.[161] The second chapter provides an interesting insight into the mindset of ordinary pirates: according to Mainwaring, they knew that, if caught, it was usually only their captain who would be hanged, while they would escape with 'a little lazy imprisonment, which is rather a charge to your Highness, than any affliction to them, since their whole life for the most part is spent but in a running Prison' (that is, their ship); Mainwaring thus recommended that they should be used as galley slaves in summertime and in winter as labourers to repair castles and coastal fortifications.[162] Such punishment was then the norm in the Mediterranean. He also offered advice on how to deal with those pirates who claimed they had been acting under duress:

> The Way in this case neither to punish the innocent, nor to let the guilty escape, is (in my conceit) to have all such committed, till a just proof can be made . . . whether they have received shares or pillage of the goods or not, more than to supply their necessary wants and wearing clothes; if they have, they are then absolutely as willing and as guilty as is the Commander.[163]

The short third chapter on pirate tactics offers only superficial insight into the well-known basics, such as the use of false flags or drags to disguise a ship's actual speed under full sail. The impression is that the former pirate Mainwaring was here playing his cards very close to his chest, careful not to give away too much information, which presumably might later have been used against him had he decided to turn pirate once more. The fourth chapter is longer, at sixteen pages, and is filled with detailed information about pirate ports and harbours, from coastal cities such as Tunis, Tripoli, Algiers and the Moroccan Salé to suitable rivers, bays or quiet coves along uninhabited coasts around the western Mediterranean, the Atlantic coasts including the Azores, the Canary Islands and Newfoundland, and the shores of England, Scotland and Ireland. In the final chapter Mainwaring offered his recommendations on how to curb piracy. '[T]rying to pull up the ladder behind him after making his own successful escape',[164] Mainwaring, after profiting from a royal pardon, counselled strongly against such leniency: 'Next, to take away their hopes and encouragements, your Highness must put on a constant immutable resolution never to grant any Pardon, and for those that are or may be taken, to put them all to death, or make slaves of them.'[165] Thankfully, King James did not follow Mainwaring's advice to the letter, thus sparing many a pirate who availed himself of the king's pardon to save himself from the gallows.

Another pirate turned pirate hunter was Sir Henry Morgan. At the end of his buccaneering days he was temporarily jailed in 1671 following his sack of Panama (see p. 112) – six months after the Treaty of Madrid. But since Morgan was able to convince the court that he had not heard of the peace treaty when he set sail for Panama, he was never charged. Instead, he was appointed lieutenant governor of Jamaica in January 1674 and knighted in November of the same year. However, Morgan's co-option was far less successful than Mainwaring's. Although his job description explicitly included curbing piracy, he chose to ignore his instructions, instead handing out privateering commissions to anybody who could pay for one – quite a lucrative side-business for him. Interestingly, he even attempted to silence his numerous critics who called him a corrupt and bloodthirsty pirate by way of a libel suit against the publishers of Exquemelin's then very popular and widely read report on the buccaneers of America. This had mixed results: Morgan was awarded £200 in damages and the promise of a retraction, but the latter never came. Be that as it may, as a pirate hunter he simply went through the motions: turning a blind eye was far more lucrative than slaughtering the goose that laid the golden egg, after all.

This brings us to yet another attempt to co-opt pirates to aid in counter-piracy operations. As we have already seen, the first big wave of piracy along Chinese coasts came in the shape of the Wako pirate fleets (see pp. 24, 42–3), whose operations resulted in the disastrous 'maritime prohibitions' passed by the Ming dynasty in the fourteenth and fifteenth centuries (see p. 45). The second big wave of Chinese piracy appeared in the middle of the seventeenth century during the transition from the disintegrating Ming to the Qing (Manchu) dynasty.[166] The ever more desperate land battles of the Ming armies against the implacable advance of the Manchus resulted in a loss of control over the southern Chinese coastal areas, with the effect that long before the final collapse of the Ming dynasty in 1662, drastic measures had to be taken to keep at least a modicum of law and order there. The answer was to co-opt Zheng Zhilong (c. 1600–1; in the West better known as Nicholas Gaspar Iquan after his conversion to Catholicism in Macao at some time during his youth), one of the most successful pirate lords, by appointing him admiral around 1628 in the hope that this lofty rank plus the access to (legal) riches would buy loyalty to the emperor.[167] Initially, this seemed to work quite well for the beleaguered dynasty; up to 1637, Zheng Zhilong successfully pacified the whole coastal region of southern China with the help of his pirate fleet that now formed part of the Imperial navy – all the while amassing more personal wealth and more followers. From 1636, however, Zheng Zhilong became ever more independent, and when he finally established himself around 1645 as the unofficial 'king of South China' or 'lord of the Straits', there was nothing the fading dynasty could do to oust him: his wealth and political clout now greatly surpassed theirs, and the Ming court knew that they needed him more than he needed them. Showered with even higher ranks and titles, and for a while actually using his own wealth, ships and soldiers to keep the Ming cause alive, Zheng Zhilong exploited his official position as far as he possibly could before finally defecting to the Manchus as the then obviously winning side around 1650.[168]

Zheng Zhilong's eldest son, Zheng Chenggong (1624–62), opted to remain loyal to the Ming. He is by far the better known of the two in the annals of piracy, although by the name Coxinga rather than his Chinese name (his Chinese title was 'lord with the imperial surname' or Guóxìngyé). It is open to debate whether he was as fervently loyal to the Ming as some sources would have it or was just a wily political actor. Even his contemporaries seemed unsure how to treat him, and what to call him: 'It was the Manchus and the Dutch who called Coxinga a pirate, the English and the Spanish who called him a king. His Chinese countrymen called him both, depending on their mood.'[169] What is not in doubt is that by seemingly raising the banner of Ming loyalism, and by engaging Qing troops in a series of battles in the region of Canton during 1650 and 1651, Coxinga gained the support of enough of the coastal population of southern China and Taiwan to be able to carve out a piratical empire there. In a sense, the Qing assisted him by passing an edict even more disastrous than the Ming 'sea bans', which made it illegal to live nearer than 30 miles from the sea, in the (vain) hope that a barren and hostile 'no-man's-land' devoid of people would put an end to piracy. All it achieved was the wholesale destruction of coastal infrastructure, thus condemning the coastal population either to mass migration or mass starvation.

However, for them there was yet another option that the new Qing administration had not considered: siding with Coxinga, whose ships ferried them across the strait to Taiwan. Of course, the ships he sent had another objective as well – to plunder and pillage: 'His raiders picked through whatever was left behind, and carried off what food and supplies they could from the abandoned villages before the Manchu demolition teams arrived.'[170] Coxinga also came to blows with the Dutch on Taiwan, eventually expelling them from the island in February 1662 after a year-long siege of Fort Zeelandia, their main stronghold. This decisive victory elevated Coxinga to the status of national hero in both the Republic of

China (Taiwan) and the People's Republic of China (PRC); propaganda prints of the Communist Party of China, for example, depict the victory over the Dutch in the usual colourful, martial style of 1950s Maoism.[171] Back in the seventeenth century the war was not, however, about early nationalism or communism: it was essentially a violent trade war. The Dutch, already well ensconced in the port cities of Malacca (in modern Malaysia) and Batavia (modern Jakarta/Indonesia), had gained a first foothold on Taiwan in 1624 against the resistance of the Spanish who already had a presence there, and gradually brought the whole island under their control, a Dutch expedition defeating the last remaining Spanish forces in 1642. For the Dutch, Taiwan was a stepping stone to the Chinese mainland, along the coasts of which they had a keen interest in acquiring fortified trading posts. Their ambition made them the natural enemies of Coxinga, who declared that 'such places as Batavia, Taiwan and Malacca are one inseparable market, and I am master of this area. I will never allow [them] to usurp my position.'[172] Coxinga did not have much time to enjoy his success over the Dutch, however: he died only four months later, in June 1662, of malaria. His lieutenants quickly became embroiled in a war of succession, with the result that the pirate kingdom created by Coxinga swiftly collapsed even before Manchu troops invaded the island in 1683. The question of whether Coxinga should be seen as a pirate, a king, or even a national hero and freedom fighter is an interesting one: again, the truth lies in the eyes of the beholder.

That one man's pirate is another man's national hero is likewise the case when it comes to the Indian pirate (or admiral) Kanhoji Angre. Here, the historico-political backdrop is the wars of supremacy fought from 1680 to 1707 on the Indian subcontinent between the Maratha confederation and the Mughal Empire.[173] Both were formidable land powers with only minimal naval assets, mainly in the shape of small, lightly armed vessels. The Maratha navy consisted of about fifty *gallivats*, galley-like vessels of about 30 to 150 tons, and a dozen or so two- or three-masted *grabs* (from the Arabic for 'raven'), weighing between 150 and 500 tons and equipped with light-calibre broadside artillery. In order to protect their own maritime trade while harassing the enemy's ships, each power entered into alliances with the Western sea powers already present on Indian shores, the more powerful Mughal Empire forming alliances with the formidable British East India Company and the Dutch, the Maratha confederation with the declining but still redoubtable Portuguese, based in Goa. However, in 1698 the Marathas also enlisted the help of Kanhoji Angre (1669–1729), a local maritime entrepreneur who already possessed a fleet composed of large and comparatively well-armed ships.[174] Angre was duly appointed admiral (*sarkhil*), made commander of the Maratha navy, and awarded a salary commensurate with his rank. Nevertheless, the Western sea powers, including the Portuguese who were technically allied with the Marathas, thought him a pirate pure and simple. As with Coxinga, whether Angre was a loyalist or simply availing himself of an opportunity to carve out his own little kingdom along the coastal plains between Goa and Bombay while his overlords were busily fighting battles on land is open to question.

Initially, the East India Company (EIC) and the Dutch, the main naval allies of the Mughals, seem to have taken little notice of Angre until in 1702 his fleet captured a small Bombay-bound EIC merchant vessel. Somewhat surprisingly, given the fact that the EIC was an ally of the Mughal Empire, and thus an enemy of the Marathas, his move against the EIC seems to have been unexpected: 'What had roused his anger against the English does not appear, but [in 1702] we find him sending word to Bombay that he would give the English cause to remember the name of Conajee Angria, a threat that he carried out only too well.'[175] In any case, from that moment on, Angre was the declared enemy of the EIC. Despite several naval expeditions against his strongholds, some of them in coop-eration with the Portuguese who also saw their own vessels frequently seized, the EIC was unable to defeat him. Even after Angre's death in 1729 his sons carried on successfully harassing maritime traffic along the western Indian coasts until February 1756 when Gheriah (modern Vijaydurg), their last fortress, fell to a joint operation of EIC naval forces and Maratha land forces. Angre's eldest son Tulaji, who had succeeded him as an admiral of the Maratha fleet, had become too independent and was by then regarded as a pirate even by his erstwhile employers.[176]

The case of Angre shows interesting parallels with Coxinga's: for the English, the Dutch and even his notional allies the Portuguese, Angre was clearly a pirate, but for the Marathas he was an admiral and naval hero. Some modern historians of India even reinvented him as 'a champion of Indian resistance to European imperialism'.[177] If one follows the reports of Angre's contemporary Lieutenant Clement Downing, a naval officer of the East India Company, the truth seems to lie somewhere in between. He acted, at least initially, on behalf of, and was sanctioned by, the Marathas. When they were distracted by their land battles against the Mughals, Angre seems to have begun to slip down the continuum from privateering to piracy.[178] What can be gleaned from his and Coxinga's stories is a lesson that had already been learned in the Carolingian Empire in the times of the Viking raids: for pirates, civil wars and the ensuing disunity are great enablers for ever larger-scale raiding – and eventually even for land-grabbing and empire-building. Meanwhile, the strategy of employing a formidable former pirate to establish law and order at sea worked only for those monarchs whose power was well entrenched and whose kingdoms were united. For all others, it was a double-edged sword.

Hunting the Hunters

Whether or not a former pirate was employed as pirate hunter, taking action against pirates at sea required a major effort: after all, the 'blue yonder' was wide, and the pirates crisscrossing it were highly mobile. There also always seemed to be an imbalance between the relatively few warships deployable as pirate hunters and the comparative multitude of pirates, who vastly outnumbered them. This imbalance is exemplified by the early eighteenth-century Royal Navy. Most readers are probably familiar with the refrain of the popular patriotic British song: 'Rule Britannia! Britannia rule the waves!' However, it was not ever thus. It was most certainly not yet the case when the Royal Navy, together with Spanish, Dutch and French warships, confronted the buccaneers in the still-contested waters of the Caribbean between 1650 and 1730. The difficulties involved in the Royal Navy's anti-piracy operations are illustrated by the fact that in the decade beginning 1716 the navy had in total an overall personnel strength of 13,000, while '1,800 to 2,400 Anglo-American pirates prowled the seas between 1716 and 1718, 1,500 to 2,000 between 1719 and 1722, and 1,000 to 1,500, declining to fewer than 200, between 1723 and 1726'.[179] However, of the 13,000 Royal Navy sailors, only a fraction were available for pirate hunting since such action was only one aspect of the navy's responsibility. Hence, the pirates played a game of 'catch me if you can' with the few warships initially dispatched to get rid of them. Moreover, many warships also tended to be too slow to intercept fast-sailing pirate vessels, and too big to pursue them into shallower waters.

Pirate hunting also depended on an intimate knowledge of local conditions: potential hiding places, islets, reefs and shoals, currents, and weather and wind patterns. Despite their few ships and crews, the Spanish *Armada de Barlovento* ('Windward Fleet'), for instance, captured scores of pirates between the mid-sixteenth and mid-seventeenth centuries in the Caribbean, being equipped with an excellent knowledge of their area of operation. In 1594, a Spanish *armadillo* or 'small flotilla' of three ships with a combined crew of 1,300 sailors, gunners and marines even managed to capture no less a pirate than Sir Richard Hawkins (*c.* 1562–17 April 1622), one of the most famous of Elizabeth I's 'gentlemen adventurers', off the coast of Peru after an epic three-day battle. Hawkins had already been at sea for about a year, probing the Spanish defences in the Caribbean and along the Atlantic and Pacific coasts of the Spanish Main (modern Latin America) to discover weak spots that would allow him to plunder and pillage targets of opportunity both at sea (merchant vessels) and on the shores (port cities and villages) when he ran into the Spanish squadron. Being vastly outnumbered on his own vessel the *Dainty* with a crew of seventy, Hawkins later wrote that the 'fight continued so hott on both sides, that the artillery and muskets never ceased to play'. Finally, the Spanish flotilla carried the day, as Hawkins frankly admitted:

> [Our] sayles being torne, our mastes all perished, our pumpes rent
> and shot to peeces, and our shippe with fourteen shott under water
> and seven or eight foot of water in the hold; many of our men being
> slaine, and the most part of them which remained sore hurt . . . our
> best course was to surrender ourselves before our shippe sunke.[180]

For these proactive counter-piracy operations, the Spanish were able to draw on the seamanship of their own local population – 'local' here meaning those resident on the Spanish Caribbean islands and along the coasts of the Spanish Main (the coastal areas of the Gulf of Mexico, Central America and the northern coast of South America).

On one occasion, the Spanish corsair Alonso de Contreras, usually active in the Mediterranean only, also lent a hand. In the summer of 1618, King Philip III appointed him commander of a small flotilla of two galleons and dispatched him to Puerto Rico to relieve its garrison, at that time under relentless attack by French, Dutch and English pirates. While lying there, Contreras was alerted to the presence of an English fleet of five vessels, led by one of the most famous pirates of those times: Sir Walter Raleigh, known to the Spanish as 'Guaterral'. Contreras later claimed that it was at that moment he determined upon capturing Raleigh. But the circumstances were not ideal when the Spaniard finally encountered the Guaterral; Contreras was in the process of escorting two unarmed merchant vessels from Puerto Rico to San Domingo, with his small fleet still in port, strengthened by yet another merchant vessel that strayed into port while he was there. Despite the protestations of the merchantmen's masters, Contreras decided to arm the three ships in his protection[181] to set a trap for Raleigh:

> When the enemy saw us, I veered away. But we fled very slowly and, in no time, our foes crowded in. Suddenly, I turned my bows and attacked. They retaliated, and, since they could handle their sails better than we could, they were able to close in or open the range at their pleasure. I could not get my claws on them.[182]

The fight itself seems to have been a desultory affair: Contreras reports musket shots being fired, but no broadsides. Finally, after one of the English captains had been killed by a lucky musket shot, 'they sailed away, realising that we were not merchantmen but warships after their blood', and Contreras's dream of capturing Raleigh came to nothing.[183]

While the Spanish were able to tweak the numbers game at least slightly in their favour by enlisting their own loyal settlers, this was not always an option in other parts of their global empire, or for other colonial empires trying to rid their waters of pirates. In the Philippines from the late sixteenth century onwards, for example, Spanish anti-piracy operations were launched from Luzon in the north against the Iranun and Balangingi based on Mindanao and adjacent islands to the south, but were always undone by too few ships and too few crew and soldiers, at least until the mid-nineteenth century, when the first steamships entered Spanish-Philippine waters. Like the East India Company's paddle steamer *Diana* a decade before (see p. 109), the *Magallanes*, the *Elcano* and the *Reina de Castilla* swiftly chased most of the pirates active in the Philippines out of the water.

The Portuguese, very thinly spread over their vast maritime empire, likewise tried to make up for their small numbers with a fierce fighting spirit and a reputation for deploying the utmost cruelty when it suited them. The Dutch, or initially rather the Dutch East India Company (Verenigde Oost-Indische Compagnie, VOC, founded in 1602), tried the very same approach in the beginning of their own colonial age, and for the very same reason. In the East Indies, however, they soon found it more convenient to fall back on the skills and knowledge of the locals they now ruled via so-called corvée (enforced) labour (the 'enforced expression of loyalty'),[184] while also appropriating local vessels for the purpose of policing their colonial waters. The regular cruises such vessels made through the South China Sea were known as *hongitochten* – 'voyages' (*tochten*) with 'local vessels' (*hongi*) – and had other purposes: not only chasing off anyone not supposed to be there (that is, illegal traders as well as pirates), but also inspecting and surveying their far-flung archipelagic possessions, particularly in regard to their loyalty to the Dutch and the potential yield of their plantations. After all, it was not the exotic scenery that had brought the Dutch to these waters, but the spices grown there, which were at this time highly prized and high-priced luxury goods. These cruises, first organised by Governor-General Jan Pieterszoon Coen (1587–1629) in the 1620s, had the primary objective of enforcing the VOC's monopoly on spices, especially the cloves grown in the Moluccas; this could involve the ruthless cutting down of clove trees, even if this condemned the local population to poverty and starvation. Compared to this, the anti-piracy aspect of such missions was a minor one.[185]

Privateers were also occasionally used as pirate hunters, even though their main role was harassing the enemy's maritime trade via commerce raiding (this *guerre de course* was the origin of the name 'corsair' for Mediterranean privateers). Hunting other privateers was a task that nobody on board a privateer coveted: as we have seen (p. 93), one of the reasons Henry 'Long Ben' Avery succeeded in instigating a mutiny and taking over the well-armed privateering ship *Charles II* from Captain Gibson was that its crew were not happy about the prospect of battling it out with equally well-armed French privateers in the Caribbean, on behalf of Spain and for little personal gain. How deadly such battles between privateers could be is illustrated by a 1601 encounter off the coast of Alexandria between a Maltese corsair ship (aboard which a nine-teen-year-old Alonso de Contreras was a humble soldier on one of his first cruises) and a huge and well-armed Turkish corsair. Guns at the ready, the Maltese captain hailed the Turkish vessel to find out if it was friend or foe: ' "Just a ship sailing the high seas," came the reply. And we knew by their insolence that they, too, were ready with their guns.'[186] After exchanging some broadsides that killed and maimed many crew members on both sides, the Maltese corsair drew alongside the enemy ship and Contreras and his fellows boarded it, even though it was already past midnight. Bitter but inconclusive hand-to-hand fighting raged for about an hour, during which the 400-strong Turkish crew had managed to counter-board, taking the Maltese corsair's forecastle before they could be driven off again. At dawn, the battle resumed, first fought hand-to-hand on the decks of both vessels, and, when this once more proved inconclusive, as a gun battle that killed and wounded many. At dawn on the second day, the Maltese captain ordered yet another assault on the Turkish ship. After three long hours of desperate fighting, the Turkish resistance faltered and the remaining crew members jumped overboard, swimming to the nearby shore. How bloody the battle was can be gleaned from the final tally of Turkish victims: according to Contreras, 'We found over two hundred and fifty dead bodies aboard.'[187]

Contreras's clash with the Turkish corsair might have been a chance encounter – he left it unclear in his memoirs whether the mission was a dedicated pirate hunting operation or not. The Royal Navy lieutenant Robert Maynard's mission in November 1718 was such an operation, though, and a very clear-cut one at that: he was tasked with capturing a specific pirate, namely Edward Teach, better known as Blackbeard.[188] Blackbeard was one of the most fearsome pirates ever: it was said that he never had to kill anyone aboard a targeted vessel since nobody dared to offer resistance. Perhaps overconfidently, Blackbeard ignored urgent warnings of imminent action against him, and Maynard managed to surprise him at anchor in the estuary of Ocracoke Island off North

Carolina on the evening of 17 November 1718.[189] The battle itself started early the following morning, when Maynard's two sloops *Jane* and *Ranger*, which were not equipped with guns, bore down on the pirate vessel. To a casual observer along the estuary, the battle must have looked like a very one-sided affair: while Maynard's crews engaged the pirates with small arms only, Blackbeard responded with broadside after broadside.[190] At one time, it appeared as if Blackbeard would triumph: one of his broadsides struck home, killing and wounding twenty of Maynard's men on the *Jane* while killing nine of the *Ranger*'s crew, including the vessel's commander, a Midshipman Hyde.[191] Seeing Blackbeard's vessel drawing alongside and suspecting another devastating broadside as a prelude to boarding, Maynard ordered his men on the *Jane* below deck, telling them 'to get their Pistols and Swords ready for close fighting, and to come up on his Command'.[192] This turned out to be a wise decision: as soon as Blackbeard's vessel was alongside Maynard's, the pirates threw several primitive hand grenades filled with 'small Shot, Slugs, and Pieces of Lead or Iron, with a quick Match in the Mouth of it'.[193] Under normal circumstances, these weapons would have killed or disabled most of the crew, but due to Maynard's foresight, nobody was injured. More decisively, seeing only Maynard and the helmsman on deck, Blackbeard gave order to board. As in the battle described by Contreras, the hand-to-hand fighting that followed was fierce, fought by fifteen pirates against thirteen pirate hunters armed with pistols, swords, cutlasses, axes and daggers. At the end of it, Blackbeard was dead, and so were eight other pirates. As Defoe has it, 'all the rest, much wounded, jump'd over-board, and called out for Quarters'.[194] Retreating to their own vessel was no longer possible, it having been boarded and captured by the *Ranger*'s remaining crew.

Not all pirates put up such a desperate fight when a pirate hunter intercepted them. Some were far too drunk even to realise what was happening, while others were caught with their ships beached for repairs. Many pirates, even greatly feared ones, seemed sometimes simply to have lost their courage. John 'Calico Jack' Rackham, one of the most infamous pirates of his day, inexplicably reacted with seeming cowardice when his ship was engaged along the northern coast of Jamaica by an English sloop under the command of pirate hunter Captain Jonathan Barnet. Rackham and his entire crew quickly surrendered without putting up much of a fight – to the derision of female crew members Anne Bonny and Mary Read (see p. 68). It's reported that, before Rackham was hanged, he was allowed to see his lover Anne Bonny one last time, 'but all the Comfort she gave him, was, that she was sorry to see him there, but if he had fought like a Man, he need not have been hang'd like a dog'.[195]

Anti-Piracy Alliances

Much better than fighting individual pirates at sea or in creeks – but also far more dangerous – was taking the fight to their bases to shut them down once and for all. The wars fought from the sixteenth to the early nineteenth centuries by various Western sea powers – initially mainly Spain and its allies Genoa and the Knights Hospitaller, later also the Netherlands, France and England/Great Britain – against the Barbary Coast corsairs of Algiers, Tripoli and Tunis offer considerable insight into the difficulties that accompanied such campaigns.

The majority of the maritime raiders operating out of those three Barbary Coast principalities were, strictly speaking, privateers: their activities were sanctioned by their rulers, and were restricted to attacking each city's respective enemies, of which there were usually many. The main income of Algiers, Tripoli and Tunis was booty, comprising goods, gold and silver (either in bars or in coins), arms and ammunition, and slaves for their bustling slave markets; without the income derived from this state-sponsored piracy, the principalities would not have been viable states,[196] and their seaborne jihads were waged against the infidels much more out of economic necessity than religious conviction (see pp. 76–7). To maximise their income, some of their raiders even made forays into the Atlantic and the North Sea; one raid carried out by Algerian corsairs in 1616 targeted the Azores,[197] while Murat Reis the Younger (formerly Jan Janszoon) operated in the North Sea for five years, his activities culminating (as we have seen, p. 108) in the sack of the Irish port of Baltimore in 1631. An even more ambitious corsairing operation in June 1627 went as far as Iceland, 5,000 nautical miles from Algiers.[198] Ships encountered in the course of such expeditions only avoided being attacked if they were flying the flag of a state that paid handsomely for what the Barbary corsairs called safe-conduct passes, and what the rulers of Algiers, Tripoli and Tunis who 'sold' those passes preferred to call 'tribute'. Modern scholars are more clear-eyed: 'nations who did not pay tribute – who did not make blackmail payments, in other words – were attacked, had their vessels and towns plundered, and crews, passengers, and coastal residents enslaved'.[199] During the sixteenth, seventeenth and eighteenth centuries, the main European trading nations of the Netherlands and Great Britain, as well as the Spanish, the French, the Danes, the Swedes, and various Italian principalities, all paid for these passes. The sums involved were substantial: 'In the 1780s Great Britain was paying Algiers around £1000 a year to maintain the peace, roughly equivalent to £1.2 million [$1.56 million] today. The Dutch paid about £24,000 and the Spanish a colossal £120,000.'[200] However, experience showed that the peace bought with money – and at times even with maritime equipment, arms and ammunition – often proved brittle and short-lived; after all, to live in peace with all trading nations would have been counterproductive for the economies of Algiers, Tripoli and Tunis.

It is thus not surprising that several major trading nations and military powers of their day attempted to occupy or at least neutralise these notorious pirate lairs, either alone or as part of a multilateral operation. Short-lived alliances to combat the Barbary Coast corsairs were formed: a combined French–Spanish naval attack on Tunis in the year 1609 was followed by a successful Dutch–Spanish attack on twenty-four Algerian corsairs in 1618, while the British attempted between 1617 and 1620 to form an alliance against Algiers with the Dutch and the Spanish.[201] This naval triple alliance was planned to a large extent by Admiral Sir William Monson, who had a good record of suppressing Irish and Scottish pirates along their respective coasts and in the Irish Sea. In his opinion, 'so many ships of his Majesty's as will carry three thousand tons burthen, and twelve hundred men; Spain and Holland sending ships to this rate will be a force sufficient to encounter the whole number of the Turkish pirates'.[202] That was, provided that two conditions were met: the first was Spanish cooperation, as the combined fleet would need to use Spanish harbours for replenishing; the second, perfect timing: since a frontal assault on Algiers with the Algerian fleet in port was deemed to be suicidal, Monson advised blockading the port after the corsairs had left, arguing that no other port they might run for, such as Tunis or Agadir, could offer the same kind of protection. This could only be accomplished by keeping the operation absolutely secret, otherwise the Algerian corsairs would simply remain in port, thus forcing the allied fleet to abandon the whole operation.[203] Monson therefore recommended 'that our ships be provided under pretence of another employment'.[204] He also stated that the combined fleet should 'be extraordinary well provided with muskets and all other munitions, and especially with dice shot to be shot out of ordnance; because, where there are many men, as commonly there be in pirates, dice shot will make a great slaughter among them'. [205] But despite James I's diplomats pulling out all the stops to make the alliance happen, mutual distrust between the Netherlands and Spain proved to be insurmountable, and the small Navy Royal (it became known as the Royal Navy only from the 1660s onwards) was left to go it alone. In 1620, a fleet under the command of Sir Robert Mansell was duly dispatched to deal with the Algerian corsairs. However, due to a combination of flawed strategy and adverse weather conditions off Algiers, little was accomplished.[206]

Despite several further efforts over the following decades to shut down the Barbary Coast ports, the situation had not really changed by the time US merchant vessels began to enter Mediterranean waters during the second half of the eighteenth century. Following the Declaration of Independence in 1776 the Americans had a problem: the British safe-conduct passes that had previously protected them no longer did so, and US diplomats had to be dispatched to negotiate with the Barbary Coast principalities. As usual, the treaties proved short-lived, with the various rulers demanding renegotiation on the least pretext. Yusuf Karamanli, pasha of Tripoli, turned out to be the greediest and the most bellicose of the lot; after his demands for additional money on top of the $40,000 (plus 'presents' of $12,000 in cash) that had been agreed upon in a treaty in November 1796 were flatly refused by the United States, he declared war on them on 26 February 1801.[207] Thus began the First Barbary War (1801–5, also known as the 'Tripolitan War')[208] – coincidentally also the first war declared on the US. The war proved inconclusive, as did the (very) short Second Barbary War of 17–19 June 1815 (also known as the 'Algerian War') which also involved Algiers and Tunis as belligerents.[209] The hostilities were, however, of great importance for the fledgling US Marines and the US Navy, allowing them to test their abilities as well as their reach.[210] The activities of the Barbary Coast states only came to an end courtesy of French imperial designs. After one of France's familiar disputes with Algiers, on 13 June 1830 a major French expeditionary force of 37,000 infantry backed up by 83 field guns landed in a bay near Algiers, routing the Algerian forces over the following six days and then laying siege to the city. After a heavy bombardment on 4 July, the ruler of Algiers, Hassan Bashaw, surrendered and was swiftly exiled by the French. They intended to remain. And not only that: once 'in possession of Algiers, the French began expanding into the interior of the country and later across much of North Africa, so inaugurating a long, bloody war of conquest which did not end until December 1847'.[211] Now without their previously enabling environment of supportive states and friendly shores, the Barbary Coast maritime raiders, both pirates and corsairs, finally faded into history.

The Apparent Demise of Piracy

As Britain's unsuccessful efforts to form a combined Anglo-Dutch-Spanish alliance against Algiers show, the fight against piracy was not just a tactical problem – it was also a political one. As with the modern war against global terrorism, wars on piracy depended on a 'coalition of the willing' to be successful. Driven by self-interest, the maritime powers of the day could play very cynical games: an English consul in Syria in 1611 observed that 'there were difficulties in the way of uniting sovereigns for the suppression of piracy; for some are not displeased that pirates exist and are glad to see certain markets harassed'.[212] The French attitude towards multinational operations against the Barbary Coast pirates is telling: in 1729, an anonymous memorandum stated rather bluntly that we 'are certain that it is not in our interest that all the Barbary corsairs be destroyed, since then we would be on a par with all the Italians and the peoples of the North Sea'.[213] This was also one of the main reasons why even the major European military powers acquiesced for so long in the tribute system: paying tribute to the Barbary Coast states was still cheaper than fitting out a naval expedition, while it also gave them a commercial edge over those poorer competitor states that could not afford to pay the tribute – with the result that their ships were regularly attacked.[214]

Furthermore, 'the great maritime nations were always suspicious of each other's intentions and were often reluctant to believe that a proposed attack on the corsairs was not a cover for some other more nefarious activity. Such suspicions were sometimes justified.'[215] Regarding the English proposal to Spain for an expedition against the Barbary corsairs at the end of April 1617, British naval historian Sir Julian Corbett wrote that an 'expedition against the Barbary corsairs became the stock diplomatic formula for covering some ulterior and sinister design'.[216] Against the backdrop of this climate of mutual distrust, it is no wonder that most of the proposed alliances against the Barbary corsairs and the ports from which they operated came to naught. Similar considerations also hampered the fight against rampant buccaneering and piracy in the Caribbean, or in the South China Sea where British, Dutch, French and Spanish colonial naval forces each organised their own unilateral anti-pirate patrols in 'their' waters, while often clandestinely supporting or at least facilitating piracy in the waters of the others.

Nevertheless, by the early twentieth century, this tit-for-tat, mercantile-focused policy had changed – and so had the international landscape. The French occupation of large parts of North Africa was symptomatic of this. Most of the major non-Western powers, that for centuries had posed a formidable challenge to European powers, were on the wane or had already collapsed. Among them were the 'gunpowder empires' – the Ottoman Empire (which for that very reason could not come to the rescue of the Barbary Coast states), the Safavid Empire in the Middle East, and the Mughal Empire in South Asia. In the age of imperialism, more and more of the shores previously offering safe havens to various pirate fleets now came under the direct control of Western sea powers, especially Great Britain. The times had changed in another way, too: after centuries of waging 'small wars' on the fringes of their spheres of influence, the old European empires had finally staked – and to a certain extent mutually accepted – their claims, and now found it more profitable to rely on maritime trade than on point-scoring and raiding via privateers or pirates. This also meant that these previously useful tools in the incessant proxy wars at sea no longer served the purpose of furthering the national interest – now quite the opposite was true. Furthermore, modern technology gradually gave the various sea powers' naval forces an edge over pirates, tribal maritime raiders such as the Iranun and Balangingi, and even the old-fashioned and obsolete war fleets of soon-to-be-colonised non-Western powers. We have seen how just one paddle steamer, the East India Company's *Diana*, reduced a marauding fleet of Iranun *prahus* to splinters (p. 109). At last, piracy seemed about to be confined to the history books.

*　*　*

How had piracy changed and developed during the period that saw the rise of European sea power? The main driving factors to turn pirate remained grievances such as poverty, unemployment and harsh living conditions on the one hand, and greed or 'the lure of easy money' on the other, with religion occasionally thrown into the mix. What made people become pirates was still a complex mixture of push-and-pull factors, the exact composition depending on local circumstances. Frequently, a certain amount of coincidence forced the hands of individuals like Zheng Yi Sao, Contreras, Le Golif or Exquemelin, and occasionally even a sense of adventure, as with Stede Bonnet or William Dampier. But these individuals were few and far between: even Elizabeth I's 'gentlemen adventurers' were driven by greed more than anything else.

Some forms of piracy persisted while others disappeared. Corsairing in the Mediterranean continued uninterrupted from the Middle Ages until the end of this period, while waves of pirates still harassed the coasts of China and haunted the waters of the South China Sea. In northern waters, small-scale piracy and privateering continued unabated, but larger-scale raiding by huge pirate fleets such as those of the Victual Brothers, or large-scale coastal raiding as conducted by the Vikings, was by now a thing of the distant past. Not that pirating had gone out of fashion in northern waters – rather, some profound changes triggered by Western colonialism and imperialism brought (one could almost say 'exported') many Western explorers, adventurers and, of course, pirates to the distant shores of the New World, those of Central and South America yielding immense treasures of gold, silver and pearls, those of the Far East luxury commodities such as spices, Chinese silks and porcelain, as well as gold, silver, diamonds, emeralds and other precious jewels. Conveniently for pirates of the period, especially those operating in Western waters, these astonishing riches were transported by Portuguese and Spanish vessels via the Atlantic from the Spanish Main or Southeast Asia to their home ports, or carried on Indian vessels plying the pilgrimage route to the Red Sea and back. Many pirates amassed riches beyond their wildest dreams, like 'Black Sam' Bellamy, Sir

Francis Drake (pirate or privateer, depending on one's view) and Thomas Tew. Tew's case, however, also demonstrates why the pirates' motto was 'a merry life but a short one': in July 1695, he died a miserable death after being grievously injured in the battle with the *Fateh Mohammed* (see p. 120), having been active as a pirate for just three years. The reason pirates in this period could strike so far away from their own bases compared to the pirates of the Middle Ages lay in the advances made since that time in the arts of navigation and shipbuilding, which made possible voyages on the high seas, say, from the Caribbean via the Atlantic to Madagascar, and from there to the Gulf of Aden or to the west coast of India and back again – a voyage known as the 'Pirate Round' and popular roughly between 1690 and 1720.

The 'Pirate Round' brings us to the most important insight into pirates between 1500 and 1914. Although the Mediterranean, the Northern seas and the Eastern seas still featured their own local types of pirates – those who were either disinclined or unable to embark on long-distance voyages, or preferred to stay close to home or to the shores where their most lucrative targets could be found – the 'Western' type of piracy went global, so to speak, helped along by the rapid expansion of the Western powers' worldwide empires. New continents were discovered and new sea routes found that connected the far-flung colonial possessions of Spain, Portugal, England, France and the Netherlands. Formerly powerful empires such as the Ottoman Empire in the Middle East, the Mughal Empire in South Asia and the Chinese Qing empire in East Asia collapsed under the relentless onslaught of various European sea powers. The endemic struggles for supremacy between these new global maritime powers, and their fight against regional states, resulted in many uncontrolled maritime spaces full of lucrative shipping – harassed both by locally operating pirates similar to those of earlier centuries and by pirates now often operating globally. It is this 'meddling in regional affairs' on a global scale that is the most striking difference from the piracy we encountered in Part I.

PART III

A Globalised World, 1914 to the Present

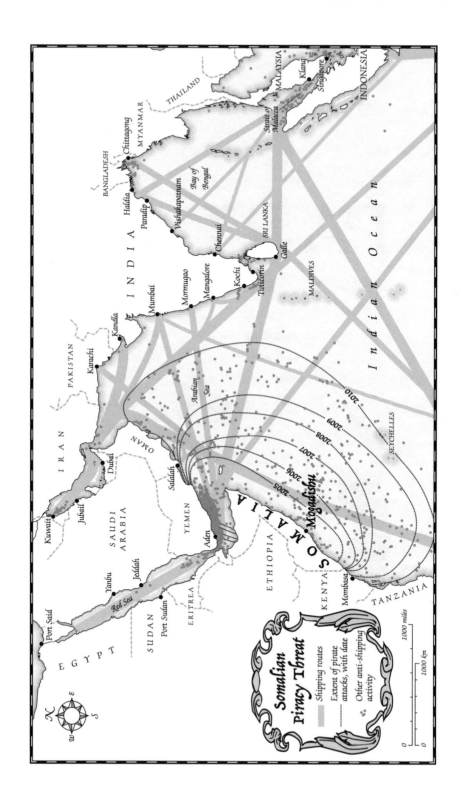

Somalian Piracy Threat

— Shipping routes
····· Extent of pirate attacks, with date
⠂⠄ Other anti-shipping activity

1000 miles
1000 km

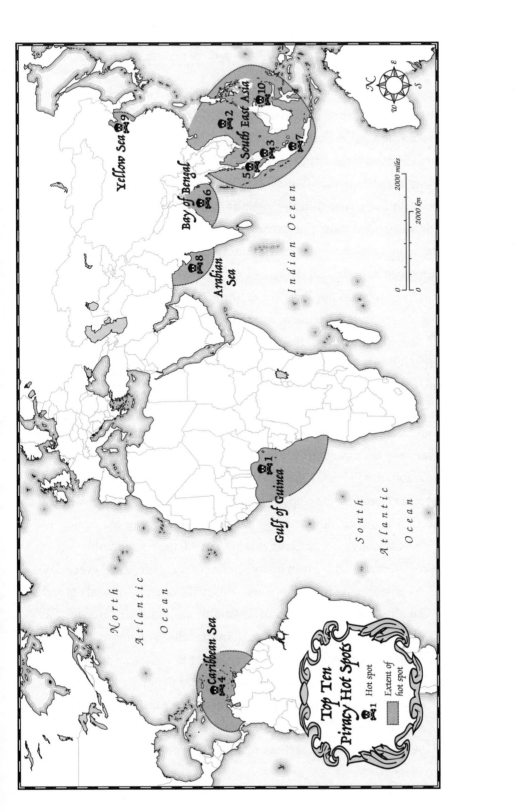

Top Ten
Piracy Hot Spots

☠1 Hot spot

▨   Extent of
    hot spot

Gulf of Guinea

☠1

Caribbean Sea
☠4

North
Atlantic
Ocean

South
Atlantic
Ocean

Indian Ocean

Arabian
Sea
☠8

Bay of
Bengal
☠6

South East Asia

☠2

☠10
☠3

☠3
5 ☠

☠7

Yellow Sea ☠9

2000 miles

2000 km

N
W   E
S

They Were Rich, We Were Poor

By now it will be obvious that being a pirate was not so much a romantic and splendid adventure as it was a rather dangerous occupation. The age-old realities (the likelihood of dying at sea, in action or of disease, or being captured by the authorities and jailed or even killed, rather than striking it rich) are mostly outcomes that modern-day pirates still face. Not much has changed in this regard. And just as in the case of their predecessors, the most important driver in the decision of individuals today to embark on a career as a pirate is a combination of push-and-pull factors such as greed and the lure of easy money, and grievance born of harsh living conditions, however defined. Notions of romanticism or a (probably misguided) sense of adventure do not normally play a role in such decisions. Not much has changed on that front either.

It should also be clear by now that greed as a motivating factor for pirates does not mean the dictionary definition of 'excessive, selfish desire for something, especially wealth and power, motivated by naked ambition'. Rather, more often than not we are talking about rational choice: why toil away for little gain when much more could be got with a little ambition and some risk? In a world of globally declining fish stocks, fishermen from less-developed countries lacking any developed welfare state find it increasingly hard to make ends meet. The temptation to explore alternative occupations making use of their seamanship is not surprising, particularly given many on the coast are presented every day with a veritable parade of container ships, bulk carriers, oil tankers and the like all carrying thousands of dollars of cash in their safes for the payment of harbour fees and wages. In Somalia, a young man in the first decade of the twenty-first century might have faced a stark choice between earning a couple of hundred dollars a month as a militiaman, and less than half that as a farmer, or turning pirate and making between £7,000 and £70,000 ($10,000–$100,000, depending on the vessel targeted and the role played) from each successful raid. The risks inherent in a life of piracy – being caught or killed in action or perishing at sea – do not seem that daunting when compared to a life that promises an average annual income of about £2,300 ($3,000) and an average life expectancy of just over fifty-five years. So why not make the best of it?

But it would be unfair to accuse those young Somali men[1] who become pirates of doing so only out of greed. At least in the case of the first wave of Somali piracy, which gradually emerged in the late 1990s, grievance was the main cause. In particular, it was the collapse of the Somali state in January 1991, and the corresponding collapse of law and order on land and at sea, that drove young Somali fishermen into piracy. Initially they organised themselves into gangs simply to defend their waters from the depredations of high-seas trawlers from all over the world which came to pursue illegal, unregulated and unreported (IUU) fishing (see pp. 163–6). These trawlers reportedly did not shy away from using violence against the usually much smaller Somali inshore fishing vessels, destroying their nets or even ramming them to force them back to shore. Thus, in the mid-1990s Somali fishermen started to organise themselves into self-help groups to fend off these aggressive intruders.

However, they quickly realised that capturing foreign vessels and holding their crews to ransom was much more lucrative than fishing – which is why in the late 1990s, these self-help groups gradually turned into pirate gangs. Interestingly, they still saw themselves mainly as defenders of their own waters, and the names they gave their pirate gangs, and the justification of their pirate attacks (at least as regards trawlers as targets), still highlighted the themes of grievance and self-defence. For example, on 15 August 2005, a pirate gang calling itself the National Volunteer Coast Guard of Somalia captured three Taiwanese-owned trawlers that were fishing in Somali waters. The pirates brazenly declared that they had not hijacked but 'impounded' these vessels, and that the $5,000 they demanded from each of the forty-eight captured crew members was not a ransom demand but a 'fine' for their participation in the crime of illegal fishing.[2] Another group using the name Somali navy also made use of the self-defence rationale – but when they hijacked the freighter MV *Semlow* on 27 June 2005, it became clear how threadbare this excuse was, and that the initial motive of grievance had already turned to greed. That the vessel was chartered by the UN World Food Programme and was transporting food aid to Mogadishu for the Somali victims of the Boxing Day tsunami of 2004 didn't stop the pirates from demanding ransom.[3]

By contrast, the Somali piracy that peaked between 2008 and 2012 does seem to have been motivated purely by greed and the lure of easy money. The 'pirate action groups' were no longer all fishermen but rather a mixture of former fishermen, valued for their nautical experience, and militiamen who were used as muscle. Reaching far out into the Arabian Sea, the pirates of this second wave were no longer simply defending their waters and no longer referred to that as a reason – the grandiose claims of the Somali Islamist guerrilla organisation al-Shabaab ('The Youth') that the pirates were 'mujahedeen at sea fighting against Western infidels' notwithstanding.[4]

Young Somali men are not the only ones who have to make hard choices in modern times. In Indonesia's troubled province of Aceh, at the northern tip of Sumatra, adjacent to the Straits of Malacca, many young Acehnese pirates might have chosen to lead far less dangerous lives as farmers or fishermen under different circumstances. The brutal three-decades-long conflict that began on 4 December 1976 between the separatist Free Aceh Movement and Indonesian armed forces meant many young Acehnese turned to piracy, before the devastation caused by the Boxing Day tsunami of 2004 and then the peace treaty of 15 August 2005 put an end to such activities.[5] After all, when the average daily wage amounted to no more than $6 (£4.60), the prospect of making between $13,000 and $20,000 (£10,000–£15,000) for just one successful raid must have seemed very appealing.[6] Due to large-scale illegal, unregulated and unreported (IUU) fishing in Indonesian waters, almost all fishing communities in this archipelagic nation of about

17,000 islands are affected by endemic poverty, so part-time piracy can be seen as a matter of survival rather than an expression of greed, as Marcus Uban, a former Indonesian pirate, emphasised: 'Just like me, many came from miserable kampong [villages]. Singapore was rich; we were poor. So, we went to pillage the areas in the vicinity of Singapore.'[7]

The Nigerian pirates currently active in the Gulf of Guinea have similar stories to tell: grievance over illegal fishing by foreign high-seas trawlers, but also over oil pollution that renders inshore fishing ever more difficult.[8] When listening to the stories of rank-and-file modern pirates, it quickly becomes clear that in those parts of the world that have not profited from globalisation and modernisation, and where abject poverty and the daily struggle for survival are still a reality, the root causes of piracy are still the same as they were a couple of hundred years ago. For these losers in the globalisation lottery, the temptation must be great to somehow get even.

There is one caveat, however: greed and grievance may explain individual choices behind the rise of modern piracy, but, as in previous centuries, this is only part of the answer as to why individuals become pirates, and not always a very convincing one. The first-wave Somali pirates' grievance-based claims of simply 'defending' their own waters against intruders, for example, shouldn't simply be taken at face value: pirates are not Robin Hoods of the sea, and many of their explanations are convenient excuses rather than honest accounts. But psychological analyses aside, what is also still required for piracy to flourish is the willingness of society at large, and of the state – or at least of powerful officials – to turn a blind eye to such activities. In Nigeria, where this nexus of pirates and officials pertains, the attempts 'to explain the problem from the angle of poverty are insufficient in the light of bad governance in Nigerian coastal states',[9] with a 'criminalisation of politics and the politicisation of crime' being behind the steady rise of piracy in the Gulf of Guinea.[10] We shall return to this issue later.

The Winds of Change

In the two previous periods we have looked at, the Northern seas and the Mediterranean were formidable piracy hot spots. Nevertheless, these areas are now virtually pirate-free. Does this mean that the push-and-pull factors in the shape of greed and grievance are no longer present there? Are the grievances of old all gone? Is piracy simply no longer profitable?

The statistics tell us that all three questions can be answered with a firm 'no'. With regard to profitability, the indications are that maritime trade is booming; with more ships plying the seas than ever before, surely that must mean the existence of tempting targets. The presence of cash in the ships' safes combined with sea lines in the confined waters of the North Sea and the Baltic Sea, or in some parts of the Mediterranean, make swift 'hit-and-run' attacks launched with speedboats both lucrative and feasible – the formidable natural ambush locations of the past have not disappeared after all.

Nor is it the case that all members of modern-day European coastal populations are so well off that piracy is inevitably viewed as too dangerous an occupation in the light of other easier and better-paying professions. There are still relatively deprived coastal communities that do not fully profit from the various economic miracles that followed the two devastating world wars, and whose populations in former times would have become pirates without much hesitation. This is especially the case for the shores of the European Mediterranean: the Greek economy, for example, is still in the doldrums after the Greek government debt crisis starting in 2010, and unemployment, in particular youth unemployment, remains very high. In the periods covered in Parts I and II, this would have been enough to result in a noticeable rise in piracy in the Aegean Sea, yet today, what could certainly be termed 'harsh living conditions' aren't making people turn pirate.

Furthermore, along the eastern shores of the Mediterranean exists a veritable 'arc of crisis' running from Syria and Libya – both of which are embroiled in civil wars – to Algeria, Tunisia and Morocco, comparatively weak states with their own groundswells of popular unrest. Plenty of grievances there too, one would have thought. Yet why are the many disadvantaged individuals in this region, with not much opportunity to succeed on the legitimate job market, not motivated to become pirates by the greed factor, either? The endemic human trafficking and smuggling of migrants across the Mediterranean into Europe[11] conducted by Middle Eastern and North African criminal networks[12] indicate that there are still some hard-nosed individuals willing to embark on at least that variant of seaborne crime. Is people trafficking so lucrative that they are simply not bothering with the presumably riskier enterprise of piracy?

Part of the answer to this question can be found in the fact that nowadays, there is effective maritime patrolling in the North Atlantic and in most parts of the Mediterranean, which renders acts of piracy less likely to occur than other forms of maritime crime, such as smuggling for example; unlike pirates, whose activities may result in frantic calls for help from the vessel under attack, human traffickers and drug smugglers conduct their businesses clandestinely, without attracting unwelcome attention. Another and probably more important part of the answer is the lack of societal approval: nowadays, being a pirate is simply no longer seen as 'doing the right thing'. The former glorification of pirates has not survived the shift of values that has taken place in almost all current states since early modern times. Where piracy does still exist, this change is nevertheless reflected in the societal composition of pirate crews, who hail almost exclusively from the bottom of the social pyramid; the times when the lower ranks of the nobility and the gentry also became pirates have long since passed. There are probably many factors behind this, among them the loss of influence of the nobility in liberal democracies. The most important reason, however, is the end of the legal variant of piracy, privateering, which was outlawed in the Paris Declaration Respecting Maritime Law of 1856; it stated unequivocally that 'Privateering is, and remains, abolished' (discussed below).[13] The illegality of privateering was further underscored by The Hague's

Declaration of 18 October 1907, the Convention Relating to the Conversion of Merchant Ships into War-Ships ('Hague VII' for short). Since then, any member of the nobility or the gentry who feels an urge to go to sea to seek fame and adventure will need to join a regular navy. Likewise, the opportunities being grabbed by today's foremost merchants are legal, not illegal, with the era of globalisation and liberalisation offering opportunity enough to get rich by maritime trade. Nowadays, they want to be seen as 'swashbuckling tycoons', not 'swashbuckling buccaneers'.

In the lands that make up the eastern Mediterranean's 'arc of crisis' today, the tradition of corsairing as a maritime extension of land-based jihad was interrupted and broken by the French conquest and colonisation of the Barbary Coast in the late nineteenth century. The sovereign secular states that gradually emerged during the twentieth century had no intention of following in the footsteps of their corsairing forefathers. In the times of Arab Socialism, Islam was deemed to be a spent force anyway. Even now, with many of these coastal states in the throes of civil war and insurgency, a return to the 'bad old days' is not on the cards – for practical reasons (almost all resources are needed for use on land), but also due to a lack of interest in such ventures and the absence of societal approval. Theoretically, this could change if a stridently Islamist faction were to win power in such a coastal state and rekindle the dormant reflex to harass non-believers at sea once again. For example, the so-called Islamic State of Iraq and Syria (ISIS) declared in 2015 that after seizing control of the land (in their case, the Mediterranean coast of Syria and the Northern Arabian Gulf coast of Iraq), they would, God willing, take to the sea in order to continue their jihad against the 'Worshippers of the Cross and the infidels [who] pollute our seas with their warships, boats, and aircraft carriers and gobble up our wealth and kill us from the sea'.[14] Whether ISIS would have done so or not is a moot point: since they lost the battle on land, the possibility of them taking to the waves anytime soon is rather remote.

The final difference that separates our time from the earlier periods of piracy is that, quite simply, societal changes over the centuries mean that fearsome tribal warrior societies such as the Vikings or the Iranun and Balangingi no longer roam the seas. The history and tradition of doing so have not been forgotten, but they are mostly commemorated in events and celebrations rather than inspiring people to take up the profession. In such events as the Jorvik Viking Festival in York or the Shetland town of Lerwick's famous Up Helly Aa festival – in which a torch-lit evening procession of several hundred men decked out in Viking costumes parades down to the harbour, where a replica of a Viking longship is burnt – the tradition of piracy has made the transition from a deadly business to colourful folklore. History was also refashioned in Indonesia, in this case into a sporting event, with the Sail Banda 2010 yacht race as a historical reference to the Dutch *hongitochten* (see p. 134). Yet despite this distancing from actuality, and the controversy caused by the former prime minister of Malaysia, Mahathir Mohamad, when he dismissively described the then incumbent prime minister, Najib Razak, as a descendant of Bugis (Malay) pirates,[15] for some Malay or Filipino fishermen piracy is still an accepted part of the culture, without much of a stigma attached; something they resort to on an ad hoc basis when industrial fishing fleets from neighbouring countries come bottom-trawling with their drag nets. The Tausugs from the island of Jolo (in the southwestern Philippines) still regard piracy as a traditional and honourable occupation that allows young men to demonstrate 'highly regarded virtues such as bravado, honour, masculinity and magnanimity'.[16] Their only nod to modern times is the fact that, unlike their forebears, they no longer embark on slave raids, and settle for commodities such as jewellery, money or weapons.[17]

ISIS's threat to take their land-based jihad to the sea shows that religion still serves as a strong instrument for 'othering', that is, for dividing 'us' from 'them', thus continuing to offer piracy a veneer of respectability, as it did in the previous two periods (see pp. 20–1 and 61). In current times, organisations such as the notorious Abu Sayyaf Group based in the southern Philippines describe themselves as militant Islamists – they ostensibly fight for a much nobler cause than simple personal enrichment, and thus appear more like a respectable guerrilla movement than a brutal criminal gang that also conducts piratical raids as part of their business model. Similarly, though Somali pirates themselves may see any vessel as a legitimate target no matter the flag it flies or the religious affiliation of its crew, as we have seen, al-Shabaab glorifies Somali pirates as defenders of Somali waters against a new generation of 'Western crusaders'. It is interesting that the centuries-old 'crusaders versus jihadists' theme still has some traction – a handy method to explain away the actions of one's own side while vilifying those of the other.

Modern Enabling Environments

As in the two previous periods we have looked at, for piracy to really flourish an enabling environment is required, such as that created by the connivance of government officials, by certain ports operating on a 'no questions asked' basis, and maybe even when some states are either uninterested in dealing with piracy or too weak to do so.

A telling example of the collusion of individual government and port officials is the case of the general cargo ship *Erria Inge*, which was captured by pirates in the Indian Ocean in 1990 and re-registered as *Palu 111*. Despite several attempts by the vessel's rightful owner to get his ship back it still managed to slip out of several ports, unchallenged by the port authorities.[18] It is an open secret that corruption is still rampant in many ports along modern sea lines of communication,[19] and it can be argued that the current problem of piracy in many waters is made worse because 'government personnel are involved in illegal activities, and rampant corruption of military and law enforcement personnel is a concern, seriously undermining efforts to combat piracy'.[20]

On the other hand, the modern global environment renders it much more difficult for ports to openly establish themselves as safe havens than was possible in previous times (see pp. 23 and 81), when state control was still weak and intermittent, or territory still contested. In northern and eastern waters, now controlled by strong, stable states, none of the formerly notorious pirate lairs such as the Cinque Ports in the UK, Baltimore in Ireland, Dunkerque (Dunkirk) in France, Rostock and Wismar in Germany, Charleston in the US or Macao in China welcomes pirates any longer, and the formerly unruly littoral regions like the Frisian coast of the North Sea (now part of the modern Netherlands and Germany) or the coasts of the Seto Inland Sea (Japan) were brought to heel a long time ago. Nowadays, a port can realistically only openly support pirates when the state to which it belongs is either a weak state (where the government is unable to effectively govern all of its territory) or a failed state (where the government has all but collapsed).

Both the Philippines and Indonesia belong to the former category. The power of the Philippine government is reasonably strong in the mainly Catholic northern part of the archipelago, centred on the island of Luzon, but does not extend to its predominantly Muslim southern part, where separatist organisations such as the Moro Islamic Liberation Front (MILF), the Bangsamoro Islamic Freedom Fighters (BIFF) and the Abu Sayyaf Group (ASG) operate (though the ASG is arguably an organised crime group that also dabbles in piracy rather than a credible Islamist separatist movement). Meanwhile, the Indonesian government's authority does not extend to all the 17,000 islands of this spread-out archipelagic state. Aggravating the situation in both countries is the relatively high level of corruption. Hence, smaller harbours and anchorages can still get away with clandestinely supporting pirates by providing them with food, fuel, arms and ammunition, and allowing them to sell their illicit goods on the black market to merchants who don't ask questions. In the case of the Philippines, in the 1980s and early 1990s this allowed notorious pirate captain Emilio Changco to operate with impunity out of Manila Bay, and thus under the very eyes of the Philippine government. His particular business model was stealing ships and their cargoes to order, his criminal customers paying $300,000 for the service: his motto was 'you choose, I steal'.[21] Changco paid hefty bribes to ensure a blind eye was turned to his activities – until the early 1990s, that is, when he made the crucial mistake of hijacking the MT *Tabango*, a tanker that belonged to the government-owned Philippine National Oil Corporation. This brazen act finally led to his arrest, and he was duly sentenced to many years in prison. In 1992, and after he had served about a year, he was shot dead under murky circumstances – allegedly when he tried to make his escape.[22]

Parts of the Riau Islands still function as pirate lairs for much the same reasons as in former times (see pp. 83–4): they are under weak Indonesian state control, and are ideally placed to monitor the maritime traffic in and out of nearby Singapore. Furthermore, the conflicted history of foreign and security relations between that modern-day independent city-state and its rather larger archipelagic neighbour makes policing these waters difficult. In 2004, when researcher Eric Frécon visited Pulau Batam, one of the Riau Islands, he discovered a pirate lair as an annexe of Kampung Hitam ('Black Village'):

[At] the end of the market road, after a small post office, a left turn leads one to a pirate den. Here lies a bay divided into three parts: One for the police, another for local prostitutes, and the last one for pirates and smugglers . . . The local police are, no doubt, fully aware of the criminal activities that exist on the island and along the Straits. In fact, in order to reach the Straits, pirates have to pass their view on their way out.[23]

The police officers' rationale in looking the other way and pocketing the bribe is easy to understand; with only two small boats, they were no match for the pirates even if they did try to pursue them.[24] Furthermore, cracking down on piracy in a close-knit society where well-connected pirates occupy important positions would be dangerous not only for the officers involved and their families but also for internal stability. Hence, a quid-pro-quo had to be found, which still existed in 2015,[25] and probably continues today:

> The local policemen do not disturb the pirates and their chiefs so long as these groups do not explicitly challenge their authority. These so-called policemen only protect prostitutes; they manage their own business while keeping a low social profile. This seems to be the price of keeping the domestic peace.[26]

As for the Indonesian government, in the grand scheme of things the activities of the Riau Islands-based pirates are hardly noticeable; international drug-smuggling networks and the Islamic terrorist movement Jemaah Islamiyah – and nowadays also the local branch of ISIS – are seen as much more formidable threats to the stability of Indonesia as a whole. The fact that the victims of the pirates are not usually Indonesian citizens but rather Singaporeans or the crews of merchant vessels on international voyages adds to this lack of urgency. It is this lack of interest, combined with the not-so-friendly relations between Indonesia and Singapore, that allows the pirates to operate from their island base with near impunity, beating a hasty retreat across the sea border back into Indonesian waters as soon as Singaporean patrol vessels appear on the horizon. Such pirates are engaging in 'state capacity arbitrage: the political and economic landscapes of different states provide different opportunities for the hijacking networks, leading them to spread their operations throughout peninsular and archipelagic Southeast Asia'.[27]

Somalia, meanwhile, is a failed state. After the collapse of its government in January 1991, the country found itself embroiled in a civil war in which various actors have continued to fight each other in ever-shifting coalitions. Although in August 2012 a federal government was finally established with the help of the UN, the EU and the African Union, only rudimentary national law enforcement structures are in place, contested by a plethora of tribal militias and the Islamist guerrilla organisation al-Shabaab. Furthermore, two of Somalia's provinces, Somaliland and Puntland, are drifting away from Somalia proper, the former as a self-declared sovereign state (albeit not recognised by the international community), the latter as a (semi-)autonomous province, and both with their own governments and security forces.

This quagmire of quickly changing alliances and allegiances allowed ports such as Kismayo, Harardhere and, in particular, Eyl to openly operate as safe havens for Somali pirates at the peak of the Somali piracy wave. These were places where hijacked ships, their hostages still aboard, could be anchored in plain sight of both Puntland officials on shore and naval officers on board the warships of various nations patrolling the coast. While the latter were unable to act due to the risk to the lives of the hostages, the former were both unable and unwilling: unable because the well-connected pirates would have been formidable opponents for the ill-equipped government forces, and unwilling because influential government officials and politicians received their share of the profits from the pirates' operations – some of which were conducted with the active financial support of certain government officials. A number of credible reports state that wealthy individuals based in Puntland's capital, Garowe, about 200 kilometres from the sea, financed diverse pirate gangs between 2008 and 2012, with the pirates in return investing substantial sums of their ransom monies in the city: the 'evidence is in the skyline: the unmistakeable Holy Day hotel for example, shaped like the hull of a ship, is owned by a famous pirate who has now transformed it into apartments'.[28] This is not to say that Puntland did nothing to curb piracy during these years: scores of pirates were arrested and jailed. But they mostly belonged to the rank-and-file. As the UN Monitoring Group on Somalia and Eritrea put it, 'top pirate leaders/organisers/investors and negotiators . . . remained undisturbed, and . . . continued to organise and manage piracy operations'.[29] In Eyl, as in Pulau Batam, as long as the pirates do not openly challenge the government, they will not be disturbed.

If law enforcers did so, domestic peace and stability would suffer – and so would a substantial side-income for conniving authorities.[30] This equilibrium could only be changed if the legitimate power-holders in Puntland came to the conclusion that even more money could be made by supporting legal trade: in that case, the pirate clans, including their leaders, would have outlived their utility.[31]

A similar enabling environment exists in the Niger Delta – an environment that can be described as a murky nexus of legal politics (Nigerian government and political parties), illegal politics (shore-based ethnic and tribal insurgency movements such as the Movement for the Emancipation of the Niger Delta – MEND), land-based organised crime, with piracy as its sea-based equivalent, and all this with a high degree of corruption at all levels thrown in for good measure. Some observers explicitly mention corruption and 'dirty deals within the Nigerian navy' as facilitators of pirate attacks.[32] In particular, Nigerian pirates' 'alliance with corrupt security agents [allows them to] hold hostages for an average of ten days while negotiating with the naval authorities and other stakeholders without being apprehended'.[33] In a faint echo of Elizabeth I's famous remark that Drake was 'her' pirate, Nigerian piracy is contingent upon the whims and needs of the various powerful stakeholders involved. William Hughes, the former head of the UK's Serious and Organised Crime Agency (now part of the National Crime Agency), stated that it is 'very difficult to deal with the indigenous law enforcement [agencies of these governments] because they're all controlled by ministers and other government officials who are all suspect, if not actively involved in [crime]'.[34] This 'active support' may well include the provision of timely intelligence and targeting information to pirate gangs, thereby allowing them to select vessels with lucrative cargo. It is thus not that surprising that port and customs officials who have access to such sensitive information are regarded with suspicion by ship owners and masters of vessels on international voyages.[35]

There is at least some good news with regard to state support for piracy: having played such a prominent role in enabling piracy in the past, currently no state actively supports pirates in order to harass the maritime traffic of its neighbours. The operative word here, though, is 'actively'. As already mentioned, some states still deem it useful to turn a blind eye to the activities of pirates operating in their waters so long as they prey on somebody else's vessels – especially if relations with this 'somebody else' are less than cordial. However, turning piracy on and off like a tap to suit the needs of the states in the moment – as was the way during the reign of Elizabeth I, when pirates were licensed and became privateers – has been a thing of the past since the outlawing of privateering in 1856. By that point the Western imperial powers had mutually accepted most of their territorial and maritime claims, with only a few regions remaining where that was not the case, so zones of contested authority where pirates could operate rapidly shrunk. The process of drawing mutually accepted borders – not only on land but also at sea – continued in the decades of decolonisation during which all remaining colonies became sovereign states. Although there are some contested maritime regions today, grey areas of disputed control and sovereignty have become fewer and fewer, while the states' power to enforce law and order not only on land but also at sea has gradually increased. Also, by the time of the Paris Declaration, the age of mercantilism, when one state's gain was the other's loss, had given way to the era of globalism and the realisation that free trade was far more profitable than piracy. Both reasons explain why none of the states formerly making good use of the 'raffish instrument of foreign policy, the privateer' does so any longer. As regards piratical states like Coxinga's and Kanhoji Angre's short-lived kingdoms (see pp. 127–8 and 128–30), the proliferation of Western-style sovereign nation-states with clearly demarcated land and sea borders explains why break-away territories no longer exist: they simply would not be recognised as sovereign independent states by any other country or any international organisation – as Somaliland, the breakaway province of Somalia, experienced[36] – and would probably even find themselves the target of a multinational coalition tasked with restoring order.

A New Raffish Instrument

In certain states a new 'raffish instrument of foreign policy' seems to have replaced privateering and piracy: high-seas trawlers, conducting what some observers call either 'fishery wars' or 'pirate fishing'.

In the period covered in Part II, colonial powers often meddled in regional affairs while also applying short-sighted mercantilist politics in which one nation's gain by definition resulted in another nation's loss. In extreme cases, central governments rode roughshod over the requirements of their own coastal fishing communities, for example by severely restricting or completely banning maritime trade, or by forcing the coastal population to move inland in order to create a cordon sanitaire. In modern times, such short-sighted mercantilist politics have been replaced by the globalisation and liberalisation of trade, while domestic politics based on radical Ming dynasty-like 'scorched earth' tactics have also been largely consigned to the history books. Nevertheless, in many regions of the world where states are still in the process of nation-building, fishing communities continue to be pushed to the fringes of mainstream society, finding themselves 'betwixt and between'.

In Southeast Asia (more precisely, the coasts of the Malay Peninsula, Singapore and the Riau Islands), a telling case in point are the remnants of the Orang Laut or 'Sea People', also known as 'Sea Gypsies'. Despite the rapid economic progress made in many Southeast Asian countries, these maritime people usually live in squalid, subsistence-level circumstances without access to national welfare policies or national healthcare – quite often, they are not even seen as 'proper' citizens of the state on whose coasts they live, and thus as fair game for exploitation.[37] The Orang Laut are just one example of the systematic disregard shown for poor fishing communities, whatever their nationality or ethnic group; recall Indonesian pirate Marcus Uban's palpable sense of not getting his fair share, and the Indonesian government's seeming lack of interest concerning the conditions on some islands far away from the political centre. Left to their own devices, routinely on the receiving end of the depredations of high-seas trawlers poaching in their traditional fishing grounds, and hailing from cultures with a not-so-distant history of maritime raiding, members of these marginalised marine communities are faced with difficult choices. Some of them may choose to move to the cities to make a living there. Others may try to find a legal hire on board a merchant vessel. And others may take to either smuggling or piracy, or both. Most of them probably take the first opportunity that presents itself. Wherever persistent piracy emerges, a weak or failed coastal state can be found, one that does not care about social welfare for its marginalised marine communities and finds it difficult to suppress illegal fishing in its own waters.

The continued meddling of extra-regional powers in regional affairs, though now happening at a far lower level than it used to in the times of colonialism and imperialism, can to a certain degree still be blamed for the persistence of opportunistic, small-scale piracy. In the case of the 2008–12 wave of Somali high-seas piracy, for instance, it can be argued that the problem began in the early 1990s, when Somali fishermen had to fight against high-seas trawlers intruding into their fishing grounds – which belong to one of the Indian Ocean's most important large maritime ecosystems (LME)[38] – in order to poach high-value fish, such as bluefin tuna, mackerel or snapper. This intrusion was a consequence of the collapse of Somalia's central government in 1991, and the country's ensuing descent into a continuing civil war; the international vessels had either no licence at all or 'licenses of dubious legality, written on ex-Somali government letterhead and signed by a warlord in Mogadishu claiming to represent the previous Barre government'.[39] The loss of law and order on land also translated into a loss of law and order at sea – an area where maintaining any meaningful form of governance is in any case a more challenging task than on land. As a consequence, Somali fishermen had to deal with an ever-rising number of high-seas trawlers from various European (e.g. France, Spain), Middle Eastern/West Asian (e.g. Saudi Arabia, Pakistan) and Far Eastern (e.g. Japan, Taiwan, Thailand) countries that systematically emptied Somali waters.[40]

It is difficult to establish hard numbers when it comes to the value of fish poached in Somali waters. Surveys quantifying marine life numbers along the coast of the country conducted 'by UN, Russian and Spanish assessors just before the collapse of the President Barre regime in 1991 estimated that at least 200,000 tons of fish per year could be harvested sustainably by both artisanal and industrial fisheries [while] Australian scientists put this figure to at least 300,000 tons'.[41] Because of the economic as well as ecological damage of illegal fishing in Somali waters, some observers do not hesitate to compare this activity to piracy, calling it 'pirate fishing':

> While biased UN resolutions, big power orders and news reports continue to condemn the hijackings of merchant ships by Somali pirates in the Indian Ocean and the Gulf of Aden, pirate fishing was and is ignored. Why are the UN resolutions, NATO orders and EU decrees to invade the Somali seas persistently failing to include the protection of the Somali marine resources from IUU violations in the same waters?[42]

There are probably many polite diplomatic answers to this straightforward question. An equally straightforward answer, however, would be to draw attention to the fact that international relations are still about national interest and not much else. It is thus not that surprising that France and Spain were the most vocal supporters of the EU's Operation Atalanta, organised in December 2008 to curb Somali piracy: the operation – which is still ongoing at the time of writing (November 2018) – was in their national interest, protecting their own fishing fleets, which operate in Somali waters.

In any case, chasing pirates out of the water is obviously only one side of the coin. It is imperative that illegal trawlers be apprehended if the international community really is interested in ending, or at least reducing, piracy – and not only in Somali waters. In Indonesia, for instance, the economic and ecological damage done by illegal fishing is so great that the government of President Widodo has ordered the Indonesian navy to sink trawlers intruding into Indonesian waters (their crews having been arrested and removed) in order to dissuade others.

The Modern Pirate Fleet

One of the most iconic lines in film history is Roy Scheider's unforgettable quip from the 1975 blockbuster *Jaws*: 'We're gonna need a bigger boat.' Until the twentieth century, many pirates would have agreed – after all, 'bigger' usually meant more space for cargo and plunder, and a longer endurance allowing for extended cruises on the high seas. Furthermore, a bigger vessel also could carry more guns, thus being capable of engaging lucrative targets even if they were well defended. Henry 'Long Ben' Avery's frigate *Fancy* – with which he captured the *Fateh Mohammed* as well as the *Ganj i-Sawai* in July 1695 (see pp. 105–6) – was such a ship. But not all pirates attempted to acquire ever-bigger vessels with ever-more firepower: indeed, those pirates who did not conduct lengthy operations on the high seas preferred vessels that were big enough to carry a fair amount of plunder but not so big and powerful as to raise suspicion. At the beginning of his career as a pirate, John Ward decided to attack a French flyboat he encountered (see above, pp. 91–2): that vessel was bigger than his, and armed with some guns as well. But Ward came to like the flyboat not because it was bigger, but because it was a harmless-looking vessel, 'as warlike as a coal scuttle'.[43] Approaching other ships in a flyboat thus rarely raised suspicion until it was too late to escape. Pierre Le Grand is another example of a pirate choosing a smaller, harmless-looking vessel instead of a bigger one with more firepower: after all, it was the 'pitiful' appearance of his small piragua that allowed him to go alongside a huge Spanish galleon unchallenged, and to quickly overwhelm its surprised crew (see pp. 99–100). The unnamed Iranun pirates who captured the Spanish colonel Ibanez y Garcia in 1857 in Philippine waters would probably have agreed with Ward's and Le Grand's choice of vessel: for the purpose of piracy, the ability to hide in plain sight in order to launch a surprise attack on unsuspecting prey was more important than sheer size and firepower.

Pirate gangs currently active in the South China Sea and the Straits of Malacca, in the Arabian Sea and in the Gulf of Guinea, also seem to have learned the lesson that 'bigger' does not necessarily mean 'better': in an era of maritime surveillance not only by sea but also by air via helicopters, maritime patrol aircrafts and even drones, the art of hiding in plain sight is more important than ever. Mimicking the behaviour of the countless inshore fishing vessels and smaller trawlers ever-present in the coastal and archipelagic waters of these maritime regions is easy: the only difference between a pirate boat and a fishing vessel is that the former is equipped with grapnels and ladders – revealing accoutrements of piratical intent – and its crew are typically armed with some assault rifles and rocket-propelled grenade launchers. The vessels' similarity makes apprehending pirates rather difficult if they are not caught in the act: all they need to do to transform themselves into apparently harmless fishermen is to throw their ladders and grapnels overboard. And in certain areas such as the Somali coast and the Gulf of Guinea, even the presence of small arms can be explained away as normal fishing crew equipment– after all, fishermen have to defend themselves against the pirates who might otherwise take their boats.

As regards the quest for 'bigger boats', this only made sense for those Somali 'pirate action groups' that extended their area of operations to the high seas between 2008 and 2012 when the phenomenon of Somali piracy reached its peak. In those years, Somali pirate action groups were found operating as far south as the entrance of the Channel of Mozambique, as far north as the Gulf of Oman, and as far east as the Laccadive Islands and the west coast of India. The most distant of these locations are more than 1,500 nautical miles from the Somali coast. Quite logically, small inshore fishing vessels or 'Boston whaler'-type fibreglass boats measuring between 3.4 and 11 metres are not suitable for the open ocean: the crew would rapidly run out of food, potable water and khat (leaves chewed for their stimulating effect), and also of fuel, as some anecdotal evidence about hapless Somali pirate gangs who used such vessels to go a-pirating on the high seas shows. While most such crews presumably perished at sea, one was picked up, half-starved and desperate for water, in the vicinity of the Laccadives by the Indian navy.[44] The better-organised Somali pirate gangs, however, did exactly what John Ward did: they 'acquired' a bigger boat, usually a high-seas trawler or a small freighter, by force, to use that vessel as a mother ship with their fibreglass skiffs in tow. Because of the ubiquity of trawlers and small tramp freighters (older vessels voyaging from port to port depending on the cargo they get, without a fixed route or timetable), the pirates were still able to hide in plain sight while drastically extending their reach. In such cases, the pirates could also 'outsource' the daily maintenance and navigational work of the vessel to its legitimate crew members, who were usually kept on board both as hostages to be ransomed and as 'human shields' to protect the pirates against counter-attacks from warships – a tactic that sometimes resulted in the death of innocents.

Guise and Guile in Modern Times

Piracy without a boat is – of course – simply not feasible. But does piracy then always involve pirates laying their hands on a suitable vessel to use as a mobile platform from which to plunder other vessels or coastal settlements? Not necessarily. In the earlier twentieth century, there were some cases when pirates did not 'acquire' a vessel, but only temporarily 'borrowed' it for the purpose of thoroughly ransacking its cargo and the valuables of those aboard. In the 1920s and 1930s, for instance, some Chinese pirates disguised themselves as seemingly innocent passengers of British mail steamers sailing in and out of Hong Kong in order to plunder them en route. The tactic was simple: the majority of the pirates boarded the vessel as regular passengers travelling in the usually crowded third class, while a select few – including the leader – had tickets for the first class. The number of pirates thus embarking varied between as few as ten and as many as sixty, and, thus spread over the ship, they were able to quickly take over both the engine room (usually in the vicinity of the third-class quarters below deck) and the bridge (usually easily accessible via the first class on the upper deck) when the attack commenced. They could then either stop the vessel or steer a course of their choosing, such as to meet up with their escape vessel. The operators of steamers quickly became familiar with this brazen type of piracy, and access to the bridge via its windows was blocked by iron grilles to prevent anybody from clambering in, while its doors were protected by armed guards.[45] But since officers had to access the bridge at predictable intervals, and since complacency is human nature, all the pirates had to do, in the aftermath of these security changes, was to wait for an opportune moment: 'then there is a shrill whistle, or a shot, or perhaps a hellish beating of the gongs. It is the signal for the attack.'[46] At a time when crews were not yet subject to vetting, and the identity of embarking passengers not checked, this was an astonishingly effective tactic: despite the security measures taken, between 1921 and 1929 about thirty vessels fell prey to such pirates,[47] who, after each successful operation, simply escaped into Chinese waters to evade British naval patrols. Like their predecessors, these pirates demon-strated an admirable ability to fully exploit the cracks of an awkward colonial arrangement in which diverging British and Chinese capabilities and political interests offered a particularly favourable enabling environ-ment for pirates.

Nowadays, prospective crew members have to undergo vetting proce-dures before they are hired, while passengers are required to present their passports or ID cards before they are admitted on board – at least in theory. Nevertheless, the chance that pirates – or terrorists, for that matter – could sneak aboard a ship unnoticed and unchallenged is still not exactly zero. In practice, not all shipping lines take precautions as seriously as they should: a thorough vetting of the crew is time-consuming, and thorough passenger checks can lead to delays – and in any case, ID cards and passports can be faked.

Pirates, or just opportunistic criminals, sneaking on board unobserved and unnoticed or entering a vessel either on a pretext or with faked credentials in order to commit what is colloquially known as 'theft at anchor' is also a serious issue for the unwary yachter – not all of whom take the threat posed by persistent piracy as seriously as they should either. There are a couple of cases of yacht piracy on record in which hired deckhands or paying charter customers turned out to be criminals, using their access to a vessel to overwhelm its owners and either tie them up or kill them outright. In the Caribbean, the reason behind such an attack is usually to acquire a suitable yacht for the purposes of smuggling drugs into the United States. In some cases, the captured vessels are never seen again. The German sloop *Nordstern IV* along with its two-man crew and four German charter customers mysteriously disappeared after it had left Antigua on 18 March 1977 for a cross-Atlantic trip to Lisbon. What makes the case rather dubious is that the owner of the sloop, also a German national, was highly indebted, and knew that his vessel would be seized by the authorities upon arrival in Portugal. More than four decades on, there remains a lot of speculation around this case. Twenty-five years after the incident, an observer of the yachter scene offered an explanation: 'In the heyday of drug smuggling between Colombia and the United States, *Nordstern IV* could have been pressed into service as a fast drug courier vessel. I believe she was hijacked by pirates and her crew liquidated.'[48]

It is not only the drugs trade that imperils yachts and yachters; in many other cases, opportunistic criminals simply sneak aboard moored yachts in small harbours where security is lax, or in bays where security is absent. In early March 2016, for example, masked gunmen boarded two German-owned yachts anchored in Wallilabou Bay off the island of Saint Vincent on the same day, in two separate incidents of 'theft at anchor'. In the first, the boat's owner Martin Griff was shot dead, while in the second,

Reinhold Zeller was injured by a gunshot to his shoulder. It is unclear whether the two incidents were committed by the same gang, and whether the victims had offered resistance.[49]

Saint Vincent is not the only place in the Caribbean where vigilance is required – rather, yachters are well advised to be cautious in the whole of the Caribbean: 'Some parts are safe as houses. In others, people could come to serious harm.'[50] The Amazon is similarly notorious for such opportunistic pirate attacks. On 7 December 2001, the famous New Zealand-born world champion yachtsman Sir Peter Blake was fatally shot on board his yacht *Seamaster* when he tried to defend himself against seven or eight armed river pirates who had managed to sneak aboard unnoticed around 10 p.m.[51] More recently, on 13 September 2017, the British kayaker Emma Kelty was killed on the banks of the Solimões River, a tributary of the Amazon, presumably by a gang of river pirates. The day before the attack, she posted a chilling message on social media that read 'Turned corner [of river] and found 50 guys in motor boats with arrows!!! . . . OK 30 guys . . . but either way . . . that's a lot of folks in one area in boats with arrow[s] and rifles.'[52] According to her own posts, Kelty, a seasoned kayaker and adventurer, had received a warning that this stretch of the river was piracy-prone at least three days before the deadly attack, but seemed to have made light of it: 'I will have my boat stolen and I will be killed too. Nice.'[53]

The carefree holiday atmosphere of the Caribbean and the breath-taking beauty of the Amazon may well make these places underestimated as piracy hot spots. Only a very few incidents make headlines in the Western media, and it is thus understandable that yachters might forget to take precautions – sometimes with lethal consequences. This lack of awareness of the dangers of piracy also seems to be shared by a number of yachters planning to sail through the South China Sea, the Straits of Malacca or the Arabian Sea, and thus through the most notorious piracy hot spots of today. Anecdotal evidence suggests that, even when yachters were aware of the threat, they held the mistaken belief that pirates would leave them in peace because there were no valuables or substantial amounts of cash on their boats; indeed, some added that the boats themselves were their only major possession. This is not the view of young Somali, Nigerian or Indonesian pirates, for whom the idea of leisurely sailing around the world in one's own boat is the epitome of being very, very rich – turning yachts and their crews into irresistible targets for them.

Shock and Awe Today

Despite all the changes that the relentless march of technology has brought to sailors and pirates alike, for the latter one important issue has not changed over the ages: the need to spot suitable prey in order to attack and overwhelm it before it can escape or – with the help of radiotelegraphy or Morse systems (from the second half of the nineteenth century to the end of the twentieth), radio (from the second half of the twentieth century onwards) or satellite phones (nowadays) – make speedy contact with authorities who could assist it. Hence, modern pirates still favour the creeks, small bays or rocky promontories which previous generations had sought out, and for the same reason: these locations allow pirates to lie in ambush, dash out and strike before the targeted vessel has time to react by speeding off or calling for help. Until the start of the Second World War, the same Greek islands in the Aegean Sea that found favour with corsairs such as Alonso de Contreras served as hiding places for the few remaining Greek and Levantine pirates. In eastern waters, some spots remain popular with pirates to this day, especially the islands of the South China Sea and the Straits of Malacca, one of the world's busiest straits as well as one of its most formidable maritime choke points.

If suitable ambush locations are unavailable, modern pirates simply continue to hide in plain sight, pretending to be just another boatload of honest fishermen trying to put food on the table while watching the merchant vessels slowly pass by with a keen eye. Before they were driven out by counter-measures (discussed below), the first wave of Somali pirates in the late 1990s loitered in the approaches of the Bab el-Mandeb in the Gulf of Aden – just as Henry 'Long Ben' Avery had done a little more than three hundred years earlier during the raid on the *Ganj i-Sawai* that made him famous (see pp. 105–6). Compared to Avery, however, the Somali pirates found far more maritime traffic on which to prey: today, some 16,000–20,000 vessels pass through these waters annually, which, like the Straits of Malacca, also belong to the world's busiest maritime highways or 'sea lines of communication' (SLOCs), to use the proper technical term. The Nigerian pirates who made a sudden appearance in the early 2000s use to their best advantage the confined waters of the Gulf of Guinea and the dense tanker traffic slowly negotiating the stationary oil and gas installations there. Having spotters and informers in relevant ports is also a great advantage for the modern-day pirates of the South China Sea, Nigeria and Somalia – the former occasionally even having informers among a targeted vessel's crew, providing them with mobile phone updates whenever possible. Meanwhile, the rise of social media and the now-habitual use of Facebook or Twitter to let people know that a ship is heading out of port A in order to be at port B at a certain time while steering a certain course, greatly facilitates modern pirates' business: 'loose lips sink ships', so to speak. By and large, however, it could still be said that 'more often than not the sighting of a fine prize probably owed more to luck and inspired guesswork than to planning'.[54]

There is another issue that modern pirates have in common with their forebears, and that is a reluctance to engage in bloody battles. Like their ancestors, modern pirates therefore employ shock-and-awe tactics in order to ensure the swift surrender and unopposed boarding of a targeted vessel. Some observers claim that modern pirates are so risk-averse that they even refrain from approaching vessels that look like they could defend themselves. For instance, a 1984 article in *The Economist* regarding pirates active in the Straits of Malacca and the South China Sea stated that since 'Israeli, Russian and American ships often carry arms, which their crews are trained to use, [they] are rarely attacked'.[55] Similarly, anecdotal evidence has it that the Somali pirate action groups also preferred to stay clear of Israeli and Russian vessels for fear of determined, and armed, resistance. They held US-flagged vessels in much lower esteem, as the attempted hijack of the *Maersk Alabama* between 8 and 12 April 2009 illustrated.[56] Given the fact that some Russian vessels were actually attacked, and that some Somali pirate action groups even attacked naval vessels by mistake – for example, the US Navy dock landing ship USS *Ashland* on 10 April 2010, and the Spanish navy oiler ESPS *Patino* on 17 January 2012[57] – one should, though, take these claims with a pinch of salt. After all, from the rather low vantage point of a small fibreglass skiff it can be quite difficult to make out the name and registration of a huge freighter or tanker before it is too late – especially around dusk or dawn.

In general, however, the risks faced by modern pirates in battling it out with their prey are generally much lower than those of their fore-bears: modern merchant vessels and their crews are typically unarmed. Modern pirates therefore find it rather easy to make use of shock and awe by way of brandishing assault rifles and rocket-propelled grenade launchers, while for the merchant vessel's crew the rationale for a quick surrender is basically the same as for crews of previous ages, armed or not: why should (usually badly paid) deckhands fight for cargo that is insured and belongs to somebody else? Even if pirates ransacked the crew's belongings there is a good chance that the insurance will pay out. And despite the terror of being subject to Somali pirates' preferred business model of kidnap for ransom, a captured crew that complied with the pirates' orders would also know that, sooner or later, the ransom would be paid and they would be released. Picking a fight with pirates is still not worth it.

The particular shock-and-awe tactics used by Somali pirates usually involve up to seven pirates acting alone in one fibreglass boat, or several boats mirroring the wolfpack-style swarming tactics of the past, albeit on a much more modest scale. In those instances, pirate action groups up to forty strong swiftly approach the targeted vessel from different angles in several boats propelled by powerful Volvo or Yamaha outboard engines. They try to force the vessel to stop by firing some salvoes of AK-47 rounds at the superstructure, occasionally followed by a rocket-propelled grenade to make an even more forceful point.[58] In many reported cases, that has proved to be enough to convince the master to heave to in order to avoid bloodshed. In November 2008, for instance, Captain Nozhkin of the Danish-flagged cargo ship *CEC Future* did so after failed attempts to outmanoeuvre Somali pirates. On the moment he spotted them on the radar screen he later said, 'It was like a firecracker had gone off in my head'[59] – illustrating just how much distress the appearance of pirate skiffs can cause even a seasoned crew on board a large vessel. The Somalis' swarming tactic wasn't always successful, though. As we saw in the Introduction, the vigorous counter-measures taken by the crew of the liner *Seabourn Spirit* on 8 November 2005, including a combination of abrupt changes of the vessel's course and speed, the use of a high-pressure hose to try to flood the pirates' two boats, and the employment of a then still rather novel 'sonic gun' (a Long Range Acoustic Device, or LRAD), carried the day.[60]

The 'Uniquely Violent Nature' of Nigerian Piracy

Compared to the 'firecracker' that went off in Captain Nozhkin's head, the fear caused by pirate skiffs when they appear on radar screens in the Gulf of Guinea is even worse: Nigerian pirates' level of violence, and their willingness to cause injury or even death to crew members not immediately complying with their orders, is much higher than that of Somali pirates. Nigerian pirates are not always primarily motivated by taking crew members hostage for ransom. Instead, general cargo vessels are ransacked for the crew's valuables and the money in the ship's safe, while oil tankers are often attacked for their cargo of refined oil, which is siphoned off by another vessel in a quick ship-to-ship transfer after the captured tanker has been made to sail to a remote and secure spot.[61] In both cases, the survival of the original crew is not required for the success of the piratical operation – a fact of which crew members sailing in these waters are very aware. Unlike their Somali and Southeast Asian counterparts who rarely risk encounters with vessels that look like they could put up a fight, Nigerian pirate groups are also known to attack merchant vessels even if they are protected by armed and well-trained security guards and to engage them in protracted firefights – so regularly that many sources comment on the 'uniquely violent nature of Nigerian pirates'.[62] During the attack on the tanker MV *SP Brussels* on 29 April 2014, for instance, a group of eight Nigerian pirates in two speedboats even forced an armed security team to take shelter, together with the crew, in the ship's citadel (a reinforced room into which a crew can retreat when under pirate attack).[63] Two of the pirates were later killed in a firefight with a vessel of the Nigerian navy that had come to the rescue of the tanker, while the remaining six were arrested.[64]

Firefights between Nigerian pirates and the country's navy are not untypical: in two incidents in August 2013 alone, pirates opened fire on Nigerian navy vessels trying to rescue ships they had captured. The second of these two incidents involved a gasoline tanker, the MT *Notre*, which was surrounded by eight Nigerian navy craft dispatched to arrest the pirates. Although a gasoline tanker is a veritable 'floating bomb' – certainly not the best platform for a protracted firefight with automatic weapons – the pirates chose to give battle anyway. Eventually, they tried to make their escape on a small boat, but to no avail: during the thirty-minute exchange of fire, twelve of the sixteen pirates were killed and their boat was sunk.[65] Such a tendency for extreme, bordering on suicidal, violence is virtually unknown in the case of Somali piracy.

Some boats under attack by Nigerian pirate skiffs may be able to take evasive options; for others such tactics are impossible: Nigerian pirates are also known to attack static offshore oil installations such as oil rigs, floating production, storage and off-loading units (FPSOs) and barges housing oil workers. Royal Dutch Shell's *Bonga* FPSO, for instance, is located 120 kilometres off the Nigerian coast and was thus thought to be safe from attack.[66] At 1 a.m. on 19 June 2008, however, about two dozen heavily armed men from the guerrilla group Movement for the Emancipation of the Niger Delta (MEND) approached on speedboats and attempted to storm the FPSO. Failing to gain access, they opened fire. Several crew members were injured but fortunately nobody was killed. The incident lasted no less than four hours without any naval vessels coming to the rescue. Unable to capture the FPSO, the MEND guerrillas then intercepted a nearby offshore support vessel and took its American master hostage – he was released a day later – to ensure their safe return to their base. Although the audacious attack on the FPSO was a failure, it nevertheless 'sent shockwaves through the oil industry', raising 'great concerns and even fears for the security of deep-sea offshore installations in the region, which had previously been considered out of reach of the militant groups'.[67] As a consequence, the oil-production of Nigeria 'dropped to its lowest level in twenty-five years and the global oil prices soared'[68] – exactly what MEND later claimed to have intended with their act of piracy, in order to force the Nigerian government to a negotiated settlement of their political demands, including an amnesty.[69] MEND is a guerrilla organisation and not a pirate gang, but nevertheless the FPSO attack could be classified as an act of political piracy: contrary to 'normal' piracy (a criminal act carried out at sea for private gain) the activities of the MEND guerrillas aimed to further the political objectives of the movement while also generating additional funds to finance its activities by way of ransom money. Fighting a guerrilla war does not come cheap, after all: arms and ammunition have to be bought, officials bribed and guerrilla fighters paid.

It is not only MEND that conducted such acts of political piracy – the Free Aceh Movement also used income derived from piracy to fund their own guerrilla war against the Indonesian government until peace was brokered in the aftermath of the Boxing Day tsunami of 2004. The noto-rious Abu Sayyaf Group's 23 April 2000 attack on a diving resort on Sipadan Island, Malaysia, during which they abducted twenty-one people (all eventually released after a ransom had been paid), could also be seen to have had political intentions: the ASG's demands included the release of the al-Qaeda-linked terrorist mastermind Ramzi Yousef and the with-drawal of Philippine forces from Jolo.[70] Yet with the ASG's abduction of the German yachter Jürgen Kantner and the murder of his wife (who allegedly tried to escape) off Tambisan, Malaysia on 6 November 2016, the intention was simply private gain. Obviously, there is not only a continuum between privateers and pirates, but also between organised crime (including piracy) and terrorism.

Modern Pirates' Modus Operandi

The Nigerian pirates' penchant for lethal violence (including firefights with security guards and Nigerian navy vessels) in contrast with the Somali pirates' typical avoidance of such encounters points to the variety of tactics used by modern-day pirates. As in the previous periods, whether lethal and gratuitous violence is inflicted or not depends to a large degree on what the pirates are after: mainly the ship's cargo and the crew and passengers' valuables, as for example were the Victual Brothers or the Golden Age pirates, or mainly passengers and crew, either to be ransomed or sold into slavery, as were the Mediterranean corsairs or the Malay pirates.

There are different ways to classify the variants of piracy used by modern pirates,[71] but, in general, they can be broken down into the following categories (in ascending order of violence): simple robbery of vessel at anchor; armed/violent robbery of vessels at anchor; armed/violent robbery of vessels underway; hijack of vessels underway in order to take hostages for ransom; and, finally, hijack of vessels to turn them into 'phantom ships' (that is, vessels 'without legal registry plying the seas for illegal purposes').[72] The cases of thefts at anchor described above belong to the category of armed/violent robberies. The *Seamaster* incident that resulted in the death of Sir Peter Blake shows that armed robberies can turn lethal – although, if everything goes as planned, the crew may not even realise that pirates have sneaked on board, stolen whatever they can lay their hands on, and then disappeared. Armed/violent robberies of vessels underway, also known as hit-and-run attacks, currently form the most frequent assault type in modern piracy. In most cases, such attacks only last between thirty minutes and an hour. The attacks carried out in the Straits of Malacca are typical of this particular modus operandi. A small boat, hiding in plain sight by mimicking the behaviour of fishing vessels, sneaks up by night in the stern wash of a merchant vessel – a notorious blind spot for the ship's radar – to draw alongside. Some of the pirates climb up to the merchant vessel's deck on ropes fastened to grapnels[73] – for the pirates, usually the most dangerous part of the raid because the risks of slipping and either getting crushed between the hull of the merchant vessel and their own boat, or getting sucked under water and into the ship's propeller, are considerable. Modern pirates thus have to be quick and nimble, and the majority are in their late teens or early twenties – an old salt like John Ward who started his piracy career on the wrong side of fifty would have had to struggle to get aboard a modern freighter in this way. The pirates are usually equipped with machetes and assault rifles, an arsenal which is more than enough to subdue the startled crew before they can even think of offering resistance. The crew are then locked up, usually in a room in the deckhouse, while the captain is frog-marched to the ship's safe to open it and hand over the cash. On average, ships on international voyages have between $30,000 and $50,000 (£23,000–£38,000) in their safes to pay for port fees or expenses for the crew. The crew's possessions also get ransacked, and everything else that is both portable and of value is taken as well. With the looting complete, the pirates quickly return to their boat, and vanish into the night. Time is of the essence: if the bridge crew of the merchant vessel manage to make a distress call before being subdued, a coastguard vessel may already be on its way. For the crew under attack, the only good news is that such incidents usually do not involve killing.

Armed/violent robberies of vessels underway may well account for the majority of modern piracy, but seafarers face more serious attacks in certain regions of the world. These are deliberate vessel hijackings – types of attack in which pirates board the targeted vessel either to take the crew hostage for ransom or to take over the vessel to steal its cargo and turn it into a 'phantom ship'. This latter variant is the most dangerous for the crew of an attacked merchant vessel: if pirates are only interested in the vessel and its cargo, then the crew are redundant. If they're lucky, they just get thrown overboard, maybe even with a life raft or two. If they are not, they are killed in cold blood – as in the MV *Cheung Son* incident (see p. 2). The next stage is that easily recognisable parts of the captured vessel, for example the funnel, are hastily repainted, while the vessel's name is overpainted or altered – sometimes including spelling mistakes. Then, the vessel is re-registered with false papers. Its cargo is sold at some small port with a 'no questions asked' policy, before the pirates sail it to another port, take on legitimate cargo under the guise of the ship's new fraudulent identity, and sell it on to someone suitably incurious – to the detriment of the rightful purchaser of the cargo, of course, who having already paid for it waits in vain at the previously scheduled port. Eventually the ship might be scuttled in an attempt to fraudulently claim insurance, or simply to get rid of the evidence if the pirates suspect their illegal activities have attracted the attention of law enforcement agencies.[74]

Capturing ships and their crews for ransom is the variant of hijacking of ships – also known as 'shipjacking' – which brought the Somali pirates to international attention between 2008–12. Somali pirates usually refrained from using lethal violence against crew members as long as they did not resist. This did not mean that the captured crew had an easy ride: some masters who refused to cooperate were shot dead in cold blood, while many more were beaten. In several incidents, as masters frantically called their companies or relatives to transmit the pirates' demands, shots were fired over their heads in order to underline the calls' urgency and to speed up negotiations that might otherwise last several months.[75] In general, however, the captives stood a good chance of eventually being freed to tell their stories: in their Somali captors' eyes they were essentially 'money on legs' and thus had to be kept alive and reasonably well. The hijacked vessels, which even included super tankers of more than 300 metres in length, were steered towards the Somali coast and anchored in plain sight, for example in the port of Eyl in Puntland or Harardhere in southern Somalia. Most of the crew were then brought to safe locations in the interior, while a number of pirates or militiamen guarded the vessels against attempts to recapture them; some original crew members were usually kept aboard as human shields. This very brazen modus operandi, unique in modern times and reminiscent of the corsairs of yesteryear, was possible only because of the collusion of port authorities, in conjunction with the absence of central state authorities that could have intervened.[76] In a sense, the enabling environment that greatly benefited the activities of the Somali pirates could be compared with that of the port cities of Algiers, Tunis and Tripoli discussed in Part II.

The best-known cases of Somali piracy in its 2008–12 heyday make for a long list, and include the French luxury yacht MY *Le Ponant* (hijacked on 4 April 2008, rescued on 12 April 2008, ransom paid: $2 million [£1.5 million]), the MV *Faina*, a 152-metre roll-on/roll-off cargo vessel (hijacked on 25 September 2008, released on 6 February 2009, ransom paid: $3.2 million [£2.45 million]), the South Korean super tanker MV *Samho Dream* (hijacked on 4 April 2010, released on 6 November 2010, ransom paid: $9.5 million [£7.3 million]), the Greek tanker MV *Irene SL* (hijacked on 9 February 2010, released on 21 December 2010, ransom paid: $13.5 million [£10.36 million]), and the Singaporean tanker MT *Gemini* (hijacked on 30 April 2011, released on 3 December 2011, ransom paid: $10 million [£7.67 million]). Although this list is far from complete, it shows how lucrative the Somali pirates' business model was – the corsairs of old would have doffed their caps to them. This also explains why the second-wave Somali pirates active from 2008 onwards were much more motivated by greed than by grievance than the earlier, first-wave Somali pirates of the late 1990s and early 2000s, and why the composition of Somali pirate groups also changed from mainly fishermen to a mixture of fishermen and militiamen. Indeed, when the news broke in Somalia about the hijack of the French luxury yacht *Le Ponant* and its thirty crew members in August 2008, which netted a ransom in the millions of dollars, not the hundreds of thousands as between 2004 and 2008, many enterprising young militiamen in their twenties and thirties flocked to the shores to join the equally young fishermen to get a piece of the action and of the ransom.[77] Also of note is that Somali pirates never attempted to offload a hijacked vessel's cargo – in the case of the MV *Faina*, that turned out to be thirty-three Ukrainian-made T–72 main battle tanks, a number of anti-aircraft guns and rocket-propelled grenades, officially destined for Kenya but probably meant to strengthen the forces of South Sudan. The pirates who attacked the MV *Faina* seemed to be as surprised as everybody else and did not touch this special cargo, notwithstanding the fact that some participants in Somalia's civil war would have been quite interested in laying their hands on such heavy weapons.

Since the Somali pirates brazenly hijacked whole ships instead of 'just' kidnapping individual crew members, they dominated international news stories for about a decade until, around 2012, they were finally chased out of the water by a multinational anti-piracy alliance – or at least that is how it looks for the time being. Nowadays, the most notorious pirates are Nigerian, on account of their use of violence, followed by the various Southeast Asian pirate gangs operating in the South China Sea and the Straits of Malacca. But, as the case of British kayaker Emma Kelty demonstrates (see p. 171), there are other manifestations of piracy that are virtually invisible so long as their victims remain as local as the pirates themselves. And these piratical activities do not even happen on the high seas or in coastal waters, as is the case in all other hot spots. Rather, they occur in the estuaries of big river systems and even along the rivers themselves.

During the Ming and Qing dynasties (see pp. 41–2 and 126–7), this kind of 'riverine piracy' was one aspect of Chinese organised piracy. Today, apart from the Amazon (see p. 171), there is one region noted for its riverine piracy that stands out: the Sundarbans, a vast coastal fresh-water mangrove swamp, formed of the deltas of the Brahmaputra, Meghna and Padma rivers that empty into the Bay of Bengal, straddling 10,000 square kilometres along the border areas of India and Bangladesh. This labyrinthine network of criss-crossing rivers, channels and rivulets, with ever-shifting mudflats, islands and mangrove forests teeming with wildlife, is a paradise for hunters and fishermen. But tigers are not the only predators on the prowl: this littoral region is a happy hunting ground to well-organised pirate groups who use the hiding places offered by this marine labyrinth to their own advantage. If they're lucky their catch of the day may consist of a coastal freighter or high-seas trawler navigating these waters, but most of the vessels they attack belong to inshore fish-ermen who are defenceless against them. In the words of one victim, 'You can fight against wild animals and shoo them away, but only a fool would think about fighting these armed robbers. A little resistance and a bullet would pierce through your head.'[78] The tactics used by these riverine pirates are quick ambush-style attacks in order to kidnap for ransom. Like the pirates operating from the Riau Archipelago, the riverine pirates of the Sundarbans make use of 'state capacity arbitrage', slipping across the India–Bangladesh border with their unfortunate hostages. Since there is no Indo-Bangladeshi agreement on the right of 'hot pursuit', and in any case with coastal law enforcement services too ill-equipped and understaffed to be able to enforce law and order in this territory, the tactic works well – the odd successful police operation notwithstanding.[79] Ransom monies demanded are usually in the range of 100,000 to 150,000 Indian rupees (£1,150–£1,920, or $1,500–$2,500).[80] Although to Western audiences this may sound rather unimpressive, this is not the case for the families of the victims: often, the ransoms are more than their annual income. But if they refuse to pay, the victim will be killed. Though it is cold comfort for the local victims, this piracy does not usually affect international shipping – which also explains why this kind of piracy remains largely unknown in the wider world.

Modern Variants of the Merry Life

While in the olden days a pirate's desired loot consisted of gold and silver, jewels and precious commodities, for the majority of modern pirates the hoped-for plunder usually consists of money in cash. Like most pirate groups in history, Somali pirates, today's top earners (at least between 2008 and 2012), also divide their particular plunder – ransom money – into shares that depend on each pirate's role in the action leading to the capture of a vessel. In the case of the attack on the MV *Lehmann Timber* in May 2008, those who participated on the seas were awarded $140,000 (£107,000) each from the ransom, while those tasked with guarding the hostages in Eyl still made $20,000 (£15,300) apiece – still more than six times the average annual income in Somalia.[81] The leader of the pirate gang, known only as Abdulkhadar (nicknamed 'Computer'), also allegedly awarded a 'performance-linked bonus' to the first pirate who climbed aboard the vessel after the forty-minute chase: a Land Cruiser worth $15,000 (£11,500).[82] This is reminiscent of the rewards for bravery in the times of the buccaneers, where the first to climb on board also got an extra part of the loot.

During their heyday, Somali pirates were elite earners – the money made by most other pirates is usually much less. Those earning in the 'mid-range' include pirates operating in the Straits of Malacca and the South China Sea who commit hit-and-run attacks to ransack the contents of ships' safes and take the valuables of their crews. Such raids may net between \$20,000–\$50,000 (£15,000–£38,000) in total – still a handy sum, but one that must be at least divided between all those participating in the attack, and some of which needs to be reserved to pay for bribes to officials and presents to village elders. The 'occasional' pirates on the lower end of the range, those who simply sneak on board anchored vessels to steal whatever they can lay their hands on, usually get away with some coils of rope, cans of paint or suchlike – again, not quite the stuff of pirate legend.

The merry life of modern pirates depends very much on the nature and, of course, on the quantity of the plunder. A successful modern-day Somali pirate would be able to afford a fairly good time at Harardhere or Eyl, where businesses from coffee shops to car dealerships are available to cater to pirates' demands. Allegedly, many successful young Somali pirates active between 2008 and 2012 spent their substantial shares of ransom money on pick-up trucks and dowries for additional wives. However, most of the tabloid stories about pirate villas, brand-new 4x4s gliding along newly paved roads and fancy new restaurants catering to pirates may well have been sensationalist embellishment of a not-so-glorious reality by a Western press with no reporters on the ground. Jay Bahadur, a freelance journalist who actually went to Eyl, scoffs at these stories:

> If Eyl was awash in pirate cash, its inhabitants were certainly hiding it well. As a pirate haven, it was a profound disappointment; conspicuously absent were the opulent mansions, wild parties, and drug-fuelled binges that the international media coverage had led me to expect.[83]

One Somali pirate at the time, however, explained how his colleagues, in anticipation of a soon-to-be-paid ransom, issued IOUs at a hefty 50 per cent interest:

As soon as the ship gets to its destination, the party is already on, the money is already flowing . . . No one knows when the ransom will come. It could take one month, two months, three months. But [the pirates] want to have fun, they want to have a car now . . . In the end, they pay double for whatever they buy on credit . . . If they want to buy a house, the regular price might be $20,000 [£15,000], but for them it's $30,000 [£23,000] or $40,000 [£30,000].[84]

Despite living in a different time, and in a different culture, Somali pirates active between 2008 and 2012 demonstrated behaviour that would have struck a chord with the pirates descending on Port Royal in the seventeenth century. At the time of writing, however, their good times are already over: due to ever-more effective patrolling conducted by a multinational naval alliance, Somali pirate action groups venture out only very rarely, and usually without success. Hence, their merry life has come to an end – at least for the time being.

Piracy and the Law

In a Western legal context, one argument that keeps reappearing time and again in relation to piracy is that pirates are *hostis humani generis*: 'enemies of all mankind'. Nowadays, this mantle seems to have passed to global terrorists such as al-Qaeda and ISIS – both targets of a continuing US-led global war on terrorism declared by President George W. Bush which commenced in the aftermath of 9/11. It should be noted that Bush's global war on terrorism was not the first such effort: that was President Theodore Roosevelt's global war on anarchist terrorism announced in 1904 after the assassination of his predecessor, President William McKinley, by an anarchist terrorist in September 1901.[85] Roosevelt's justification for that war is interesting:

Anarchy is a crime against the whole human race and all mankind should band against the anarchist. His crime should be made an offense against the law of nations, like piracy and that form of manstealing known as the slave trade; for it is of far blacker infamy than either. It should be so declared by treaties among all civilised powers.[86]

In order to drive home the seriousness of this at-the-time novel menace to his audience, Roosevelt was using the then well-known threats posed by pirates and slavers. When, a century later, Bush sought to rally the world to fight his war on global terrorism, he also referred to slavery and piracy when he promised to use 'the full influence of the United States, and working closely with allies and friends, to make clear that all acts of terrorism are illegitimate so that terrorism will be viewed in the same light as slavery, piracy, or genocide: behaviour that no respectable government can condone or support and all must oppose'.[87]

In both speeches, the idea of 'enemies of all mankind' shines through. Although in its original Roman context the meaning may have been a bit different from our modern interpretation,[88] this is how pirates were seen by Western sea powers from early modern times onwards. A description of piracy offered by one of the leading jurists of his day, English barrister William Blackstone (1723–80), is typical:

> The crime of piracy, or robbery and depredation on the high seas, is an offence against the universal law of society; a pirate being . . . *hostis humani generis*. As therefore he has renounced all the benefits of society and government, and has reduced himself . . . to the savage state of nature, by declaring war against all mankind, all mankind must declare war against him: so that every community hath a right, by the rule of self-defence, to inflict punishment on him, which every individual would in a state of nature have been otherwise entitled to do.[89]

This issue poses a rather interesting legal problem on how to deal with pirates, in domestic as well as international law. In classic, pre-modern

(Western-origin) international law, for instance, pirates were situated somewhere between mere criminals and proper military enemies. First, they 'were criminals in the sense that they were not associated with a state for any public purpose (but rather came together for purposes of "wrong-doing"), and they were military enemies in the sense that through their interference with free trade and commerce, they had declared war upon all mankind'.[90] This implies that they could be treated either as criminals or as combatants, depending on the circumstances in which they were encountered. But second, far from being the enemies of all mankind, pirates quite often enjoyed at least the tacit support of certain port author-ities, and even states themselves (such as England in its incessant wars, declared or not, against Spain). After all, piracy was big business, and pirates could be used as deniable tools for a naval proxy war, weakening the enemy.[91] And third, it did not escape the attention of law experts that it was not so much a different modus operandi that distinguished priva-teers from pirates as that the former carried out their operations sanc-tioned by a state while the latter did so without it.[92] This argument leads to a logical question: 'If two practices are distinguishable only *in nomine* and with regard to state sanction, how can one be "heinous" or "revolting" and the other perfectly respectable?'[93]

As a result, states were often not on the same page when it came to effectively combating piracy multilaterally. Rather, many states frequently found it in their national interest to obstruct and undermine the unilateral efforts undertaken by the rival sea powers of the day. Today, alliances against piracy are still hampered by mutual distrust lying beneath the surface, while an additional problem is states' different operational prac-tices and varying ideas about human rights. For example, while the European Union and the United States hold firm to the UN's Universal Declaration of Human Rights (at least before the Trump administration pulled out of it), others are far less squeamish in their approach. The recapture on 6 May 2010 of the Russian-owned tanker MV *Moscow University*, which had been taken over by pirates just a day earlier, by a

Russian naval infantry commando is a case in point. Although official Russian sources claimed that the surviving pirates had the bad luck to 'perish at sea' after being sent back to their home shore in an inflatable boat, other sources maintained that they might well have been summarily executed – an interpretation that was given some weight by then Russian president Dmitri Medvedev's rather dark comment on the very day of the recapture that 'we'll have to do what our forefathers did when they met the pirates'.[94]

We have seen what 'our forefathers' did to pirates when, rather than offering them amnesties or using them as a tool in their incessant wars, they tried to bring them to justice. There were many ways to dispatch pirates, very much depending on what kind of lethal punishment a culture deemed acceptable. Whatever form of execution was used, it was normal to turn these grisly events into public spectacles in order to dissuade anyone from following in the pirates' footsteps. In our more civilised times, the death penalty, where it still exists, is usually no longer carried out in the open. What remains the same is that states are not always keen to bring apprehended pirates to justice. For instance, financial consider-ations going hand-in-hand with human rights issues often dissuaded affected states from bringing captured Somali pirates to justice during their heyday. An official from the US Department of State told the author, only half in jest, why that was:

> Consider we want to open a court case against a couple of appre-hended pirates. We have to bring them to the United States, obvi-ously. But not only them: we also have to fly in their lawyers, the victims, the witnesses other than the victims, representatives of the ship owners, their lawyers, and so on. We have to hire translators as well. We have to pay for whatever is needed to give them a fair hearing. Then they get probably sentenced, and do some time in one of our prisons. And when they are done serving, they probably end up driving taxis in New York.[95]

Of course, costly court cases could not always be avoided – especially not in the high-profile examples of the *Maersk Alabama* (see pp. 5–6) and the attack on the US Navy's USS *Ashland* (LSD–48) in the early morning of 10 April 2010, after pirates had mistaken it for a merchant vessel.

The same aversion to bringing pirates to costly justice can be found in other states as well. One reason is that, fundamentally, states' domestic criminal laws are no longer built to deal with the resurgence of the particular crime of piracy, since it seemed to have disappeared as a phenomenon more than a century ago. Principles known in Western legal tradition since Roman days as *nullum crimen sine lege* (no crime without law) and *nulla poena sine lege* (no punishment without law) mean that without such legal apparatus, piracy can neither be deemed a crime nor punished. Tellingly, even if a country's statutes codify acts of piracy, they are not necessarily drawn upon. For example, paragraph 316c of the German criminal code punishes an attempt to take unlawful control of a civil vessel with a prison sentence of five years – a section that was used for the very first time in November 2010 in a case against ten Somali pirates who had seized the German freighter MV *Taipan* that April. As many observers pointed out, this was the first German trial of pirates in four hundred years.[96] It is thus not unfair to say that many courts are currently out of practice when it comes to dealing with piracy cases.

There is another reason for this reluctance to bring pirates to justice: various EU states do not want to allow apprehended pirates to be brought on board their warships for fear that they might use this golden opportunity to apply for asylum – which is their right, according to EU law. For that reason, and until the EU concluded cooperation agreements concerning the prosecution and imprisonment of pirates with Kenya and the Seychelles,[97] a practice known as 'catch and release' was common: apprehended pirates who were not caught in the act were simply disarmed and then sent back to their own shores in their own boats, thus enabling them to try their luck again as soon as the warship had disappeared. Of course, as the MV *Moscow University* incident suggests, for one reason or another not all pirates seem to have made it home.

Citadels and Robot Ships

Piratical attacks on land targets are now exceedingly rare and restricted to only a very few locations. In Europe, the inhabitants of German coastal towns and villages no longer need to be on the lookout for Vikings, and Frisia is no longer subject to the 'usual surprise attacks' as one of the chronicles of the day sardonically put it. In the Mediterranean, the few remaining Martello towers (see p. 46) now serve as interesting landmarks for tourists and not for protection: the corsairs and pirates have disappeared there as well. The end of this endemic threat also resulted in a swift repopulation of the coasts, with people gradually moving back from the better protected interior to the seaboard, from where fishing and trading are so much easier. The same is true of the coastal areas of China and Japan: people there are able to go about their daily business without fear of being abducted by pirates appearing like a bolt out of the blue. There too, watchtowers and fortifications are now must-see tourist destinations. And along Latin American and Caribbean coasts, villagers and town-dwellers no longer fear attacks by British sea dogs or their French and Dutch equivalents. But there is no rule without an exception: in some locations, the threat of piracy is not completely gone. As we have seen, there are still attacks on yachts lying at anchor in the Caribbean, and riverine pirates can still be found on the Amazon in Brazil or the Sundarbans between India and Bangladesh. There, remaining vigilant is still the order of the day – especially when policing at sea is ineffective, be it due to a lack of funds and equipment or, indeed, to corruption.

When it comes to defences against pirates at sea, an obvious choice for merchantmen has for a long time been sailing together in convoys: as already discussed, some degree of safety could be found in numbers. More recently, faced with the threat of Somali piracy on the high seas, the

European Naval Force (EU NAVFOR) deployed to protect Europe's most important sea lines of communication (SLOC) to Asia swiftly took action to reintroduce convoys for voyages through the pirates' favoured area of operation – the Gulf of Aden and the northern part of the Arabian Sea. In December 2008, EU NAVFOR's newly established Maritime Security Centre – Horn of Africa (MSC–HOA)[98] started organising group transits through a protected maritime corridor:

> The concept of 'group transits' differs from the traditional convoy system (which restricts the speed of the convoy to that of the slowest ship) in that the transiting merchant vessels are given staggered start times and then monitored through the corridor. Ships are timed to arrive and pass together through the area of highest risk in the company of escorting warships.[99]

Despite the staggered start times, and the deployment of a number of helicopters (admittedly, initially rather limited),[100] the group transit system had a fatal weakness. As demonstrated by a number of successful pirate attacks on ships in convoy in the transit corridor, the window of opportunity for deploying decisive anti-piracy measures (such as anti-boarding teams of naval commandos arriving by helicopter or speedboat) was just eight minutes – that is, the time from when a ship spotted approaching pirates, who until then had perhaps been masquerading as nearby fishing vessels, to when the pirates would be clambering on board and taking hostages. In many cases this window was simply too narrow to take effective action. So, as in previous centuries, the captains of fast ships realised joining a group transit sailing through Somali waters was not necessarily the best choice; they preferred to trust to the superior speed of their vessel. For this reason, container ships on international voyages hardly ever bothered to join such convoys; Somali piracy statistics showed that no vessel with a speed of 18 knots or above had ever been boarded, and modern container vessels can go much faster than that.[101] Superior speed did not always protect a vessel from running into an ambush, however, and it also did not help much when the port of call was situated right in the middle of piracy-prone waters. This is what Captain Richard Phillips of the MV *Maersk Alabama* discovered on 8 April 2009 (see pp. 5–6) when Somali pirates suddenly launched a speedboat from their innocent-looking mother ship, the hijacked Taiwanese trawler FV *Win Far 161*. Although the container ship had successfully thwarted a previous attack aided by a choppy sea that prevented the small skiff from catching it, this time, circumstances were against them: the sea was calm.[102] Nevertheless, sailing in group transits or trusting to a ship's superior speed, combined with mental preparation and a keen look-out, remain cost-effective passive counter-measures that make life more difficult for pirates.

To better prepare seafarers against the endemic Somali piracy of 2008–12, MSC–HOA published a compendium of best-management practices (BMP) for merchant vessels which listed all recommended defensive counter-measures. After an overview of Somali piratical activities the booklet then talks the reader through risk assessment, typical Somali pirate attacks, incident reporting procedures, company and ship master's planning, ship protection measures, how to react when under attack, how to react should pirates manage to take control, how to react in the event of military counteractions, and post-incident reporting. In its appendices, it also offers special advice for fishing vessels and for leisure craft including yachts. Although the recommendations are not mandatory, the authors make very clear that the potential consequences of not following them may be severe: 'There have been instances of pirates subjecting their hostages to violence and other ill treatment.' They also point out that the average length of a hostage situation after the capture of a vessel was seven months, and that a military response to rescue the crew of a captured vessel was not guaranteed. But, finally, the authors emphasise that the ultimate responsibility for how to prepare or how to act rested with the vessel's master: 'Nothing in this booklet detracts from the Master's overriding authority to protect his crew, ship and cargo.'[103]

The first security measure recommended in the BMP booklet is enhanced watchkeeping, including radar watch, and increased vigilance as soon as piracy-prone waters are entered. The 'Mark I Eyeball' (i.e. the naked eye) – also, of course, used by modern crews' predecessors – should preferably be augmented by the use of binoculars and, if possible, night-vision optics. In an era of high-tech, starting with the importance of watchkeeping may seem a bit odd, but the MSC–HOA leaves no doubt as to its importance: 'A proper lookout is the single most effective method of ship protection where early warning of a suspicious approach or attack is assured, and where defences can readily be deployed.'[104]

The booklet then moves on to recommend measures to protect the bridge from pirates' rifle- and RPG-fire, for instance by adding extra metal sheets and sandbags or donning Kevlar jackets and helmets (preferably in a non-military colour to avoid being mistaken for soldiers). Access doors and hatches should be secured or locked, not only those leading to the bridge but throughout the vessel, while tools and equipment should be safely stowed away. Furthermore, physical barriers such as judiciously deployed razor wire, metal grilles topped with spikes or even electrified fences (depending on the vessel type) should be considered to render boarding more difficult. Fire hoses or, if and when available, foam monitors and water cannon should also be kept at the ready in order to prevent pirates from boarding and to swamp their skiffs. To monitor pirates' moves after boarding, CCTV should be available, supported by upper-deck lighting. Should all counter-measures fail, a safe muster point or citadel, defined in the booklet as a room 'designed and constructed to resist a determined pirate trying to gain entry for a fixed period of time'[105] and usually equipped with a two-way external communication/radio system in order to call for help, should be available where the crew can take refuge: without crew members as hostages and human shields the pirates would be extremely vulnerable to counter-attack and unable to navigate the vessel into their own waters. Here, the authors warn that the 'whole concept of the Citadel approach is lost if any crew member is left outside before it is secured'.[106] As the case of the MV *Maersk Alabama* shows (see pp. 5–6), this is indeed an important point.

The BMP booklet also covers active counter-measures, such as deploying armed private maritime security contractors or making use of military vessel protection detachments (VPDs) – although the authors emphasise that they neither recommend nor endorse that course of action, and that the use of such personnel must come as an additional layer of security and not in lieu of the recommended passive measures.[107] For certain vessels, those either carrying valuable cargo or that are slow and thus easy targets, the protection offered by VPDs or private armed security guards makes sense. However, VPDs are not readily available, while private maritime security contractors are expensive – which is why even during the height of the Somali piracy crisis ship operators were none too keen to take this particular course of action. However, it did not escape notice that in the particular case of Somali pirates, no ship that had armed guards on board was ever hijacked; after some salvoes were fired at them, pirates usually went to look for an easier target. Unsurprisingly, several maritime experts suggested that crew members themselves should be armed: surely having 'specially trained security teams from the ship's crew, led by a highly trained licensed officer'[108] available on board would be much cheaper than hiring private contractors. Support for the idea of arming the crews themselves mainly came from the US where the attitude to the private possession of firearms is much more relaxed than, say, in western Europe. In May 2009, for example, in the light of the threat posed by the Somali pirates in general, and the *Maersk Alabama* incident in particular, the chief executive officer of Liberty Maritime Corporation, an American commercial shipping company, 'respectfully request[ed] that Congress consider clearing the obstacles that currently block ship owners from arming our vessels'.[109] Other counter-piracy specialists, in particular non-US ones, were far less sanguine, while the International Maritime Organisation was initially adamantly opposed to the idea of arming crews.[110]

There are three main arguments against arming crews. First, to equip crew members with assault rifles is pointless unless they are trained to use them. Although not too difficult to accomplish, weapons-training would interfere with their normal duties and put an additional burden on those who already have plenty of work to do, modern merchant vessels being even more economically crewed than their predecessors were. Second, crew members of merchant vessels are, as in previous centuries, civilians, not auxiliary marines, and thus quite unlikely to be prepared to die for a cargo that does not belong to them. Third, there are several legal obstacles to overcome, especially the laws of coastal states governing the possession and use of weapons. For instance, in many coastal states it is illegal to possess 'weapons of war', a category that includes not only heavy weaponry like artillery and tanks but also simple assault rifles. Several private security contractors have ended up in jail after unwittingly violating such local laws. Of course, these problems can be overcome, either by bilateral or multilateral negotiations between affected states, or by the inventive solutions of the private security industry: 'arsenal ships', for example, are deployed in international waters at the entry and exit points of high-risk areas, where arms can be borrowed and returned, or armed guards be taken on board. A cheaper and more common solution if approaching the sovereign waters of a coastal state with a restrictive approach to the possession of firearms is simply to throw the weapons overboard.

Not all pirates are as squeamish as the Somalis in the face of counter-fire. Many Nigerian pirates think nothing of engaging in a firefight, even if, as we have seen, the opponent is the Nigerian navy or the field of battle is a tanker carrying aviation fuel; and the ferocity of their fighting on one occasion forced even private security contractors to take shelter in a targeted vessel's citadel (see p. 176). Having armed personnel on board is not necessarily a panacea against piracy, and may even lead to other problems. For example, as the BMP booklet states, it is the prerogative of the ship's master to decide what kind of counter-measures should be implemented – but would private security guards on board a ship attacked by pirates accept the master's orders to lay down their arms and surrender, knowing very well that they might be executed by the marauders, or would they brush aside the master's lawful authority and fight? Again, it is clear that an approach that at first glance may seem wise in fact presents a number of issues.

Modern technology may soon come to the rescue – at least in the West. For some years now there has been talk within the shipping industry of making use of 'robot ships' to transport goods – that is, unmanned vessels either controlled remotely from a station on land or navigating autonomously along pre-set routes. The two main rationales for the development of such ships – improved safety on the one hand, and reduced operating costs with no crew to pay and support on the other – have nothing to do with piracy. However, as one report points out, remote-controlled and autonomous vessels 'will also mitigate the piracy threat by being designed to be difficult to board at sea. If successfully boarded, control of the vessel can still be denied. Lack of crew makes them a less attractive target as there is no one to be held hostage for ransom.'[111]

In 2017, the British-Norwegian firm Automated Ships Ltd commissioned the design of an unmanned autonomous robot ship, which will be built over the next couple of years. Named *Hrönn*, the vessel will service offshore wind farms as well as oil and gas platforms.[112] And Automated Ships Ltd is not alone – Rolls-Royce plc, for example, is also currently developing a vessel that 'looks like a cross between a gigantic torpedo and a metal whale [and] has about as much in common with modern-day cargo ships as today's ships have with the *Mayflower*'.[113] The company clearly have Somali pirates' tactics in mind when they assess the advantages of uncrewed autonomous vessels over conventional, crewed ships:

The target is actually attractive to pirates because it is manned. The pirates can hold hostages for ransom. An unmanned vessel would be a lower priority target. If a boat was to be attacked by pirates, we could shut off all the power and propulsion, make it harder for pirates to bring the vessel and its cargo ashore. We can alert the authorities and install homing technology so the ship automatically travels to a predesignated safe port.[114]

Unmanned vessels are not quite the 'silver bullets' that they may appear to be for countering piracy, while also improving safety and cutting costs. As an EU research project named Maritime Unmanned Navigation through Intelligence in Networks (MUNIN) shows, the use of autonomous vessels would not be feasible in congested, high-density-traffic waters, such as the approaches of a port, where an onboard crew would still be required to ensure timely reactions to ever-changing navigational situations; while remote-controlled ships remain unfeasible for the time being due to restricted satellite bandwidth in certain maritime regions.[115] Furthermore, until such a time as these robot vessels have become inexpensive enough to penetrate down the strata of the maritime transport sector, pirates will simply change their targets, attacking the ships of the more lowly operators who usually man older vessels of little more than scrap value. Piracy would thus cease to be a problem for developed countries whose shipping companies could afford the state-of-the-art vessels, yet though it would vanish from Western radar screens, it would not disappear in reality.

It should be noted that all of the passive and active security measures mentioned above are aimed at improving the safety and security of merchant vessels. In the case of leisure craft or of cruise liners, MSC–HOA's recommendations are less useful. For instance, it is well-nigh impossible for crew and passengers of such vessels to assemble in a citadel: yachts do not have the space for one, and cruise liners would need several of them to accommodate their hundreds or even thousands of passengers and crew – which also begs the question of how a timely evacuation into these safe rooms could be organised. For yachts, the most sensible course of action is simply to stay out of piracy-prone waters altogether. The International Maritime Organisation does not mince its words in that regard: all 'sailing yachts under their own passage should remain out of the High Risk Area or face the risk of being attacked and pirated for ransom'.[116] One would think that this warning, here referring to Somali waters, would be clear enough, and that common sense would result in its application to other piracy hot spots such as the South China Sea. But as already discussed (see pp. 171–2), anecdotal evidence collected by the author shows that often the threat is met with yachters' ignorance of the dangers or blind confidence that with nothing to steal they have nothing to fear.

Cruise liner operators, however, took swift action in the aftermath of the *Seabourn Spirit* incident, scrutinising the security measures inaugurated in the wake of the *Achille Lauro* hijack of October 1985.[117] Top-of-the-line cruise liners operated by leading companies were carrying security personnel on board well before the advent of Somali piracy, and some of these vessels were also protected by LRADs or 'sonic guns' just like the *Seabourn Spirit*. But against the backdrop of the emergence of Somali high-seas piracy and the persistence of piracy in the South China Sea and the Straits of Malacca, additional measures have been adopted. Some are in line with the recommendations of MSC–HOA, such as 24/7 watchkeeping, preparedness for a sudden increase in speed to outrun approaching pirates, and having fire hoses at the ready to repel boarding attempts. Others include observing radio silence and the institution of a blackout from dusk to dawn – measures that obviously require the understanding and cooperation of passengers. For example, the July 2017 voyage of the Princess Cruises vessel *Sea Princess* from Sydney to Dubai saw the captain ordering a ten-day blackout and a dusk-to-dawn shut-down when the ship entered the Indian Ocean, during which activities on deck such as parties or films were forbidden, and lights were dimmed to minimise the ship's visibility as much as possible. Passengers had to take part in a compulsory anti-piracy drill and were given specific advice on how to react in case of an attack. Those who had outside cabins 'were told to close and lock their balcony doors, then lock the entrance door to their cabin and take shelter in the corridors [as that] would put two metal doors between passengers and pirates'.[118] These measures certainly put a temporary chill on the party atmosphere, and were indeed 'taken out of an abundance of caution and not in response to a specific threat', as a spokesperson for the company put it.[119] But erring on the side of safety and security is arguably better than just trusting to luck.

Hunting Pirates at Sea

Active pirate hunting at sea has always seemed to have been beset by a mismatch in numbers: too few warships tasked with patrolling too vast maritime regions to hunt too many pirates. Even though the advent of steam-powered vessels gave pirate hunters an enormous technological edge over pirates (see p. 142), this numbers game could not be solved. The same initial mismatch between pirates and pirate hunters also hampered the anti-piracy measures launched to combat the Somali pirates in several multinational ventures in the early twenty-first century, such as the European Union's Operation Atalanta,[120] NATO's Operation Ocean Shield[121] and the Combined Task Force (CTF) 151.[122] Most of the warship-deploying countries also took part in related international governance and counter-piracy mechanisms such as the Contact Group on Piracy off the Coast of Somalia (CGPCS) and Shared Awareness and Deconfliction (SHADE).[123]

On paper, this sounds like a sizeable armada was cruising up and down the coast of Somalia, rendering piracy well-nigh impossible. The reality, however, was very different. For instance, Operation Atalanta started with only three or four warships, a dozen or so helicopters and two maritime patrol aircraft (MPAs); Operation Ocean Shield consisted of three to five NATO warships 'at any point of time';[124] and CTF 151 commenced operations with three US Navy warships and a dozen helicopters.[125]

Hence, when faced with a proposal tabled in November 2009 by the Spanish navy to blockade the 3,300-kilometre Somali coast in order to solve the piracy problem by keeping pirates out of the water – in fact a time-honoured counter-piracy measure – the Royal Navy commander Mike Jager, well aware of the comparatively small number of warships that were then available for the task, quipped that it was equivalent to 'policing the East Coast of America with five police cars'.[126] Although blockading the coast was unfeasible, the idea was then put forward that the warships blockade the most notorious Somali ports in an effort to prevent pirate action groups from operating from them. But with the realisation that Somali pirates did not require sophisticated port infra-structure to launch their raids – for those equipped with fibreglass boats, any stretch of beach would do, while for those operating from mother ships, they could allegedly make use of certain Yemeni harbours to replenish their supplies – hence, even this watered-down counter-measure was eventually discarded.

Instead, the MSC–HOA established the secure maritime transit corridor (see p. 192) to reduce the size of the area that had to be patrolled, and for the first time since the Second World War warship-protected convoys were formed. Unlike their predecessors, these modern pirate hunters could also draw on 'eyes in the sky' to facilitate their task: while land-based maritime patrol aircraft and ship- or land-based unmanned aerial vehicles (UAVs), colloquially known as drones, greatly facilitated early threat detection, more ship-based armed helicopters became avail-able that could be deployed against Somali pirate action groups from the bigger warships on patrol, which in most cases also generally allowed for a quick response. Usually, suspected pirate vessels were stopped, boarded and inspected by vessel boarding, search and seizure (VBSS) teams, often covered by an armed helicopter. If evidence of criminal intent – such as arms and ammunition, ladders, grapnels – was found then the crew of the suspicious vessel was apprehended for further investigation and their boat sunk by gunfire.[127]

Modern weaponry and surveillance technology notwithstanding, fighting pirates remains a risky and daring business, especially when it comes to recapturing hijacked vessels. The fight against Somali piracy offers some instructive examples. The recapture of the tanker MV *Moscow University* in May 2010 (see pp. 188–9), for instance, saw a commando of Russian special forces abseil from a helicopter and quickly overwhelm the eleven pirates after a short, intense firefight during which one pirate was killed. None of the commandos was injured, and nor were any crew members; unlike the *Maersk Alabama* incident where the pirates had managed to capture the vessel's master (see pp. 5–6), the *Moscow University*'s crew had all barricaded themselves in two citadels (the radar room and the engine room) when their vessel was boarded, thus staying out of harm's way while also denying the pirates hostages to be used as human shields. An even more daring operation was carried out on 16 September 2008 by the French navy's Commando Hubert in the Gulf of Aden to rescue the two-person crew of the sailing yacht SY *Carré d'As IV,* held hostage on board by seven pirates. In order to approach the vessel unobserved, the French commandos parachuted into the sea some distance from the yacht and stealthily swam up to it. As planned, they took the pirates by surprise: one of them was shot dead, while the remaining six wisely surrendered. The two hostages were not harmed.

Operations of this kind do not always end in success. On 9 April 2009, about 20 nautical miles off the coast of Somalia, a French commando operation to recapture the pirated yacht SY *Tanit* and five hostages on board resulted in the death not only of two pirates but also of the yacht's skipper, Florent Lemaçon, who was caught in the crossfire.[128] Even worse, US Navy forces' attempt on 22 February 2011 to recapture the pirated sailing yacht SY *Quest*, which had been held by a gang of nineteen pirates since 18 February, led to the death of all four hostages, all of them US citizens. Whether the hostages died during the pirates' firefight with the approaching US Navy boarding team (as the surviving pirates claimed), or were shot dead in cold blood, perhaps to avenge the three Somali pirates killed when the *Maersk Alabama* incident came to its dramatic conclusion in April 2009, is unclear. According to US Navy reports, the special operations boarding team had only taken action when they saw a burst of gunfire on board the yacht – which would support the possibility of a revenge killing.[129] In any case, the pirates' plan had already gone awry well before the fatal firefight: they had intended to transfer the hostages and themselves to a nearby mother ship and to ditch the vulnerable yacht immediately after the successful hijack. But the mother ship had made off at the first sight of the approaching US Navy vessels, thus marooning the nineteen pirates with little food or drinking water on the tiny *Quest*.[130]

Due to the grave risk to the lives of hostages of pirated vessels, some counteractions have been cancelled at the planning stage. The German freighter MV *Hansa Stavanger* and its crew of twenty-five were captured by Somali pirates on 3 April 2009, just five days before the *Maersk Alabama* drama commenced. Although the maritime unit of the German federal police special force GSG–9 was rushed to the scene to mount a rescue operation, the operation was called off at the last moment: the number of pirates was unclear, but was estimated to be thirty or more – overwhelming them quickly enough to save the lives of all hostages hence posed a challenge from the outset. Furthermore, of the twenty-five crew members held hostage, at least six had been intentionally kept out of sight, probably below deck, in order to render a rescue operation more difficult. It was thus estimated that even in the best circumstances, these six hostages at least, and probably also several GSG–9 members, would either be killed or injured during the counter-raid.[131] With the benefit of hindsight, and keeping in mind Murphy's Law (everything that can go wrong will go wrong), the decision to cancel the mission was probably a good one: even though the *Hansa Stavanger* crew had to endure four months of captivity, they and their vessel were finally released on 3 August, after a ransom of $2 million (£1.53 million) had been paid.[132]

The lack of vessels available to deal with piracy is a problem that could be solved, or at least mitigated to a certain extent, by a maritime variant of the UAVs or drones discussed above. For instance, the *Protector* unmanned surface vehicle (USV), a highly manoeuvrable 30-foot rigid-hull inflatable boat capable of a speed of up to 50 knots, was developed by the Israeli defence provider Rafael in the early 2000s and is currently in service in Israel, Mexico and Singapore. It is equipped with a sophisticated surveillance system and a weapons station usually armed with a machine gun. Although its developers primarily had naval force protection in mind, this USV could also be adapted for use in piracy suppression operations, for surveillance purposes and for investigating potential threats.[133] But whether the *Popular Mechanics* headline 'Robot Boats Hunt High-Tech Pirates on the High-Speed Seas' will ever come true remains to be seen – at the moment, this is nothing more than speculation.[134]

Counter-Measures on Pirate Shores

Before the twentieth century, the best, though not necessarily the easiest, way to end piracy emanating from clearly identifiable locations once and for all was to prevent the pirates operating out of them – either by sending naval forces to destroy these locations or by invading the whole area and establishing a colonial regime. The latter course of action produced more durable results, while the former usually proved to be only a temporary setback for pirates: the failure to shut down the ports of Algiers, Tripoli and Tunis with bombardment are good examples of that (see pp. 138–9).

Nevertheless, the magnitude of Somali piracy during the peak years of 2008–12 resulted in some lobbying within various Western navies for anti-piracy operations to take place on Somali shores as well, in addition to the counter-measures taken at sea. These proposed strikes, though intended to be limited in scope and reach, would have had the aim of disrupting the pirates' land-based infrastructure, for instance by destroying their vessels, and of either arresting or 'eliminating' those leaders of pirate gangs who had come to the attention of Western intelligence services. Those in favour of such a robust course of action drew attention to the fact that such missions were already part and parcel of counter-terrorism operations against al-Shabaab (nowadays allied with al-Qaeda), and that similar raids had already been undertaken in the context of anti-piracy missions, for example in the aftermath of the *Le Ponant* hijack: immediately after the ransom had been paid and the thirty hostages released, French commandos swooped in just as the pirates tried to make off into the desert. Some of the ransom money was recovered, and six pirates were captured and up to three more may have been killed and a few others injured, although French sources still deny this.[135]

Various Western naval forces also considered the feasibility of recapturing hijacked vessels moored in plain sight in Somali ports, but due to the risk posed to hostages onboard the idea was quickly discarded. Targeted strikes against pirate leaders or attacks against the pirates' infrastructure were likewise deemed risky. After all, even the best-planned strike might cause collateral damage, the unintended deaths of innocent bystanders or the destruction of infrastructure belonging to non-pirates. In the light of experiences in Afghanistan, where many counter-strikes had gone awry, a consensus emerged among the naval decisionmakers involved that hitting the wrong targets could result in a new wave of al-Shabaab recruits – motivated not for any lofty religious reasons but rather simple revenge.

After long deliberation, in March 2012 the EU adopted a watered-down version of the various recommendations for anti-piracy operations on land and permitted limited operations against identified pirate targets on Somalia's 'coastal territory and internal waters'. Two months later, the first land strike was carried out under EU NAVFOR (aka Operation Atalanta) – a strafing run of a single Tiger attack helicopter operating from the French amphibious assault ship *Dixmude*. The damage caused by this somewhat underwhelming operation was limited: half a dozen pirate skiffs were put out of commission.[136] Of note is the negative media coverage the operation received, essentially arguing that the strike might trigger an escalation of violence and that subsequent operations might be 'met with an arsenal of anti-aircraft guns and missiles'.[137] Fortunately, this was not the case, but the negative public response highlighted the EU's general reluctance to get drawn into yet another interminable land conflict.

However, land strikes were only one aspect of Operation Atalanta's comprehensive approach to solving the problem of Somali piracy – an approach that explicitly acknowledged the necessity of tackling its root causes 'by contributing to the social and economic development of Somalia, concentrating on three sectors of cooperation: governance, education, and the productive sectors, particularly rural development'.[138] Furthermore, due to the immense costs involved in keeping warships on patrol in Somali waters – vessels that were then also not available for operations elsewhere – in 2011 the EU also encouraged regional counter-piracy approaches via a 'regional maritime capacity building' programme, focusing on 'strengthen[ing] the sea-going maritime capacity of Djibouti, Kenya, Tanzania and the Seychelles' (states in close proximity to the piracy hot spot), and on 'train[ing] and equip[ping] the Coastal Police Force in the Somali regions of Puntland, Somaliland and Galmudug, as well as train[ing] and protect[ing] judges in the Somali region of Puntland'.[139]

These initiatives make for impressive reading, and look like a comprehensive package. Implementing them, however, will be tricky. First, developing such durable solutions will not come cheap and will take considerable time; as of the time of writing (November 2018), there is not much progress to report. Second, IUU fishing conducted by vessels hailing from several EU countries poses a huge problem for Somali fishermen, and this root cause must also be addressed. Whether France and Spain, the two EU member states most heavily involved in IUU, would be willing to tackle an issue when it would be actively working against their own interests to do so, remains to be seen. Currently, the Somali pirates are lying low – less because of ambitious regional initiatives launched by the EU, and more because of the increasingly effective passive and active counter-measures deployed at sea, enhanced by more effective pirate hunting by various Western and non-Western navies, which has chased the pirates out of the waters for the time being. Whether they stay out of the waters for good, at least as pirates, is unclear at the moment: if the promised capacity-building comes to naught, and if the warships of various extra-regional powers that still patrol Somali waters are withdrawn, then piracy will surely return. The two pirate attacks reported in 2017 (both vessels boarded by pirates but recaptured), and the two in 2018 (both failed), are rather ominous signs in this regard.[140]

In other regions, especially the South China Sea, the Straits of Malacca and the Gulf of Guinea, pirates are still active. Although in general the recommendations of MSC–HOA's best management practices (see pp. 193–7) make good sense for these piracy hot spots as well, some elements need to be adapted to the local environment. For example, the recommended active onboard counter-measures, especially those involving armed guards, need to be considered against the fact that many Nigerian pirate gangs think nothing of getting involved in protracted firefights. It should also be noted that attacks on inshore targets, or even patrolling within Nigeria's sovereign waters, are out of the question for any would-be international armada; this course of action was only possible in Somali waters because the transitional federal government granted permission for international actors to enter sovereign Somali territory for that purpose. Thus far, Nigeria has refused to do this. In the Gulf of Guinea, then, a local solution that harnesses the capabilities of all local littoral states to form an effective regional anti-piracy regime will be necessary.

In the east, the fairly effective Malacca Strait Patrols (MSP) – anti-piracy patrols conducted by Malaysian, Singaporean, Thai and Indonesian warships – along with the broader Regional Cooperation Agreement on Combating Piracy and Armed Robbery against Ships in Asia (ReCAAP)[141] which includes twenty Southeast and East Asian states, have been promoted by the International Maritime Organisation as blueprints for regional anti-piracy operations elsewhere – especially in the Gulf of Guinea. The adoption of the Djibouti Code of Conduct on 29 January 2009 by Djibouti, Ethiopia, Kenya, Madagascar, the Maldives, the Seychelles, Somalia, the United Republic of Tanzania and Yemen was certainly a major step in the right direction.[142] According to this code, the member states are mandated to cooperate in investigating, arresting and prosecuting pirates including those persons facilitating such acts (for example, by financing pirate operations); to stop and search, and if necessary seize, suspected pirate vessels; to rescue ships or individuals under attack by pirates; to conduct shared operations, including operations with warships of extra-regional powers; and, finally, to share intelligence regarding piracy.[143] But again, as in the case of the EU's 'regional maritime capacity building' programme, it turned out that signing a document is one thing, trying to implement its lofty provisions quite another. At the moment, it does not look as if these lofty aims and objectives have been reached, or that even a little dent has been made in the depredations of Nigerian pirate gangs, who continue to prey on vessels and even on offshore oil installations pretty much at their leisure.

CONCLUSION

Back with a Vengeance

Like pirates returning to port at the end of a long journey and taking stock of the treasure they have amassed, what can the centuries of pirate history we have surveyed tell us about who the pirates were, how their contexts made their activities possible, why it was so difficult to counter them, and what lay behind the emergence, growth, maturity and decline of piracy across the world?

The career of a sea robber, irrespective of period and region, was not for the timid or for those beset with moral qualms. Indeed, most would-be pirates probably faltered at the first hurdle – simply by not daring to become pirates. Those who did become pirates then faced a steep learning curve; some probably lost courage and either deserted or were rejected by their comrades for incompetence or cowardice, if they did not perish in an early raid or a shipwreck. But, by and large, it is fair to say that most of those who overcame the first hurdle also overcame the second and became reasonably good at what they did. Like any other career, that of piracy tends to gradually 'socialise' new recruits into their new profession, so that what at first appears peculiar and new, or terrifying, dangerous and gruesome, gradually comes to feel normal. This is important: our gut feeling is to empathise with the victims of piracy and the horrors they had to live through – if they survived their ordeal. It is more difficult to identify and empathise with pirates themselves, such as the cold-blooded killers of the crew of the MV *Cheung Son* or the Somali or Nigerian pirates of today who, after their capture, usually strike observers as rather forlorn, ragged figures. These are far from the romantic, swashbuckling and largely fictional rogues portrayed by Hollywood. Yet it is possible to at least sympathise with the former Acehnese pirate Marcus Uban when he said in defence of his piratical activities that 'Singapore is rich, we are poor'.

Perhaps it is even possible to accept the defence frequently offered by many captured pirates (and by some revisionist scholars as well) that 'there was no choice'. Even overlooking the spuriousness of that defence, it is still quite a leap from that point to portraying pirates, historical as well as modern, as noble 'social bandits'.[1] Some modern sociological works on the Golden Age pirates do precisely that, though they also make some good arguments. One leading scholar, for example, focuses especially on the quasi-democratic relationship between pirate captain and crew.[2] And it is indeed true that Golden Age pirates elected their captains on a 'one man, one vote' basis, and he could enforce discipline, and a certain course of action, only after deliberations or 'parleys' with all crew members, culminating in a vote. Even a pirate captain as fearsome as Blackbeard occasionally had to resort to cajole his mutinous crew into following his plans. This quasi-democratic approach probably contributed to the romantic notion prevalent in the general readership, and even in parts of scholarship, of pirates being swashbuckling, dashing and larger-than-life 'princes of the sea'.

However, these Golden Age 'princes' were hardly emblematic of pirates at the time. For one thing, privateers and corsairs seemed to have been much more disciplined – although cases in which captains had to hold parleys with their crew are not unknown. Chinese pirate fleets on the other side of the world enforced a strict Imperial navy-style hierarchy, with severe discipline, as the eyewitness Richard Glasspoole observed: 'any transgressions [were] immediately punished, which, as their vessels are filled with their families, men, women, and children, seems almost incredible'.[3] The Iranun and Balangingi pirates infesting Southeast Asian waters, meanwhile, were organised in a quasi-feudal or tribal structure, similar to the earlier more northerly Vikings or the Orang Laut in the Straits of Malacca. It is obvious that 'one size fits all' explanations are bound to fail, and that romantic Western notions of piracy hide more than they reveal: 'being a pirate' is not only about egalitarianism and proto-democracy, but also, depending on region, strict hierarchies and severe discipline. And when it comes to pirates' modi operandi, it is not only about ship-to-ship encounters involving one or two pirate vessels and one treasure ship, but also, again depending on the region, about large-scale operations of hundreds of ships and thousands of pirates, laying waste to whole coasts, and even to the interior via navigable river systems.

Regarding the often-mentioned justification that 'there was no choice', it should be clear by now that sea raiding, both sanctioned and unsanctioned, does not exist in a vacuum. Rather, the phenomenon and its ebbs and flows are closely connected to the prevailing circumstances on land, and in particular in coastal areas, since these are the regions where those with essential mariner skills can be found. Although there are variations over the centuries and across different regions, in general it is fair to say that piracy is rooted in marginalised segments of a population and, in some regions, in specific marginalised communities, usually situated on the periphery of 'polite', 'civilised' mainstream society. Even today, such maritime communities living in squalid, subsistence-level circumstances still exist. The Southeast Asian Orang Laut would be but one example.[4] The outcome of such neglect is predictable: those disenfranchised parts of the population sooner or later start looking for a way out of their misery. Becoming a pirate is one possible, and sometimes very obvious, choice.

Of course, this does not mean that all pirates are innocent victims of circumstances outside of their control, motivated by 'grievance' alone. Arguably, 'greed' in the shape of the perennial 'lure of easy money' is always present as well – often being (or at least becoming) the dominant factor. In the case of modern Somali pirates, for example, the original motivating factor of 'grievance' – large-scale illegal fishing in their waters – swiftly gave way to 'greed' – the hope of getting rich quick, after the hijack of the French luxury yacht MY *Le Ponant* in April 2008 brought in a $2 million (£1.53 million) ransom. The widespread coverage of the incident resulted in a modern maritime equivalent of the California Gold Rush: many young militiamen who had never even seen the sea before flocked to the shores to get a piece of the action, and a share of the loot. Of course, it may well be that many of them only occasionally participated in a raid, drifting in and out of piracy depending on how their wheels of fortune turned. Many such opportunistic pirates could probably be resocialised if they were presented with a choice. However, as with land-based criminality, there will always be a core group of hard-nosed career criminals committed to their own shot at the merry life – which also means that piracy will stay with us probably as long as there is maritime trade, robot ships notwithstanding.

If states really want to reduce the scourge of piracy, they will have to begin on land: 'because pirates – like all other people – must live on the land, it is on the land that they must be stopped; naval power alone is not sufficient to fight piracy'.[5] Establishing (in the case of weak states like the Philippines or Indonesia) or re-establishing (in the case of failed states like Somalia) law and order on land is the logical first step. Although this is not easy to accomplish, in the case of Somalia there is a glimmer of hope: here, the breakaway province of Somaliland and the semi-autonomous province of Puntland have successfully re-established a fair degree of law and order, thus effectively curbing the piracy that emanates from their shores. Law and order on land, however, is not the only answer. With regard to marginalised fishing communities, specialised welfare programmes need to be developed to improve peoples' lives and present them with a true choice as to which career to follow: in the 1970s, Malaysia inaugurated a poverty-eradication programme that was specifically targeted at small-scale fishermen for that very reason.[6] Notwithstanding the programme's much discussed shortcomings, such as mismanagement of funds or rivalries between various government authorities, piracy vanished from Malaysia's coasts. Ironically, although Malaysian fishermen are no longer the perpetrators of acts of piracy, they still continue to fall victim to Indonesian pirates coming from the other side of the Straits of Malacca; so far, the Indonesian government has not yet launched its own version of the programme.

This implies that when it comes to effectively tackling piracy, outside powers – and not only one's immediate neighbours – have a role to play too. Indeed, the meddling of external players in particular regional affairs is also a trigger for the emergence and persistence of piracy. Foreign incursions into regional coastal states' zones of influence were most pronounced in the ages of colonialism and imperialism. For instance, the eighteenth-century wave of maritime raiding in Southeast Asian waters was largely triggered by the continuous forceful attempts of Western colonial powers, especially the Dutch, to destroy all local competition – attempts that resulted in a near complete disruption of centuries-old maritime trade networks. And, regarding the Malay pirates of the eighteenth and nineteenth centuries, it should not be forgotten that it was 'the greed of the European powers' in the South China Sea that made them so (see pp. 89–90).[7] Even today, interference in regional affairs in the shape of illegal fishing operations carried out by foreign high-seas trawlers in Somali, Philippine and Indonesian waters is still to a large extent to blame for the persistence of piracy in those countries. Anti-piracy patrols are thus only one side of the coin: illegal fishing must also be targeted in order to give local fishermen a fair chance of earning a living without having to resort to smuggling or piracy.

The fight against piracy is not only a tactical and operational problem, it is also a political one. Just like the current war on global terrorism, wars on piracy depend on a 'coalition of the willing' to be successful. In the past, forming a meaningful alliance against pirates always turned out to be a nearly impossible mission – after all, trade was usually seen as a zero-sum game, where one nation's gain was another's loss. The attempts of the Hanseatic League to form an alliance against the Victual Brothers at the end of the fourteenth century are a case in point (see pp. 53–4 and 59), as is James I of England's attempt to form a naval triple alliance with Spain and the Netherlands against Algiers between 1617 and 1680 (see pp. 138–9). However, in today's globalised world, reliant on just-in-time deliveries and the smooth functioning of the maritime transport chain, viewing trade as a zero-sum game no longer makes any sense. Take the case of Somali piracy, which swiftly progressed from opportunistic coastal piracy affecting only a few vessels to organised high-seas piracy first in the Gulf of Aden and then in the Arabian Sea as a whole, presenting a veritable threat to European maritime supply chains. The EU, particularly its major sea powers of the United Kingdom, France and Spain, thus made efforts to 'securitise' piracy, that is to 'promote' it from being mere seaborne crime to a global security threat potentially in league with terrorism – efforts that resulted in the deployment of European Union and NATO naval squadrons, followed by warships of other stakeholder nations such as Japan, South Korea, China, Russia and India. (It's likely that for some of these navies, other motives also played a role, such as learning how to operate in waters far away from their own bases, mastering the art of replenishing at sea, as well as familiarising themselves with the maritime and meteorological conditions of the Arabian Sea – and of course being able to show their flag as a form of naval diplomacy.)

A rather more interesting approach to tackling piracy might come with the return of privateering. Though this was outlawed in the nineteenth century (see pp. 153 and 162), the US declined to ratify the Paris Declaration, or any other treaty specifically outlawing the practice of privateering itself, because it then still depended on privateers to strengthen its modest navy in case of war. Although the US did formally abolish privateering during the 1899 Spanish-American War,[8] Article 1, Section 8 (Powers of Congress: Enumerated Power) of the US Constitution still includes the 'right to grant Letters of Marque and Reprisal' just after the right to 'define and punish piracies and felonies committed on the high seas'.[9] This fact has implications for the fight against Somali and Nigerian pirates, and the emergence of private maritime security companies: it could result in a return of privateering through the backdoor via the now common practice of outsourcing ever more core services of the state, including those services related to the Weberian concept of 'the monopoly of the legitimate use of physical force in the enforcement of its order'.[10] Indeed, in the aftermath of 9/11, US congressman Ron Paul raised the matter of privateering in Congress by introducing the Marque and Reprisal Act of 2001, which would have enabled the US president to issue commissions against specified terrorists. In 2009, when Somali pirates expanded their operations onto the high seas, Paul suggested issuing such letters to combat the Somali pirate action groups as well. His idea came to naught, but it raised the question of the efficacy of privatising the suppression of piracy at sea and along the coasts; in an era of steadily dwindling state budgets and concomitantly shrinking naval forces (at least among the long-established Western sea powers), it might be a tempting option.

At the moment, the brief of private maritime security companies is rather limited: the provision of armed security guards to ships with high-value cargos sailing into piracy-prone waters, or to oil rigs and FPSOs situated in these waters. Against the current backdrop of piracy in the Gulf of Guinea, the Straits of Malacca and the South China Sea, and of the risk posed by the still-existing Somali pirates who are presently lying low, the private maritime security industry is booming.[11] Some of the more enterprising companies have already mooted plans that include progressing from reactive to proactive security, including active pirate hunting. So far, however, this step has not been taken – mainly due to states' differing laws regarding the carrying of weapons and the difficulty of pursuing pirate vessels deep into coastal waters in an era when the sovereign rights of states are held supreme. As in the case of Singapore, Malaysia and Indonesia, for each country to grant permission to the others for their warships to enter their sovereign waters in pursuit of pirate vessels is a matter that still requires more trust and confidence – the combined patrolling notwithstanding. Likewise, India would not allow the intrusion of private pirate hunters into its sovereign waters; the Indian navy and the Indian Coast Guard have already intercepted vessels with armed guards on board as soon as they strayed into Indian territory. Clearly, outsourcing the fight against pirates to private firms as modern-day privateers would require much persuasion and negotiation.

Looking at piracy across the world and through time we can discern the broad trajectories of the 'piracy cycle' – that is, the emergence, growth, maturity and decline of piracy in a given region. As the large-scale operations of the Vikings, the Iranun and Balangingi and the Chinese pirate fleets demonstrate, piracy usually starts small but, given the opportunity, it grows in strength and size to sometimes become a truly formidable political force. In a sense, this also echoes the motto of Sir Francis Drake: *Sic parvis magna* – 'Greatness from small beginnings'. If piracy remains unchecked at its early stage, what began as opportunism may rapidly escalate to organised maritime raiding. Once defending forces are greatly weakened, and the seats of political and military power close to collapse, the previously seasonal marauders become long-time occupiers and state-builders in their own right – like the Vikings. This development can be likened to the growth phase of the 'piracy cycle':

> First a few individuals from amongst the inhabitants of the poorer coastal lands would band together in isolated groups owning but few vessels apiece and attack the weakest merchantmen . . . Next would come the period of organisation, when big pirates either swallowed up the little pirates or drove them out of business. These great organisations moved on such a scale that no group of trading ships, even the most heavily armed, was safe from their attack.[12]

If the attacked state successfully counter-attacked, then the surviving pirates would be sent 'scurrying back once more to the status of furtive footpads of the sea whence they had arisen',[13] and the piracy cycle started again.

So, what can be done to end the piracy cycle? As we have seen, unfortunately most of the root causes of piracy are still present. Ironically, this means that developing a 'recipe' *for* piracy is actually easier than offering one *against* it. A (by now) familiar list of ingredients required to keep the piracy cycle going has in fact been offered:

> Take a maritime geography, which favours local outlaws and dis-favours distant law enforcers. Add the chance of enormous profit and little risk. Mix it generously with strife, internal and external. Avoid maritime law enforcement capacity, and do not add common law! Corruption helps for spicing! Make it hot.[14]

We have seen all of these elements at work in the previous chapters. Quite logically, then, the 'counter-recipe' must try to eliminate all these ingredients. Most importantly, to deal with pirates on land and at sea, in all current piracy hot spots a functioning regime of maritime law and order is required, to increase the risk to pirates while decreasing their profits. This of course requires the political will of coastal states as well as a certain maritime capacity in the shape of suitable vessels and personnel. As the cases of Somali piracy and piracy in the Gulf of Guinea highlight, none of that can be taken as a given. With regard to the developed nations so dependent on uninterrupted maritime trade, the political will to tackle this problem also often seems to be largely absent: as long as 'our' ships and crews, 'our' cargoes, and 'our' sea lines of communication – 'our' maritime highways – are not affected, it's not 'our' problem – it's 'theirs'. There is also no real political will to tackle illegal fishing, the other side of the pirate coin – very visible in the case of Somali piracy, and also one of the causes of piracy in the South China Sea. As long as that does not change, piracy is here to stay – which also means that for years or even decades to come, people from various regions will choose to go a-pirating, for all the reasons they always have.

Glossary

Angre, Kanhoji   Maratha admiral (1669–1729), considered a pirate by the English and Portuguese. Born *c.* 1669, died 4 July 1729

argosy   large seventeenth-century Venetian cargo vessel of up to 1,500 tons

Avery, Henry 'Long Ben'   pirate captain, famous for the capture of the *Ganj i-Sawaj* in July 1695. Born 20 August 1659, died *c.* 1714

Balangingi   ethno-linguistic group of the Sulu Archipelago in the Philippines, notorious for piracy in the eighteenth and nineteenth centuries

Barbary Coast   European term used from the early sixteenth century until the early nineteenth century for the North African coastal regions (modern Libya, Algeria, Tunisia and Morocco)

Barbary corsairs   term used for corsairs and pirates operating from the Barbary Coast principalities Algiers, Tripoli and Tunis between the early sixteenth and the early nineteenth centuries

Bonnet, Stede   wealthy landowner on Barbados who turned pirate out of boredom. Born *c.* 1688, died 10 December 1718 (hanged)

Bonny, Anne   female pirate, partner of *John Rackham*. Born *c.* 1698, died in April 1782

buccaneer   from the French *boucanier* ('those who use a boucan', i.e. a wooden frame for drying meat). Term for French, English and Dutch pirates and privateers active in the Caribbean in the seventeenth and eighteenth centuries, preying on Spanish shipping and on Spanish coastal settlements

Bugis   ethno-linguistic group of the Malay Peninsula and Sumatra, notorious for piracy in the eighteenth and nineteenth centuries

chain shot   special ammunition for muzzle-loaded cannon of the age of sail, usually consisting of two half-balls linked with a chain, used primarily to cut through the rigging and sails of targeted vessels, and also to maximise injuries among exposed crew members

Cinque Ports confederation of the English ports of Hastings, New Romney, Hythe, Dover and Sandwich plus the 'antient' towns of Rye and Winchelsea. Notorious pirate lairs in the twelfth and thirteenth centuries

cog large single-masted cargo vessel of up to 200 tons, used in the North Sea between the tenth and the fourteenth centuries

Contreras, Alonso de Spanish corsair active for Spain as well as the Knights Hospitaller in the Mediterranean. Born 6 January 1582, died in 1641

corsair from the French *corsair*, i.e. a commerce raider who takes part in *guerre de course* (cruiser war/commerce raiding). Synonym for privateer, and mostly used to describe privateers active in the Mediterranean. Term describes both the person engaged in this practice and the vessel itself

Coxinga Western name for the Chinese pirate lord Zheng Chenggong (son of *Zheng Zhilong*), who fought for the Southern Ming and carved out his own (short-lived) kingdom. Born 27 August 1624, died 23 June 1662

Drake, Sir Francis the most famous and most successful of Queen Elizabeth I's 'gentleman adventurers'. Born *c.* 1540, died 26 January 1596

drogue device used to slow down a vessel, often improvised with cables, sail canvass or mattresses and fixed to the stern of the vessel – used by pirates to mislead the crews of targeted ships as to the real speed their own vessel could achieve

dromond large medieval merchant galley used in the Mediterranean

East Indiaman generic name for usually large and well-armed sailing vessels of various European East India Companies

Eustace the (Black) Monk medieval pirate and privateer. Born around 1170, died 24 August 1217 in the battle of Sandwich

Exquemelin, Alexandre French buccaneer and writer. Born *c.* 1645, died in 1707

flyboat light, shallow-draught cargo vessel of up to 200 tons of the sixteenth and seventeenth centuries

freebooter from the Dutch *vrijbuiter*, i.e. someone who practises piracy. Synonym for pirate

galleon   three- to four-masted sailing vessel widely used between the sixteenth and eighteenth centuries by various sea powers as armed cargo vessel or warship

galley   oar-propelled vessel with slender hull and low freeboard. Mainly used in the Mediterranean as warship

Hanseatic League   medieval confederation of North German port cities along the coasts of the North Sea and the Baltic

hongitochten   Dutch seventeenth-century anti-piracy and monopoly-enforcement cruises in the South China Sea

IMB   International Maritime Bureau. Department of the International Chamber of Commerce specialising in maritime crime including piracy and insurance fraud

Iranun   ethno-linguistic group of Mindanao in the Philippines. In the eighteenth and nineteenth centuries notorious pirates

IUU   illegal, unregulated and unreported fishing. Called 'pirate fishing' by some observers

junk   Chinese sailing vessel, single-masted or multi-masted depending on the size – in the times of Zheng He's expeditions, allegedly up to 400 feet or 124 metres (more realistically up to 250 feet or 76 metres)

Le Golif, Louis   French buccaneer, also known as 'Borgnefesse.' Born *c.* 1640, date of death unknown

Likedeeler   from the Dutch meaning 'equal sharers'. Successors to the Victual Brothers, active in the Baltic Sea and the North Sea from 1398 (first mention of the term) until 1401

Mainwaring, Sir Henry   English pirate turned pirate hunter under King James I. Born *c.* 1586, died in 1653

Morgan, Sir Henry   English pirate (buccaneer) turned pirate hunter; lieutenant governor of Jamaica. Born *c.* 1635, died 25 August 1688

MV *Cheung Son*   Chinese cargo vessel hijacked by pirates (twelve Chinese nationals and one Indonesian) on 16 November 1998

MV *Maersk Alabama*   American container vessel captured by Somali pirates on 8 April 2009

MV *Moscow University*   Russian tanker hijacked by Somali pirates but recaptured by Russian special forces on 6 May 2010. Pirates said to 'have perished at sea'

Nuestra Señora de la Concepción   Spanish galleon captured by Sir Francis Drake on 1 March 1579 in the Pacific on its way from Manila to Acapulco

Operation Atalanta   European Union anti-piracy operation off Somalia/Horn of Africa, commencing on 8 December 2008, still ongoing as of December 2018

Operation Ocean Shield   NATO anti-piracy operation off Somalia/Horn of Africa, commencing on 17 August 2009, terminated on 15 December 2016

Orang Laut   Malay term, lit. 'Sea People'. Active in the Straits of Malacca between the eighth and thirteenth centuries, either in the service of the rulers of Srivijaya or as pirates for their own gain

Pero Niño, Don   early fifteenth-century Castilian corsair, commissioned for pirate hunting and commerce raiding. Born 1378, died 17 January 1453

pinnace   small vessel kept aboard bigger vessels as a shuttle or tender

piracy   action of committing robbery, kidnap, or violence at sea or from the sea without lawful authority and for private gain

piragua   also rendered as 'pirogue'. A type of small, fast shallow-draught boats including canoes and dugouts

pirate   someone engaging in piracy as defined above

prahu   Malayan multi-hull fast vessel propelled by oars and/or sails

privateer   contraction of 'private' and 'volunteer'. Term describes either a privately operated warship or someone commissioned as a commerce raider – i.e. a 'pirate with a licence'

Rackham, John   also known as 'Calico Jack'. Pirate captain, active 1717–20. Born 26 December 1682, died 18 November 1720 (hanged)

Raleigh, Sir Walter   one of Queen Elizabeth I's 'gentleman adventurers'. Born *c.* 1552, died 29 October 1618 (beheaded)

Read, Mary   female pirate, sailing with *Anne Bonny* and *John Rackham*. Born *c*. 1690, died 28 April 1721 (of fever while imprisoned)

Sea Dayak   also known as Iban. Branch of the ethno-linguistic group of the Dayaks of Borneo (Kalimantan), notorious for piracy in the eighteenth and nineteenth centuries

Seabourn Spirit   cruise liner, unsuccessfully attacked by Somali pirates in November 2005

Teach, Edward   pirate captain, better known as Blackbeard. Born *c*. 1690, died 22 November 1718 (killed in action)

Victual Brothers   German: *Vitalienbrüder*. Pirate guild active in the Baltic and North Seas at the end of the fourteenth century, first as privateers in service of the Duke of Mecklenburg, then as pirates

Wako   also translated as 'wokou'. Pirates active along the coasts of China, Korea and Japan, mainly between the fourteenth and sixteenth centuries. Usually organised in large fleets

Ward, John   English privateer who 'turned Turk' and became a notorious Tunisian corsair. Born *c*. 1553, died *c*. 1622

Xu Hai   originally a Buddhist monk in a famous Chinese temple. Turned pirate for unknown reasons and joined the Wako. Date of birth unknown, died 29 September 1556 (in battle with another Wako faction)

Zheng He   Chinese admiral who led seven major naval expeditions into the Indian Ocean between 1405 and 1433. Defeated the fleet of Chinese pirate Chen Zuyi in early 1407 at the end of the first expedition. Born 1371, died *c*. 1433 or 1435

Zheng Zhilong   Chinese pirate lord, co-opted by the Southern Ming as admiral. Defected to the Manchu in 1650. Born 1604, died in 1661

Endnotes

INTRODUCTION: THE SUDDEN RETURN OF PIRACY

1. Burnett, *Dangerous Waters*, 224.
2. On this stereotyping, see for example Ritchie, 'Living with Pirates'.
3. At that time owned by Seabourn Cruise Line. In April 2015, the vessel was sold to Windstar Cruises and rechristened *Star Breeze*.
4. See, for example, *Scotland on Sunday*, 'Pirates Attack Luxury Cruise Ship', 6 November 2005. See also Lehr and Lehmann, 'Somalia: Pirates' New Paradise', 4–5.
5. Rediker, *Villains of All Nations*, 175.
6. Y.H. Teddy Sim criticises this 'great men' approach, which by its very nature glosses over the probably more mundane experiences of the less prominent pirates – arguably the bulk of them. However, for illustration purposes, these 'great men' stories work rather well. See Sim, 'Studying Piracy', 5 (note 13).
7. Mann, *The Sources of Social Power*, vol. 1, 2.
8. Buzan and Little, *International Systems*, 257.
9. My emphasis; 'piracy, n.', *OED Online*; online at http://www.oed.com/view/Entry/144486 (accessed 17 September 2018).

PART I: DISTINCT REGIONS, AD 700 TO 1500

1. Antony, *Like Froth*, 89.
2. Kaiser and Calafat, 'Violence, Protection and Commerce', 71–2.
3. Saxo Grammaticus, *Gesta Danorum*, XIV, 15.5.
4. *Detmar Chronicle*, as quoted in Puhle, *Die Vitalienbrüder*, 50 (translation mine).
5. Ibid., 151–2.
6. Since the relevant parts of the so-called *Hanserecesse* – the archives of the Hanseatic League including all reports, missives, treaties and suchlike – covering the last decade of the fourteenth century, and thus the origin of the Victual Brothers, perished in the Great Fire of Hamburg of May 1842, we cannot do more than speculate.
7. Puhle, *Die Vitalienbrüder*, 41–2.
8. 'Ghibellines' (Italian: 'Ghibellini') is the name of a pro-imperial political faction in twelfth–fourteenth-century Italy that supported the Emperor against the Pope. According to the *Encyclopeadia Britannica*, the name comes from the placename 'Wibellingen' (modern German: Waiblingen) where Conrad III of Hohenstaufen had a castle. The Ghibellines' pro-papal opponents were known as the Guelfs – an Italian rendering of the German dynasty of the Welfs who, as bitter rivals of the Hohenstaufen, supported the Pope against the Emperor. See the entry 'Guelf and Ghibelline', https://www.britannica.com/event/Guelf-and-Ghibelline
9. Heers, *Barbary Corsairs*, 28, 34–5.
10. Ibid., 36.
11. Ibid., 28–9. See also Setton, *The Catalans in Greece*.
12. Puhle, *Die Vitalienbrüder*, 33.
13. Quoted in ibid.
14. Ibid., 61–3.
15. To avoid misunderstandings, it should be noted that we are talking here about individual monks from mendicant orders – not about professional 'warrior monks' such as the Christian Knights Templar and Knights Hospitaller, or the Buddhist Sōhei.

16. Burgess, *Two Medieval Outlaws*, 7–8.
17. Matthew Paris, as quoted in ibid., 34.
18. Hucker, 'Hu Tsung-hsien's Campaign Against Hsu Hai', 280.
19. Ibid.
20. Levathes, *When China Ruled the Seas*, 185.
21. Chin, 'Merchants, Smugglers, and Pirates . . .', 50–2.
22. On social bandits, see Hobsbawm, *Bandits*.
23. Hedeager, 'From Warrior to Trade Economy', 84.
24. Ibid.
25. Foote and Wilson, *The Viking Achievement*, 229.
26. As quoted in Bradford, *Mediterranean*, 361.
27. Abulafia, *The Great Sea*, 279.
28. Ibid.
29. Diaz de Gamez, *The Unconquered Knight*, 54.
30. For the nationalities, see Abulafia, *The Great Sea*, 415.
31. On Umur Pasha and the quote from the *Destan d'Umur Pasha*, see Heers, *Barbary Corsairs*, 48–50.
32. Amirell and Müller, 'Introduction: Persistent Piracy', 4.
33. Meier, *Seafarers*, 153.
34. As quoted in Higgins, 'Pirates in Gowns and Caps', 30.
35. Shapinsky, 'Japanese Pirates and Sea Tenure' (unpaginated).
36. Ibid.
37. Antony, *Like Froth*, 30.
38. Turnbull, *Pirate of the Far East*, 7; Farris, *Heavenly Warriors*, 242.
39. Wilson, *Empire of the Deep*, 14.
40. Hobsbawm, *Bandits*, 27.
41. On that, see Barrett, 'What Caused the Viking Age?'
42. Pryor, *Geography, Technology, and War*, 99.
43. As quoted in Gosse, *The History of Piracy*, 1.
44. Abulafia, *The Great Sea*, 271, 274.
45. A long, exhaustive and authoritative treatment of Chinese ship types can be found in Needham, *Science and Civilisation in China*, vol. 4, part 3, 379–699.
46. Adorno, as quoted in Heers, *Barbary Corsairs*, 33.
47. Ibid., 33–4.
48. Ibid.
49. Tenenti, *Piracy and the Decline of Venice*, 5.
50. Polo, *The Travels of Marco Polo*, 290.
51. Ibid.
52. Polo seems to use the term 'corsair' as a substitute for 'pirate'.
53. Pryor, *Geography, Technology, and War*, 76–7.
54. Diaz de Gamez, *Unconquered Knight*, 95.
55. Earle, *Corsairs of Malta and Barbary*, 140–1.
56. Turnbull, *Pirate of the Far East*, 47.
57. All quotes on this encounter are from Hermann and Edwards (trans.), *Orkneyinga Saga*, 173–7.
58. Ibid., 177.
59. Diaz de Gamez, *Unconquered Knight*, 73.
60. Also 'arquebuses', from German *Hakenbüchse* meaning 'hook gun'. These heavy firearms were discharged while resting either on a fork rest or on a steady platform such as a wall or battlement, in the latter case steadied by a hook protruding from the barrel – hence the name.
61. Reimar Kock, as quoted in Puhle, *Die Vitalienbrüder*, 43–4 (translation mine).
62. Zimmerling, *Störtebeker & Co*, 85.

63. Reimar Kock, as quoted in Puhle, *Die Vitalienbrüder*, 44 (translation mine).
64. *Annals of St-Bertin*, 39.
65. Ibid., 53.
66. Ibid., 63.
67. Ibid., 64–5.
68. Kennedy, *Mongols, Huns and Vikings*, 188.
69. Magnusson, *Vikings!*, 31.
70. *Anglo-Saxon Chronicle*, in Somerville and McDonald (eds), *The Viking Age*, 230.
71. Foote and Wilson, *The Viking Achievement*, 229.
72. Simeon of Durham, *History of the Church of Durham*, 35–6.
73. Magnusson, *Vikings!*, 31–2.
74. Morris, 'The Viking Age in Europe', 99.
75. Batey and Sheehan, 'Viking Expansion and Cultural Blending', 128.
76. As quoted in Price, ' "Laid Waste, Plundered, and Burned" ', 119–21.
77. *Riben ʒhuan* ('Treatise on Japan'), as quoted in Turnbull, *Pirate of the Far East*, 25–6.
78. Levathes, *When China Ruled the Seas*, 185–6.
79. Ibid.
80. Hucker, 'Hu Tsung-hien's Campaign Against Hsu Hai', 289–90.
81. Turnbull, *Pirate of the Far East*, 48.
82. Leeson, *Invisible Hook*, 116.
83. On the change of policy, see Lim, 'From Haijin to Kaihai', especially 20–2.
84. L. de Mas-Latrie, as quoted in Heers, *Barbary Corsairs*, 51.
85. On these towers, see for example Clements, *Towers of Strength*.
86. Turnbull, *Pirates of the Far East*, 48–50.
87. As Magnus Magnusson points out, the original version of the famous prayer line was probably *'summa pia gratia nostra conservando corpora et custodita, de gente fera Normannica nos libera, quae nostra vastat, Deus, regna'*, or 'Our supreme and holy Grace, protecting us and ours, deliver us, God, from the savage race of Northmen which lays waste our realms'. See Magnusson, *Vikings!*, 61.
88. Eickhoff, 'Maritime Defence of the Carolingian Empire', 51–2.
89. *Royal Frankish Annals*, as quoted in Somerville and McDonald (eds), *The Viking Age*, 245.
90. *Annals of St-Bertin*, 37.
91. Ibid.
92. Ibid.
93. Ibid., 98, 100, 118, 127, 130–1.
94. Ibid., 224.
95. Price, ' "Laid Waste, Plundered, and Burned" ', 120.
96. Kennedy, *Mongols, Huns and Vikings*, 193.
97. Braudel, *The Mediterranean and the Mediterranean World*, vol.1, 298.
98. Heers, *Barbary Corsairs*, 53. Bombards were early versions of cannon.
99. Convoys as defensive measures against pirates in the Mediterranean can be traced back to the Greek and Phoenician city-states of antiquity.
100. Lane, 'Venetian Merchant Galleys', 182.
101. Ibid., 189.
102. Diaz de Gamez, *Unconquered Knight*, 59.
103. Ibid., 68.
104. Teichmann, *Stellung und Politik der hansischen Seestädte*, 59.
105. Ibid., 64.
106. Ibid., 66.
107. Zimmerling, *Störtebeker & Co*, 180–5.
108. Levathes, *When China Ruled the Seas*, 98.
109. Dreyer, *Zheng He*, 55.
110. Matthew Paris, *Matthew Paris's English History*, 413.
111. Riley-Smith, *The Knights Hospitaller in the Levant*, 224.

112. Bradford, *Mediterranean*, 359.
113. Heers, *Barbary Corsairs*, 55.
114. Bradford, *Mediterranean*, 358; Heers, *Barbary Corsairs*, 55.
115. Heers, *Barbary Corsairs*, 56.
116. On the Knights Hospitaller on Rhodes, see for example Luttrell, *The Hospitallers at Rhodes, 1306–1412*, and Rossi, *The Hospitallers at Rhodes, 1421–1523*.
117. Teichmann, *Stellung und Politik*, 74.
118. Ibid., 78; see also Puhle, *Die Vitalienbrüder*, 97–102.
119. Turnbull, *Pirate of the East*, 13.
120. Ibid.
121. Ibid.
122. Hellyer, 'Poor but Not Pirates', 118.
123. Gosse, *History of Piracy*, 22.

PART II: THE RISE OF EUROPEAN SEA POWER, 1500 TO 1914

1. As quoted in Defoe, *General History*, 244.
2. Braudel, *The Mediterranean*, vol. 1, 432–3, 519.
3. Mueller and Adler, *Outlaws of the Ocean*, 298.
4. Ibid.
5. Bak, *Barbary Pirate*, 18.
6. Antony, *Like Froth*, 73.
7. Murray, 'Cheng I Sao', 258.
8. Antony, *Like Froth*, 92.
9. Defoe, *General History*, 165.
10. On women and piracy, see for example Appleby, *Women and English Piracy*; Klausmann, Meinzerin and Kuhn, *Women Pirates*; or, more generally on women and violence, Sjoberg and Gentry, *Mothers, Monsters, Whores*.
11. Wintergerst, *Der durch Europam lauffende*, 7–8.
12. Contreras, *Adventures*, 10.
13. Ibid., 13.
14. Le Golif, *Memoirs of a Buccaneer*, 28.
15. Ibid., 30–1.
16. Exquemelin, *Buccaneers of America*, part 1, 1–22.
17. Ibid., 21–2.
18. Bak, *Barbary Pirate*, 21.
19. On Ward, see ibid., especially 24, 36 passim.
20. On Frobisher, see for example Best, *A true discourse*. For a modern biography, see for example McDermott (ed.), *The Third Voyage of Martin Frobisher*.
21. Bicheno, *Elizabeth's Sea Dogs*, 159.
22. Number one was Samuel 'Black Sam' Bellamy, with about $120 million. See Woolsey, 'Top-Earning Pirates'.
23. Andrews, *Elizabethan Privateering*, 100.
24. Ibid.
25. As quoted in Reid, 'Violence at Sea: Unpacking "Piracy" ', 17.
26. Defoe, *General History*, 72.
27. Craig Cabell et al. argue that he did so to find Blackbeard who had betrayed him and seek revenge: see Cabell, Thomas and Richards, *Blackbeard*, 91, 94–5.
28. Preston and Preston, *Pirate of Exquisite Mind*, 74.
29. Cordingly, *Pirate Hunter*, 7–8.
30. As quoted in Andaya and Andaya, *History of Malaysia*, 130.
31. The Iranun are a seafaring ethnic group from Mindanao in the southern Philippines.

32. Warren, *Iranun and Balangingi*, 43–4.
33. Antony, 'Turbulent Waters', 23.
34. Andrews, *Elizabethan Privateering*, 15.
35. His hatred for the Spanish went back to the disastrous battle of San Juan de Ulúa (modern Veracruz, Mexico) on 23 September 1568 between an English squadron – of one of whose vessels Drake was master – under the command of Sir John Hawkins, and a Spanish fleet whose commander, Don Francisco Luján, allegedly broke a truce, as the defeated English had it after the incident. A short description of the battle can be found in Coote, *Drake*, 38–41; for more details, see Unwin, *Defeat of John Hawkins*, 189–212.
36. On this framing, see also Coote, *Drake*, 110–11.
37. Senior, *Nation of Pirates*, 43.
38. As quoted in Lunsford-Poe, *Piracy and Privateering*, 121.
39. Abulafia, *The Great Sea*, 647.
40. Conrad, *The Rescue*.
41. Warren, *Iranun and Balangingi*, 398. In the 1920 edition of Conrad's novel, the quote can be found on p. 263.
42. As quoted in Reid, 'Violence at Sea: Unpacking "Piracy" ', 19 (emphasis mine).
43. On Morgan, see for example the short biography of Breverton, *Admiral Sir Henry Morgan*.
44. Preston and Preston, *Pirate of Exquisite Mind*, 179–80.
45. Gosse, *The Pirates' Who's Who*, 10.
46. Lunsford-Poe, *Piracy and Privateering*, 152. Lunsford-Poe just mentions a 'Grave of Ormond', but if the date she provides is correct, it must have been James Butler, 1st Duke of Ormond.
47. Gosse, *The Pirates' Who's Who*, 10.
48. Senior, *Nation of Pirates*, 56. There is a back-story to this little port, which was sacked by a Barbary Coast corsair, Murat Rais, in June 1631; on that, see Ekin, *The Stolen Village*.
49. Mainwaring, 'Of the Beginnings', 15–16.
50. As quoted in Senior, *Nation of Pirates*, 54.
51. Talty, *Empire of Blue Water*, 40.
52. Lane, *Blood and Silver*, 105.
53. Zahedieh, 'Trade, Plunder, and Economic Development', 215.
54. Petrucci, 'Pirates, Gunpowder, and Christianity', 62.
55. Antony, *Like Froth*, 125.
56. Chin, 'Merchants, Smugglers, and Pirates', 50.
57. Petrucci, 'Pirates, Gunpowder, and Christianity', 65.
58. The Malay/Indonesian term 'pulau' simply means 'island'.
59. Atsushi, 'The Business of Violence', 135.
60. On the history of Macao, see Porter, *Macau, the Imaginary City*.
61. Grog is an alcoholic drink made of (hot) water and rum, with sugar or spices occasionally added.
62. Antony, *Like Froth*, 129.
63. Wang, *White Lotus Rebels*, 86.
64. Antony, *Like Froth*, 127–9.
65. Bicheno, *Elizabeth's Sea Dogs*, 155.
66. As quoted in Tinniswood, *Pirates of Barbary*, 17.
67. Childs, *Pirate Nation*, 2, 4; see also Ronald, *The Pirate Queen*.
68. Williams, *Sir Walter Raleigh*, 233.
69. Paul Sellin asserts in his interesting book on Raleigh that he actually found a substantial gold mine and simply fell prey to court corruption: see Sellin, *Treasure, Treason and the Tower*.
70. Lunsford-Poe, *Piracy and Privateering*, 3.
71. Earle, *Sack of Panama*, 92.
72. Lunsford-Poe, *Piracy and Privateering*, 110.
73. Ibid., 115.
74. Lizé, 'Piracy in the Indian Ocean', 81.

75. Wilson, *Empire of the Deep*, 105.
76. Ibid., 26.
77. On this, see Warren, *The Sulu Zone 1768–1898*.
78. Van der Cruysse, *Siam & the West*, 199–201.
79. The account of this incident is based on the description in ibid., 412–14. For a primary source written by Samuel White's brother George, see White, *Reflections on a Scandalous Paper*. See also Collis, *Siamese White*.
80. Senior, *Nation of Pirates*, 27.
81. Mainwaring, 'Of the Beginnings', 14.
82. Bak, *Barbary Pirate*, 43.
83. Ibid., 44–5.
84. Barbour, 'Dutch and English Merchant Shipping', 280.
85. Bak, *Barbary Pirate*, 61.
86. Senior, *Nation of Pirates*, 27.
87. Defoe, *General History*, 50.
88. According to a 1696 English East India Company petition reproduced in Jameson, *Privateering and Piracy*, 109. Defoe, however, claims the vessel's name was *The Duke*; see Defoe, *General History*, 50.
89. Ibid., 50–1.
90. Contreras, *Adventures*, 47, 49.
91. Ibid., 50.
92. Defoe, *General History*, 204.
93. Duguay-Trouin, *Les campagnes de Monsieur Duguay-Trouin*, 21.
94. Contreras, *Adventures*, 53.
95. Consul General Thomas Baker, as quoted by Tinniswood, *Pirates of Barbary*, 266.
96. Defoe, *General History*, 234.
97. Ibid., 217.
98. Hakluyt, *Principal Navigations, Voyages, Traffiques*, 817 (adapted into modern English).
99. Ibid.
100. Wintergerst, *Der durch Europam lauffende*, 10–14.
101. Exquemelin, *Bucaniers of America*, part 1, 82.
102. Ibid.
103. Ibid.
104. The forename of the captain seems to have gone unreported. On the captain's name, Harry Kelsey opines that 'San Juan is an unusual form for a Spanish name, even in an era when Spanish practice was less rigid than it is today. In addition, Antón would be the likelier spelling.' See Kelsey, *Sir Francis Drake*, 465 (endnote 114).
105. Bicheno, *Elizabeth's Sea Dogs*, 146.
106. Antony, *Like Froth*, 111.
107. Warren, *Iranun and Balangingi*, 269.
108. As quoted in ibid., 270–1.
109. Padfield, *Guns at Sea*, 29–39, 51–6.
110. Childs, *Pirate Nation*, 63.
111. Ibid., 62–3.
112. According to Corbett, it was a merchant galleass (*galeazze di mercantia*): see Corbett, *England in the Mediterranean*, vol. 1, 14.
113. Tinniswood, *Pirates of Barbary*, 36.
114. Chain shots were two half-balls chained together, used as short-range anti-personnel ammunition or to shred sails and cut the rigging of masts.
115. As quoted in Tenenti, *Piracy and the Decline of Venice*, 77–8.
116. Defoe, *General History*, 53.
117. Cordingly, *Life Among the Pirates*, 35.
118. Ibid. Other sources put the individual shares at about $500,000: see Rogoziński, *Honor Among Thieves*, 89–90.

119. On Manila galleons, see Schurz, *The Manila Galleon*, 161–77.
120. Pretty, 'The Admirable and Prosperous Voyage', 108.
121. Ringrose, *Bucaniers of America*, vol. 2, 30.
122. Little, *Sea Rover's Practice*, 6.
123. Earle, *Pirate Wars*, 105.
124. Warren, *Iranun and Balangingi*, 268–9. On the ships of the East India Company, see Sutton, *Lords of the East* (especially the chapter 'The Ships', 37–52).
125. Earl, *The Eastern Seas*, 376.
126. See Warren, *The Sulu Zone 1768–1898*, 170 (footnote).
127. Warren, *Iranun and Balangingi*, 273.
128. Rutter, *Pirate Wind*, 38.
129. Warren, *Iranun and Balangingi*, 271–2.
130. Rutter, *Pirate Wind*, 20.
131. O'Kane, *The Ship of Sulaimān*, 232.
132. On that raid, and the fascinating back-story to it, see Ekin, *The Stolen Village*.
133. Exquemelin, *Bucaniers of America*, part 1, 114–15.
134. Earle, *Pirate Wars*, 95.
135. Masefield, *On the Spanish Main*, 202.
136. Earle, *Pirate Wars*, 128.
137. As quoted in Antony, *Like Froth*, 119–20.
138. See 'Mr Brooke's Memorandum on the Piracy of the Malayan Archipelago', in Keppel, *Expedition to Borneo*, 290.
139. Ibid.
140. Earle, *Pirate Wars*, 128.
141. De Bry, 'Christopher Condent's *Fiery Dragon*', 107.
142. Exquemelin, *Bucaniers of America*, part 1, 106–7 (spelling modernised).
143. Ibid., 107 (spelling modernised).
144. Contreras, *Adventures*, 36.
145. Antony, *Like Froth*, 143.
146. Le Golif, *Memoirs of a Buccaneer*, 227.
147. Ibid., 225.
148. Murray, 'Cheng I Sao in Fact and Fiction', 260.
149. Antony, *Like Froth*, 48–9.
150. Le Golif, *Memoirs of a Buccaneer*, 228.
151. Woolsey, 'Top-Earning Pirates'.
152. Exquemelin, *Bucaniers of America*, part 2, 2–3.
153. Woolsey, 'Top-Earning Pirates'.
154. Exquemelin, *Bucaniers of America*, part 2, 56–7.
155. As quoted in Earle, *Pirate Wars*, 29.
156. Rediker, *Villains of All Nations*, 5.
157. Earle, *Pirate Wars*, 23.
158. For possible reasons, see for example Tinniswood, *Pirates of Barbary*, 75–6.
159. Mainwaring, 'Of the Beginnings', 10.
160. Mainwaring, *Life and Works of Sir Henry Mainwaring, Vol. I*, 31.
161. Mainwaring, 'Of the Beginnings', 15–16.
162. Ibid., 19.
163. Ibid., 23.
164. Tinniswood, *Pirates of Barbary*, 82–3.
165. Mainwaring, 'Of the Beginnings', 42.
166. Antony, 'Piracy on the South China Coast', 36.
167. Sazvar, 'Zheng Chenggong', 164.
168. Ibid., 165.
169. Clements, *Coxinga*, 5.
170. Ibid., 186.

171. On Zheng Chenggong as a national hero in China (both the People's Republic of China and Taiwan), see Sazvar, 'Zheng Chenggong', 201–30.

172. As quoted in Clements, *Coxinga*, 159.

173. On the history of the Marathas, see for example Gordon, *The Marathas 1600–1818*.

174. Risso, 'Cross-Cultural Perceptions of Piracy', 303.

175. Biddulph, *Pirates of Malabar* and *An Englishwoman in India*, 27.

176. Weber, 'The Successor States', 205.

177. Risso, 'Cross-Cultural Perceptions of Piracy', 305. However, she is mistaken in attributing this to K.M. Panikkar, who mentions Angre only once (on p. 94, not p. 74 as Risso claims), and in a rather neutral way. See Panikkar, *Asia and Western Dominance*, 94.

178. Downing, *Compendious History of the Indian Wars*, 20–2.

179. Rediker, *Between the Devil and the Deep Blue Sea*, 256.

180. Hawkins, *Observations of Sir Richard Havvkins Knight*, 213–14, 221–2.

181. Unfortunately, Contreras doesn't provide any details about the arms he is talking about – but since he in all probability had neither the time nor the resources to equip these merchantmen with cannon, I assume he means firearms – which would also explain why there were no broadsides fired . . .

182. Contreras, *Adventures*, 137–8.

183. Ibid., 138.

184. Chauvel, *Nationalists, Soldiers and Separatists*, 20

185. Parthesius, *Dutch Ships in Tropical Waters*, 41–2.

186. Contreras, *Adventures*, 21.

187. Ibid. Contreras remains silent about his own casualties, however.

188. On this, see for example Cabell, Thomas and Richards, *Blackbeard*, 3, 135–7; Konstam, *Blackbeard*, 233–7, 275–80.

189. This is Defoe's version of the event – Angus Konstam has it that Blackbeard only discovered Maynard's two sloops when they entered the inlet early the next morning due to his failure to keep lookouts: see Konstam, *Blackbeard*, 245–6.

190. Defoe, *General History*, 80.

191. Ibid., 81.

192. Ibid.

193. Ibid.

194. Ibid., 82

195. Ibid., 165.

196. Tinniswood, *Pirates of Barbary*, 10.

197. Hebb, *Piracy and the English Government*, 2.

198. On this raid, see Tinniswood, *Pirates of Barbary*, 131–2.

199. Little, *Pirate Hunting*, 205.

200. Tinniswood, *Pirates of Barbary*, 278.

201. Earle, *Pirate Wars*, 71.

202. Oppenheim, *Naval Tracts of Sir William Monson*, vol. 3, 80.

203. Ibid., 82–3.

204. Ibid., 82.

205. 'Dice shot were square pieces of iron used under the same conditions as the later grape shot and they are often mentioned among artillery stores in the reigns of Henry VII and Henry VIII and occasionally during the reign of Elizabeth': ibid., 81 (footnote).

206. Hebb, *Piracy and the English Government*, 134.

207. Lambert, *Barbary Wars*, 92, 101.

208. The First Barbary War is the topic of Wheelan, *Jefferson's War*.

209. On that war, see for example Lambert, *Barbary Wars*, 179–202.

210. Fremont-Barnes, *Wars of the Barbary Pirates*, 7–8.

211. Ibid., 87.

212. As quoted in Earle, *Pirate Wars*, 72.

213. As quoted in ibid., 73.

214. Tinniswood, *Pirates of Barbary*, 279.
215. Earle, *Pirate Wars*, 72.
216. Corbett, *England in the Mediterranean*, vol. 1, 52.

PART III: A GLOBALISED WORLD, 1914 TO THE PRESENT

1. Somalia is a very patriarchal society, and female fighters, or female pirates, do not currently exist.
2. The vessels were released in September 2005 for a total ransom of about $500,000 – sources are unclear on the exact sum.
3. On that, see for example Lehr and Lehmann, 'Somalia – Pirates' New Paradise; Westberg, 'Bloodshed and Breaking Wave: The First Outbreak of Somali Piracy'.
4. Lehr, 'Somali Piracy and International Crime', 125.
5. Schuman, 'How to Defeat Pirates'.
6. Simon, 'Safety and Security in the Malacca Straits', 35.
7. Frécon, 'Piracy and Armed Robbery at Sea Along the Malacca Straits', 71.
8. Pérouse de Montclos, 'Maritime Piracy in Nigeria', 535–41.
9. Jimoh, 'Maritime Piracy and Violence Offshore in Nigeria', 7–8.
10. Ibid. Also see Pérouse de Montclos, 'Maritime Piracy in Nigeria', 535.
11. On illegal migration and migrant smuggling from the Middle East and North Africa via the Mediterranean to Europe, see for example Triandafyllidou and Maroukis, *Migrant Smuggling*.
12. On these networks, see for example BBC, 'Migrant crisis'.
13. Ronzitti, *The Law of Naval Warfare*, 64.
14. As quoted in Cigar, 'Jihadist Maritime Strategy', 7.
15. Bernama, 'Zahid: Indonesia's Veep Hit by "Bugis Pirate" Remark'.
16. Koburger, 'Selamat Datang, Kapitan', 69.
17. Ibid.
18. Stewart, *Piraten*, 379–81.
19. HSBC Economist Intelligence Unit, 'Pirates of the Ports'.
20. Liss, 'Challenges of Piracy in Southeast Asia'.
21. Stewart, *The Brutal Seas*, 29.
22. Ibid., 30–1.
23. Frécon, 'Piracy and Armed Robbery', 73.
24. Ibid., 73–4.
25. Koh, 'Drop in piracy in regional waters'.
26. Frécon, *Piracy and Armed Robbery*, 77.
27. Hastings, 'Geographies of State Failure and Sophistication in Maritime Piracy Hijackings', 220.
28. Hansen, 'Somali Pirates are Back'.
29. United Nations Monitoring Group on Somalia and Eritrea, *Report of the Monitoring Group on Somalia and Eritrea*.
30. At the time of finalising this book (November 2018), pirate activity is still much reduced due to heavy naval patrolling, but their leaders continue to occupy influential positions – both in society in general and in the political-administrative system.
31. This, at least, is the opinion of a Puntland official (who prefers to remain anonymous), expressed in a phone call with the author in July 2017.
32. Pérouse de Montclos, 'Maritime Piracy in Nigeria', 536; Jimoh, 'Maritime Piracy and Violence Offshore in Nigeria', 20.
33. Ibid., 9
34. Murphy, 'Troubled Waters of Africa', 71–2.
35. A similar argument is made in ibid., 73.

36. Lacey, 'The Signs Say Somaliland, but the World Says Somalia'.
37. Young, *Contemporary Maritime Piracy in Southeast Asia*, 63.
38. On Somali piracy, see Lehr, 'Somali Piracy and International Crime'.
39. Coffen-Smout, 'Pirates, Warlords and Rogue Fishing Vessels in Somalia's Unruly Seas'.
40. Lehr and Lehmann, 'Somalia: Pirates' New Paradise', 12.
41. Mwangura, 'Somalia: Pirates or Protectors?'.
42. Ibid.
43. Barbour, 'Dutch and English Merchant Shipping', 280.
44. As virtually all experts agree, it is impossible to quantify some aspects of Somali piracy – many of the numbers bandied around are simply made up, or, at best, more or less educated guesses.
45. Lilius, *I Sailed With Chinese Pirates*, 2.
46. Ibid., 5.
47. See the list in ibid., 7–10.
48. Hympendahl, *Pirates Aboard!*, 23–7.
49. *iWitness News*, 'Murder of German Sailor "Another Nail" in St. Vincent's "Economic Coffin"'.
50. As quoted in Beeson, 'Is Piracy Still a Threat to Ocean Cruisers?'.
51. *NZ Herald*, 'Sir Peter Blake Killed in Amazon Pirate Attack'.
52. As quoted in Phillips, Gayle and Swanson, ' "I Will Have my Boat Stolen" '.
53. As quoted in ibid.
54. Senior, *Nation of Pirates*, 59.
55. *The Economist*, 'When Pirates Are Not So Bold'.
56. On that incident, see Captain Richard Phillips's report, published in Phillips and Talty, *A Captain's Duty*.
57. Associated Press, 'Somali pirate gets life in prison for attack on US Navy ship'; Bockmann, 'EU Navy Has Gunfire Exchange With Somali Pirates'.
58. See, for example, UN Monitoring Group on Somalia and Eritrea, *Report of the Monitoring Group on Somalia and Eritrea*, 34–5.
59. As quoted in Eichstaedt, *Pirate State: Inside Somalia's Terrorism at Sea*, 67.
60. Lehr and Lehmann, 'Somalia: Pirates' New Paradise', 1–22.
61. On Nigerian pirate tactics, see Kamal-Deen, 'Anatomy of Gulf of Guinea Piracy', 104.
62. See, for example, Bridger, 'West African Piracy: Extreme Violence and Inadequate Security'.
63. *Shipping Position Online*, 'SP Brussels Attack'. See also Bridger, 'The World's Most Violent Pirates'.
64. *Shipping Position Online*, 'SP Brussels Attack'.
65. Osinowo, 'Combating Piracy in the Gulf of Guinea', 3.
66. On this attack, see Kashubsky, 'Offshore Energy Force Majeure', 20–6.
67. Ibid., 20.
68. Kamal-Deen, 'Anatomy of Gulf of Guinea Piracy', 98.
69. Ibid.
70. See, for example, Hajari, 'Bungles in the Jungle'.
71. For an overview, see Oceans Beyond Piracy, 'Definition/classification of piracy'.
72. Peter Unsinger, as quoted in Herbert-Burns, 'Compound Piracy at Sea in the Early Twenty-First Century', 113. The classification can be found in ibid., 98.
73. For more details, see Herbert-Burns, ibid., 104–11.
74. Herbert-Burns also draws attention to acts of 'self-piracy – i.e. acts in which the original crew of the vessel turns its own ship into a phantom ship, either on their own initiative or on the say-so of the vessel's owner. But since this has to do more with insurance fraud than with piracy, this case is excluded here. See Herbert-Burns, ibid.
75. Instructive with regard to the rather dubious role of some negotiators is the case of Somali negotiator Ali Mohammed Ali who was negotiating between the pirates who on 7 November 2008 had captured the Danish-flagged cargo vessel *CEC Future* and the ship's owners, and

who was brought to court by the US government as a 'pirate conspirator'; in February 2014, the charges were dropped, however. See for example Schuler, 'US to Drop Charges Against *CEC Future* Pirate Negotiator', and Dickson, 'The Pirate Negotiator'.

76. Whether the newly established federal government, at the time of writing still embattled in their own capital Mogadishu, can change that remains to be seen.

77. Age range as reported in Hunter, 'Somali Pirates Living the High Life'.

78. As quoted in Pandey, 'Pirates of the Bay of Bengal'.

79. See, for example, Bagerhat Correspondent, 'Sundarbans Pirates' Ringleader Held', and Chakma, 'Maritime Piracy in Bangladesh'.

80. Pandey, 'Pirates of the Bay of Bengal'.

81. Bahadur, *Deadly Waters*, 197; Bahadur, however, seems to mix up two hijackings that occurred in the same month: that of the Jordanian-flagged MV *Victoria* on 17 May (not on 5 May as he states) by pirates based on Hobyo, and that of the German-owned and German-flagged MV *Lehmann Timber* on 28 May. Since this latter vessel was indeed hijacked by a pirate group operating from Eyl, this seems to be the vessel he is referring to. In this case, the ransom was $750,000.

82. Ibid., 194.

83. Ibid., 176–7.

84. Ibid., 197.

85. On the war, see Jensen, 'The United States, International Policing and the War against Anarchist Terrorism, 1900–1914'.

86. As quoted in ibid., 19.

87. As quoted in Thorup, 'Enemy of Humanity', 401–11.

88. An interesting discussion of this expression and its meaning can be found in Gould, 'Cicero's Ghost'.

89. William Blackstone, as quoted in ibid., 32.

90. Heinze, 'A "Global War on Piracy"?', 50.

91. Peter Earle comes to the same conclusion: see Earle, *Pirate Wars*, xi.

92. Gould, 'Cicero's Ghost', 34.

93. Ibid.

94. As reported, for example, by the *Telegraph*, 'Russia Releases Pirates Because They "Too Expensive to Feed" '.

95. Private conversation, December 2008.

96. Ebert, 'Deutschland macht Seeräubern den Prozess'. The International Tribunal for the Law of the Sea at Hamburg is responsible for adjudicating disputes arising out of the UN Law of the Sea Convention as a part of International Law. Its jurisdiction does not include criminal matters such as piracy.

97. On the different possible legal mechanisms to deal with today's pirates, see for example Kraska, *Contemporary Maritime Piracy*, 168–82; and on the persistent problems of bringing them to justice, see for example Kontorovich, ' "A Guantanamo on the Sea" '.

98. For further information, see MSC–HOA, 'The Maritime Security Centre – Horn of Africa'.

99. Maritime Foundation, 'Tackling piracy in the Gulf of Aden'.

100. Ibid.

101. On the 18 knots and above factor, see MSC–HOA, *BMP 4*, 7. How fast the various classes of modern container vessels can go is treated confidentially by their operators in order to deny their competitors a possible edge.

102. See, for example, the report in *MEBA*, 'Don't Give Up the Ship!'.

103. MSC–HOA, *BMP 4*, vi, 1, 2.

104. Ibid., 23–4.

105. Ibid, 38.

106. Ibid.

107. Ibid., 39–40.

108. Kuhlmann, 'Piracy: Understanding the Real Threat', 36.

109. As quoted in the *Washington Times*, 'Arming Sailors'.
110. Ibid.
111. Connett, 'Robot Ships'.
112. Ibid.
113. Andrews, 'Robot Ships and Unmanned Autonomous Boats'.
114. As quoted in ibid.
115. Ibid. Also see MUNIN, 'Munin Results'.
116. IMO, *Somali Piracy Warning for Yachts*.
117. On this incident, see Bohn, *The Achille Lauro Hijacking*.
118. Ahluwalia, 'Cruise Liner on Journey from Sydney to Dubai Turns into "Ghost Ship"'.
119. Pearlman, 'Cruise Passengers Ordered to Switch off Lights and Music at Night'.
120. Operation Atalanta is formally known as European Union Naval Force (EU NAVFOR) Somalia. It started on 8 December 2008 and is still continuing at the time of writing (November 2018). The operation focuses on vessels bound for Somali ports, and also monitors fishing operations in Somali waters. See EU NAVFOR Somalia, 'Mission'.
121. Operation Ocean Shield was a NATO initiative, with several non-NATO navies contributing to the effort as well. Starting on 17 August 2009, it focused on protecting vessels that transported food aid for the World Food Programme to the region, and thus could not avoid sailing through Somali waters. Operation Ocean Shield was terminated on 24 November 2016 due the drastically reduced number of pirate attacks, both successful and attempted. See Maritime Security Review, 'NATO ends Ocean Shield'; Bueger, ' "Ocean Shield" Achieved its Mission'.
122. CTF 151 was set up in January 2009 as a multinational task force in accordance with the United Nations Security Council Resolutions (UNSCR) 1816, 1838, 1846, 1851 and 1897. At the time of writing (November 2018), CTF 151 is under the command of Rear Admiral Saw Shi Tat, Republic of Singapore Navy. For further information, see Combined Maritime Forces, 'CTF 151: Counter-piracy'; Combined Maritime Forces, 'Singapore Takes Command of Counter Piracy Combined Task Force 151'.
123. Foreign and Commonwealth Office (UK), 'The International Response to Piracy'.
124. NATO, 'Operation Ocean Shield'.
125. BBC, 'US to lead new anti-pirate force'. Later, the number of warships deployed, and especially the number of shipborne helicopters, increased for all three operations.
126. As quoted in Lehr, 'Maritime Piracy as a US Foreign Policy Problem', 215.
127. See, for example, Kontorovich, 'A Guantanamo Bay on the Sea'.
128. Curtenelle, 'Uncertainty Surrounds Death in French Piracy Raid'.
129. Nagourney and Gettleman, 'Pirates Brutally End Yachting Dream'.
130. Wadhams, 'American Hostage Deaths: A Case of Pirate Anxiety'.
131. *Spiegel Online*, 'Mission Impossible: German Elite Troop Abandons Plan to Free Pirate Hostages'.
132. The ship's master, Krzysztof Kotiuk, wrote a book (in German) on the ordeal. See Kotiuk, *Frohe Ostern Hansa Stavanger*.
133. Konrad, 'The Protector'.
134. Sofge, 'Robot Boats Hunt High-Tech Pirates'.
135. BBC, 'France Raid Ship after Crew Freed'.
136. Pflanz and Harding, 'Europe's Mainland Attack Will Escalate Conflict'.
137. Ibid.
138. EU NAVFOR, *EU Naval Operation Against Piracy*, 7.
139. Ibid.
140. For the two attacks in 2017, see BBC, 'Somali pirates suspected of first ship hijacking since 2012'; MAREX, 'Chinese Navy Hands Pirates Over to Somali Authorities'. For the two attacks in 2018, see *gCaptain*, 'Chemical Tanker Attacked by Pirates Off Coast of Somalia'; Schuler, 'Hong Kong-Flagged Bulk Carrier Attacked by Pirates Off Somalia'.
141. Ministry of Foreign Affairs (Japan), *Regional Cooperation Agreement on Combating Piracy and Armed Robbery against Ships in Asia*.

142. The Comoros, Egypt, Eritrea, Jordan, Mauritius, Mozambique, Oman, Saudi Arabia, South Africa, Sudan and the United Arab Emirates joined later
143. IMO, *Djibouti Code of Conduct*.

CONCLUSION: BACK WITH A VENGEANCE

1. See Hobsbawm, *Bandits*.
2. Marcus Rediker's most important book in this regard is undoubtedly *Villains of All Nations*. On seamen in general, see his earlier work *Between the Devil and the Deep Blue Sea*.
3. As quoted in Murray, 'Cheng I Sao', 273.
4. Young, *Contemporary Maritime Piracy in Southeast Asia*, 63.
5. Lambert, 'The Limits of Naval Power', 173.
6. On that programme, see Ghee, 'Conflict over Natural Resources in Malaysia', 145–81.
7. Rutter, *Pirate Wind*, 26.
8. Anderson and Gifford, 'Privateering and the Private Production of Naval Power', 119.
9. 'Constitution of the United States and the Declaration of Independence' (2009 edition), 6; online at http://frwebgate.access.gpo.gov/cgi-bin/getdoc.cgi?dbname=111_cong_documents&docid=f:sd004.111.pdf (accessed 26 September 2018).
10. Weber, *Theory of Social and Economic Organization*, 154.
11. See, for example, Isenberg, 'The Rise of Private Maritime Security Companies'.
12. Gosse, *History of Piracy*, 1–2.
13. Ibid.
14. Mueller and Adler, *Outlaws of the Ocean*, 288.

Bibliography

Abulafia, David. *The Great Sea: A Human History of the Mediterranean*. London: Oxford University Press, 2013.

Abu-Lughod, Janet L. *Before European Hegemony: The World System AD 1250–1350*. New York and London: Oxford University Press, 1989.

Ahluwalia, Ravneet. 'Cruise Liner on Journey from Sydney to Dubai Turns into "Ghost Ship" for 10 Days to Stop Pirate Attack'. *Independent*, 9 August 2017; online at http://www.independent.co.uk/travel/news-and-advice/cruise-pirates-drill-sea-princess-ghost-ship-blackout-sydney-dubai-indian-ocean-a7884211.html (accessed 2 December 2018).

Al-Qāsimī, Sultan Muhammed. *The Myth of Arab Piracy in the Gulf*. Dover, NH: Croom Helm, 1986.

Amirell, Stefan Eklöf and Leos Müller. 'Introduction: Persistent Piracy in World History', in Stefan Eklöf Amirell and Leos Müller (eds): *Persistent Piracy: Maritime Violence and State-Formation in Global Historical Perspective*, 1–23. London: Palgrave Macmillan, 2014.

Andaya, Barbara Watson and Leonard Y. Andaya. *A History of Malaysia*. London and Basingstoke: Macmillan, 1982.

Anderson, Gary M. and Adam Gifford Jr. 'Privateering and the Private Production of Naval Power'. *Cato Journal*, vol. 11, no. 1 (Spring/Summer 1999), 99–122.

Anderson, John. *English Intercourse with Siam in the Seventeenth Century*. London: Kegan Paul, Trench, Trubner & Co., 1890.

Andrews, Crispin. 'Robot Ships and Unmanned Autonomous Boats'. *Engineering and Technology*, 12 September 2016; online at https://eandt.theiet.org/content/articles/2016/09/robot-ships (accessed 2 December 2018).

Andrews, Kenneth R. *Elizabethan Privateering: English Privateering during the Spanish War 1585–1603*. Cambridge: Cambridge University Press, 1964.

Andrews, Kenneth R. (ed.). *English Privateering Voyages to the West Indies: Documents Relating to English Voyages to the West Indies from the Defeat of the Armada to the Last Voyages of Sir Francis Drake, Including Spanish Documents Contributed by Irene A. Wright*. Cambridge: Published for the Hakluyt Society at the University Press, 1959.

Anglo-Saxon Chronicles. Translated and collated by Anne Savage. London: Book Club Associates, 1983.

Annals of St-Bertin: Ninth-Century Histories, vol. 1. Translated and annotated by Janet L. Nelson. Manchester: Manchester University Press, 1991.

Antony, Robert J. *Like Froth Floating on the Sea: The World of Pirates and Seafarers in Late Imperial South China*. China Research Monograph 56. Berkeley, CA: University of California Berkeley, Institute of East Asian Studies, 2003.

— 'Introduction: The Shadowy World of the Greater China Seas', in Robert J. Antony (ed.): *Elusive Pirates, Pervasive Smugglers: Violence and Clandestine Trade in the Greater China Seas*, 1–14. Hong Kong: Hong Kong University Press, 2010.

— 'Piracy on the South China Coast through Modern Times', in Bruce A. Elleman, Andrew Forbes and David Rosenberg (eds): *Piracy and Maritime Crime: Historical and Modern Case Studies*, 35–50. Newport, RI: Naval War College Press, 2010.

— 'Turbulent Waters: Sea Raiding in Early Modern Southeast Asia'. *The Mariner's Mirror*, vol. 99, no. 1 (February 2013), 23–38.

— 'Maritime Violence and State-Formation in Vietnam: Piracy and the Tay Son Rebellion, 1771–1802', in Stefan Eklöf Amirell and Leos Müller (eds): *Persistent Piracy: Maritime Violence and State-Formation in Global Historical Perspective*, 113–30. London: Palgrave Macmillan, 2014.

Appleby, John C. *Women and English Piracy, 1540–1720: Partners and Victims of Crime*. Woodbridge: Boydell Press, 2013.

Arnold, James A. 'From Piracy to Policy: Exquemelin's Buccaneers and Imperial Competition'. *Review: Literature and Arts of the Americas*, vol. 40, no. 1 (2007), 9–20.

Associated Press. 'Somali pirate gets life in prison for attack on US Navy ship'. *Navy Times*, 26 April 2017. https://www.navytimes.com/news/your-navy/2017/04/27/somali-pirate-gets-life-in-prison-for-attack-on-us-navy-ship/ (accessed 2 December 2018).

Atsushi, Ota. 'The Business of Violence: Piracy around Riau, Lingga, and Singapore, 1820–40', in Robert J. Antony (ed.): *Elusive Pirates, Pervasive Smugglers: Violence and Clandestine Trade in the Greater China Seas*, 127–141. Hong Kong: Hong Kong University Press, 2010.

Augustine of Hippo. *The City of God against the Pagans*, book IV. Edited and translated by R.W. Dyson. Cambridge: Cambridge University Press, 1998 (originally published AD 426).

Bach-Jensen, Richard. 'The United States, International Policing and the War against Anarchist Terrorism, 1900–1914'. *Terrorism and Political Violence*, vol. 13, no. 1 (Spring 2001), 15–46.

Bagerhat Correspondent. 'Sundarbans Pirates' Ringleader Held with Arms, Claims RAB'. *News Bangladesh*, 20 August 2015; online at http://www.newsbangladesh.com/english/Sundarbans-pirates-ringleader-held-with-arms-claims-RAB/6046 (accessed 2 December 2018).

Bahadur, Jay. *Deadly Waters: Inside the Hidden World of Somalia's Pirates*. London: Profile Books, 2011.

Bak, Greg. *Barbary Pirate: The Life and Crimes of John Ward*. Stroud: The History Press, 2010.

Barbour, Violet. 'Dutch and English Merchant Shipping in the Seventeenth Century'. *Economic History Review*, vol. 2, no. 2 (January 1930), 261–90.

Barker, Andrew. *A True and Certaine Report of the Beginning, Proceedings, Ouerthrowes, and now Present Estate of Captaine Ward and Danseker, the Two Late Famous Pirates*. London: William Hall, 1609 (e-book).

Barrett, James H. 'What Caused the Viking Age?' *Antiquity*, vol. 82 (2008), 671–85; online at https://www.cambridge.org/core/services/aop-cambridge-core/content/view/9AAD15 7E488AF39555B64D3529944D43/S0003598X00097301a.pdf/what_caused_the_viking_age. pdf (accessed 2 December 2018).

Batey, Colleen E. and John Sheehan. 'Viking Expansion and Cultural Blending in Britain and Ireland', in William W. Fitzhugh and Elisabeth I. Ward (eds): *Vikings: The North Atlantic Saga*, 127–41. Washington, DC and London: Smithsonian Institution Press in association with National Museum of Natural History, 2000.

BBC. 'I Beat Pirates with a Hose and Sonic Cannon'. 17 May 2007; online at http://news.bbc. co.uk/1/hi/uk/6664677.stm (accessed 2 December 2018).

—— 'France Raid Ship after Crew Freed'. 12 April 2008; online at http://news.bbc.co.uk/1/hi/world/africa/7342292.stm (accessed 2 December 2018).

—— 'Air raid kills Somali militants'. 1 May 2008. http://news.bbc.co.uk/1/hi/world/africa/7376760.stm (accessed 2 December 2018).

—— 'US to lead new anti-pirate force'. 8 January 2009. http://news.bbc.co.uk/1/hi/world/africa/7817611.stm (accessed 2 December 2018).

—— 'Profile: Saleh Ali Saleh Nabhan'. 15 September 2009. http://news.bbc.co.uk/1/hi/8256024. stm (accessed 2 December 2018).

—— 'Somali Pirate Leader "Big Mouth" Arrested in Belgium "Sting" '. 14 October 2013; online at http://www.bbc.co.uk/news/world-europe–24519520 (accessed 2 December 2018).

—— 'Ahmed Abdi Godane: Somalia's killed al-Shabaab leader'. 9 September 2014. https://www. bbc.co.uk/news/world-africa–29034409 (accessed 2 December 2018).

—— 'Migrant crisis: Who are Africa's people smugglers?' 23 April 2015. https://www.bbc.co.uk/news/world-europe–32381101 (accessed 2 December 2018).

—— 'Somali pirates suspected of first ship hijacking since 2012'. 14 March 2017. https://www. bbc.co.uk/news/world-africa–39264343 (accessed 2 December 2018).

Beeson, Chris. 'Is Piracy still a Threat to Ocean Cruisers?' *Yachting Monthly*, 14 October 2016; online at http://www.yachtingmonthly.com/cruising-guides/piracy-still-threat-ocean-cruisers–52973 (accessed 2 December 2018).

Bernama. 'Zahid: Indonesia's Veep Hurt by "Bugis Pirate" Remark'. *Free Malaysia Today*, 21 October 2017; online at http://www.freemalaysiatoday.com/category/nation/2017/10/21/indonesias-vice-president-hurt-by-bugis-pirate-remark-says-zahid (accessed 2 December 2018).

Bernard, W.D. *Narrative of the Voyages and Services of the Nemesis from 1840 to 1843, and of the Combined Naval and Military Operations in China: Comprising a Complete Account of the Colony of Hong-Kong and Remarks on the Character & Habits of the Chinese.* London: Henry Colbourn, 1845 (2nd edition).

Bernstein, William. *A Splendid Exchange: How Trade Shaped the World.* London: Atlantic Books, 2008.

Best, George. *A True Discourse of the Late Voyages of Discoverie, for the Finding of a Passage to Cathaya, by the Northwest, under the Conduct of Martin Frobisher Generall: Divided into Three Bookes.* London: Henry Bynnyman, 1578 (e-book).

Bialuschewski, Arne. 'Between Newfoundland and the Malacca Strait: A Survey of the Golden Age of Piracy, 1695–1725'. *The Mariner's Mirror,* vol. 90, no. 2 (2004), 167–86.

— 'Pirates, Markets and Imperial Authority: Economic Aspects of Maritime Depredations in the Atlantic World, 1716–1726'. *Global Crime,* vol. 9, issue 1–2 (2008), 52–6.

Bicheno, Hugh. *Elizabeth's Sea Dogs: How the English Became the Scourge of the Seas.* London: Conway, 2012.

Biddulph, John. *The Pirates of Malabar* and *An Englishwoman in India Two Hundred Years Ago.* London, Smith, Elder & Co., 1907; online at https://archive.org/details/piratesofmalabar00bidd (accessed 17 September 2018).

Binkley, Beatriz and Laura Smith. 'Somali Pirates: The Anatomy of Attacks'. *International Security Blog,* Matthew B. Ridgway Center for International Security Studies, 28 September 2010; online at http://research.ridgway.pitt.edu/blog/2010/09/28/pirate-attacks (accessed 2 December 2018).

Bjørgo, Tore. 'Introduction', in Tore Bjørgo (ed.): *Root Causes of Terrorism: Myths, Reality and Ways Forward,* 1–15. London and New York: Routledge, 2005.

Bockmann, Michelle Wiese. 'EU Navy Has Gunfire Exchange with Somali Pirates'. *Bloomberg Business Week,* 15 January 2012. https://archive.is/20120720192950/http://www.businessweek.com/news/2012–01–13/eu-navy-has-gunfire-exchange-with-somali-pirates.html (accessed 2 December 2018).

Bohn, Michael K. *The Achille Lauro Hijacking: Lessons in the Politics and Prejudice of Terrorism.* Dulles, VA: Brassey's, 2004.

Bouchon, Geneviève. 'The Maritime Economy and the Trading Companies', in Claude Markovits (ed.): *A History of Modern India, 1480–1950,* 132–49. London: Anthem Press, 2004.

Boxer, Charles R. *The Portuguese Seaborne Empire, 1415–1825.* London: Hutchinson, 1969.

Bracewell, Catherine W. *The Uskoks of Senj. Piracy, Banditry, and Holy War in the Sixteenth-Century Adriatic.* Ithaca, NY and London: Cornell University Press, 2010.

Bradford, Alfred S. *Flying the Black Flag: A Brief History of Piracy.* Westport, CT and London: Praeger, 2007.

Bradford, Ernle. *Mediterranean: Portrait of a Sea.* London: Penguin Books, 2000.

Braudel, Fernand. *The Mediterranean and the Mediterranean World in the Age of Philip II.* Berkeley, Los Angeles and London: University of California Press, 1995 (2 vols).

Breverton, Terry. *Admiral Sir Henry Morgan: The Greatest Buccaneer of Them All.* Pontypridd: Wales Books, 2005.

Bridger, James. 'West African Piracy: Extreme Violence and Inadequate Security'. *gCaptain,* 12 May 2014; online at http://www.gcaptain.com/west-african-piracy-extreme-violence-inadequate-security/ (accessed 2 December 2018).

— 'The World's Most Violent Pirates'. *USNI News,* 21 May 2014; online at http://news.usni.org/2014/05/12/worlds-violent-pirates (accessed 2 December 2018).

British Forces TV. 'Anti-Piracy Success Puts Funding at Risk', 30 November 2012; online at https://youtu.be/60HLTHbqyOw (accessed 2 December 2018).

Bromley, J.S. 'Outlaws at Sea, 1660–1720: Liberty, Equality, and Fraternity among the Caribbean Freebooters', in C.R. Pennell (ed.): *Bandits at Sea: A Pirates Reader*, 169–94. New York and London: New York University Press, 2001.

Bueger, Christian. ' "Ocean Shield" Achieved its Mission'. *The Maritime Executive*, 2 January 2017. https://www.maritime-executive.com/blog/ocean-shield-achieved-its-mission (accessed 2 December 2018).

Burg, B.R. *Sodomy and the Pirate Tradition: English Sea Rovers in the Seventeenth-Century Caribbean*. New York and London: New York University Press, 1995.

Burgess, Glyn S. *Two Medieval Outlaws: Eustace the Monk and Fouke Fitz Waryn*. Cambridge: D.S. Brewer, 1997.

Buzan, Barry and Amitav Acharya (eds). *Non-Western International Relations Theory: Perspectives on and Beyond Asia*. London and New York: Routledge, 2010.

Buzan, Barry and Richard Little. *International Systems in World History: Remaking the Study of International Relations*. New York: Oxford University Press, 2000.

Cabell, Craig, Graham A. Thomas and Allan Richards. *Blackbeard. The Hunt for the World's Most Notorious Pirate*. Barnsley: Pen & Sword Books, 2012.

Campbell, Penny. 'A Modern History of the International Legal Definition of Piracy', in Bruce A. Elleman, Andrew Forbes and David Rosenberg (eds): *Piracy and Maritime Crime: Historical and Modern Case Studies*, 19–32. Newport, RI: Naval War College Press, 2010.

Cannon, Henry L. 'The Battle of Sandwich and Eustache the Monk'. *English Historical Review*, vol. 27, issue 108 (1912), 649–70.

Capp, Bernard. 'Whetstone, Sir Thomas'. *Oxford Dictionary of National Biography*. Oxford: Oxford University Press, 2004; online at www.oxforddnb.com/view/article/51090 (accessed 2 December 2018).

Casson, Lionel. *Ships and Seafaring in Ancient Times*. London: British Museum Press, 1994.

Chakma, Anurag. 'Maritime Piracy in Bangladesh'. *International Policy Digest*, 24 June 2014; online at http://www.internationalpolicydigest.org/2014/06/24/maritime-piracy-bangladesh/ (accessed 2 December 2018).

Chakrabarty, Dipesh. *Provincializing Europe*. Princeton, NJ: Princeton University Press, 2000.

Chalk, Peter. *Grey-Area Phenomena in Southeast Asia: Piracy, Drug Trafficking and Political Terrorism*. Canberra Papers on Strategy and Defence, no. 123, 1997.

Chase, Kenneth. *Firearms. A Global History to 1700*. Cambridge: Cambridge University Press, 2003.

Chauvel, Richard. *Nationalists, Soldiers and Separatists: The Ambonese Islands from Colonialism to Revolt 1880–1950*. Leiden: Koninklijk Instituut voor Taal-, Land-, en Volkenkunde, 1990 (2nd edition).

Childs, David. *Pirate Nation: Elizabeth I and Her Royal Sea Rovers*. Barnsley: Seaforth Publishing, 2014.

Chin, James K. 'Merchants, Smugglers, and Pirates: Multinational Clandestine Trade on the South China Coast, 1520–50', in Robert J. Antony (ed.): *Elusive Pirates, Pervasive Smugglers: Violence and Clandestine Trade in the Greater China Seas*, 43–57. Hong Kong: Hong Kong University Press, 2010.

Chomsky, Noam. *Pirates & Emperors: International Terrorism in the Real World*. Brattleboro, VT: Amana Books, 1990.

Christensen, Arne Emil. 'Ships and Navigation', in William W. Fitzhugh and Elisabeth I. Ward (eds): *Vikings: The North Atlantic Saga*, 86–97. Washington, DC and London: Smithsonian Institution Press in association with National Museum of Natural History, 2000.

Cigar, Norman. *The Jihadist Maritime Strategy: Waging a Guerrilla War at Sea*. Middle East Studies Monograph 8. Quantico, VA: Marine Corps University, May 2017; online at https://www.hsdl.org/?abstract&did=800948 (accessed 2 December 2018).

Clarke, Ronald and Derek Cornish. 'Modeling Offenders' Decisions: A Framework for Research and Policy'. *Crime and Justice: An Annual Review of Research*, vol. 6 (1985), 147–85.

Clements, Jonathan. *Coxinga and the Fall of the Ming Dynasty*. Phoenix Mill: Sutton Publishing, 2005.

Clements, William H. *Towers of Strength: Martello Towers Worldwide.* London: Pen & Sword, 1998.

Coffen-Smout, Scott. 'Pirates, Warlords and Rogue Fishing Vessels in Somalia's Unruly Seas'. *Chebucto Community Net,* undated. http://www.chebucto.ns.ca/~ar120/somalia.html (accessed 2 December 2018).

Colás, Alejandro and Bryan Mabee (eds). *Mercenaries, Pirates, Bandits and Empires: Private Violence in Historical Context.* London: Hurst & Company, 2010.

Collier, Paul and Anke Hoeffler. 'Greed and Grievance in Civil War'. Policy Research Working Paper 2355. The World Bank Development Research Group, May 2000; online at http://documents.worldbank.org/curated/en/359271468739530199/pdf/multi-page.pdf (accessed 2 December 2018).

Collis, Maurice. *Siamese White.* London: Faber and Faber, 1936.

Combined Maritime Forces. 'CTF 151: Counter-piracy'. *Combined Maritime Forces* (CMF), undated. https://combinedmaritimeforces.com/ctf–151-counter-piracy/ (accessed 2 December 2018).

— 'Singapore Takes Command of Counter Piracy Combined Task Force 151'. *Combined Maritime Forces* (CMF), 1 July 2018. https://combinedmaritimeforces.com/2018/07/01/singapore-takes-command-of-counter-piracy-combined-task-force–151/ (accessed 2 December 2018).

Connett, David. 'Robot Ships to Transform Life on the Ocean Waves'. *i Newspaper,* 3 June 2017; online at https://www.pressreader.com/uk/i-newspaper/20170603/282299615132458 (accessed 2 December 2018).

Conrad, Joseph. *The Rescue.* London: J.M. Dent and Sons, 1920.

Contreras, Alonso de. *The Adventures of Captain Alonso de Contreras: A 17th Century Journey.* Translated and annotated by Philip Dallas. New York: Paragon House, 1989 (originally published 1633).

Coote, Stephen. *Drake: The Life and Legend of an Elizabethan Hero.* London: Simon & Schuster, 2003.

Corbett, Julian S. *England in the Mediterranean: A Study of the Rise and Influence of British Power within the Straits 1603–1713,* vol. 1. London, New York and Bombay: Longmans, Green, and Co., 1904.

Cordingly, David. *Life Among the Pirates: The Romance and the Reality.* London: Abacus, 2011.

— *Pirate Hunter of the Caribbean: The Adventurous Life of Captain Woodes Rogers.* New York: Random House, 2012.

Cordingly, David (ed.). *Pirates. Terror on the High Seas – From the Caribbean to the South China Sea.* East Bridgewater, MA: World Publications Group, 2007.

Croft, Adrian. 'World Must Not Let up Pressure on Somali Pirates – NATO'. *Reuters,* 17 December 2017; online at http://uk.reuters.com/article/2012/12/17/uk-somalia-piracy-idUKBRE8BG10U20121217 (accessed 2 December 2018).

Dampier, William. *A New Voyage Round the World: Describing Particularly . . .* London: James Knapton, 1697–1703 (3 vols; e-book).

Davies, Wendy (ed.). *From the Vikings to the Normans* (The Short Oxford History of the British Islands Series). Oxford: Oxford University Press, 2003.

Davis, Ralph. *The Rise of the English Shipping Industry in the Seventeenth and Eighteenth Centuries.* London: Macmillan & Co., 1962.

de Bry, John. 'Christopher Condent's *Fiery Dragon*', in Russell K. Skowronek and Charles R. Ewen (eds): *X Marks the Spot: The Archaeology of Piracy,* 100–30. Gainesville, FL: University Press of Florida, 2006.

Defoe, Daniel. *A General History of the Pyrates.* Edited and with a new postscript by Manuel Schonhorn. Mineola, NY: Dover Publications, 1999 (originally published 1724).

Dermigny, Louis. *La Chine et l'Occident. Le Commerce à Canton au XVIIIe siècle, 1719–1833. Tome 1.* Paris: S.E.V.P.E.N, 1964 (4 vols).

Diaz de Gamez, Gutierre. *The Unconquered Knight: A Chronicle of the Deeds of Don Pero Niño, Count of Buelna.* Woodbridge: Boydell Press, 2004 (reprint of the 1928 edition, original manuscript *c.* 1449).

Dickson, Caitlin. 'The Pirate Negotiator'. *Daily Beast*, 14 November 2013; online at http://www.thedailybeast.com/articles/2013/11/14/the-pirate-negotiator.html (accessed 2 December 2018).

Dow, George F. and John H. Edmonds. *The Pirates of the New England Coast 1630–1730*. Mineola, NY: Dover Publications, 1996 (originally published 1923).

Downing, Clement. *A Compendious History of the Indian Wars; with an Account of the Rise, Progress, Strength, and Forces of Angria the Pirate*. London: T.C. Cooper, 1737.

Dreyer, Edward L. *Zheng He: China and the Oceans in the Early Ming Dynasty – 1405–1433*. New York: Pearson Longman, 2007.

Dugaw, Dianne. *Warrior Women and Popular Balladry, 1650–1850*. Cambridge: Cambridge University Press, 1989.

Duguay-Trouin, René. *Les campagnes de Monsieur Duguay-Trouin: descrites et illustrées pour servir l'instruction des Jeunes Marins du Roy*. Paris: Le Gouaz, undated (reprinted 1957).

Dutton, Yvonne M. 'Maritime Piracy and the Impunity Gap: Domestic Implementation of International Treaty Provisions', in Michael J. Struett, John D. Carlson and Mark T. Nance (eds): *Maritime Piracy and the Construction of Global Governance*, 71–95. London and New York: Routledge, 2013.

Earl, George Windsor. *The Eastern Seas: Or, Voyages and Adventures in the Indian Archipelago, in 1832–33–34, Comprising a Tour of the Island of Java – Visits to Borneo, the Malay Peninsula, Siam . . .* London: Wm H. Allen and Co., 1837 (Ulan Press OCR manuscript).

Earle, Peter. *Corsairs of Malta and Barbary*. London: Sidgwick & Jackson, 1970.

— *The Sack of Panama*. London: Jill Norman & Hobhouse, 1981.

— *The Pirate Wars*. London: Methuen, 2004.

Ebert, Frank. 'Deutschland macht Seeräubern den Prozess'. *Legal Tribune Online*, 22 November 2010; online at https://www.lto.de/recht/hintergruende/h/moderne-piraterie-deutschland-macht-seeraeubern-den-prozess/ (accessed 2 December 2018).

The Economist. 'When Pirates Are Not So Bold'. 6 October 1984.

Eichstaedt, Peter. *Pirate State: Inside Somalia's Terrorism at Sea*. Chicago, IL: Lawrence Hill Books, 2010.

Eickhoff, Ekkehard. 'Maritime Defence of the Carolingian Empire', in Rudolf Simek and Ulrike Engel (eds): *Vikings on the Rhine: Recent Research on Early Medieval Relations between the Rhinelands and Scandinavia*, 51–64. Vienna: Fassbaender, 2004.

Ekin, Des. *The Stolen Village: Baltimore and the Barbary Pirates*. Dublin: The O'Brien Press, 2008.

Eklöf, Stefan. *Pirates in Paradise: A Modern History of Southeast Asia's Maritime Marauders*. Copenhagen: NIAS Press, 2006.

Elleman, Bruce A., Andrew Forbes and David Rosenberg. 'Introduction', in Bruce A. Elleman, Andrew Forbes and David Rosenberg (eds): *Piracy and Maritime Crime. Historical and Modern Case Studies*, 1–18. Naval War College Newport Papers 35. Newport, RI: Naval War College Press, 2010.

Englert, Anton and Athena Trakadas (eds). *Wulfstan's Voyage: The Baltic Sea region in the Early Viking Age as Seen from Shipboard*. Roskilde: Viking Ship Museum, 2009.

EU NAVFOR. *Media Information: EU Naval Operation Against Piracy*, 10 April 2012; online at http://eunavfor.eu/wp-content/uploads/2012/04/20120410_EUNAVFOR_Media_Brochure.pdf (accessed 2 December 2018).

— 'Mission'. Undated. https://eunavfor.eu/mission/ (accessed 2 December 2018).

Exquemelin, Alexandre. *Bucaniers of America, or, A true Account of the Most Remarkable Assaults Committed of Late Years upon the Coasts of the West-Indies by the Bucaniers of Jamaica and Tortuga, both English and French*. London: William Crooke, 1684.

Fa-Hsien. *The Travels of Fa-Hsien (399–414 AD), or Record of the Buddhistic Kingdoms: Re-translated by H.A. Giles, M.A.* Cambridge: Cambridge University Press, 1923.

Farris, William Wayne. *Heavenly Warriors: The Evolution of Japan's Military, 500–1300*. Cambridge, MA and London: Harvard University Press, 1995.

Fenton, James. 'Sailing By: James Fenton on Sex Slavery on the High Seas'. *Guardian*, 25 February 2006; online at http://www.theguardian.com/books/2006/feb/25/featuresreviews.guardianreview34 (accessed 2 December 2018).

Fernández-Armesto, Felipe. *Civilizations: Culture, Ambition, and the Transformation of Nature*. New York: The Free Press, 2001.

Fitzhugh, William W. and Elisabeth I. Ward (eds). *Vikings: The North Atlantic Saga*. Washington, DC and London: Smithsonian Institution Press in association with National Museum of Natural History, 2000.

Foote, Peter and David M. Wilson. *The Viking Achievement: The Society and Culture of Early Medieval Scandinavia*. London: Sidgwick & Jackson, 1970.

Foreign and Commonwealth Office (UK) and Rt Hon Alistair Burt MP. 'International action against piracy', 21 January 2013; online at https://www.gov.uk/government/speeches/international-action-against-piracy (accessed 2 December 2018).

Forte, Angelo, Richard Oram and Frederik Pedersen. *Viking Empires*. Cambridge: Cambridge University Press, 2005.

Frank, Roberta. 'Viking Atrocity and Skaldic Verse: The Rite of the Blood Eagle'. *English Historical Review*, vol. 99, no. 391 (April 1984), 332–43.

Frécon, Eric. 'Piracy and Armed Robbery at Sea along the Malacca Straits: Initial Impressions from Fieldwork in the Riau Islands', in Graham G. Ong-Webb (ed.): *Piracy, Maritime Terrorism, and Securing the Malacca Straits*, 68–83. Singapore: ISEAS, 2006.

Freeman, Donald B. *The Straits of Malacca: Gateway or Gauntlet?* Montreal: McGill-Queens University Press, 2003.

Fremont-Barnes, Gregory. *The Wars of the Barbary Pirates: To the Shores of Tripoli – The Rise of the US Navy and Marines*. Oxford: Osprey Publishing, 2006.

Gardiner, Robert (ed.). *The Heyday of Sail: The Merchant Sailing Ship 1650–1830*. London: Brassey's/Conway Maritime Press, 1995.

gCaptain. 'Chemical Tanker Attacked by Pirates Off Somalia'. 23 February 2018. https://gcaptain.com/chemical-tanker-attacked-by-pirates-off-somalia/ (accessed 2 December 2018).

Geiss, Robin and Anna Petrig. *Piracy and Armed Robbery at Sea: The Legal Framework for Counter-Piracy Operations in Somalia and the Gulf of Aden*. Oxford and New York: Oxford University Press, 2011.

Ghee, Lim Teck. 'Conflict over Natural Resources in Malaysia: The Struggle of Small-Scale Fishermen', in Lim Teck Ghee and Mark J. Valencia (eds): *Conflict over Natural Resources in South-East Asia and the Pacific*, 145–81. Singapore: Oxford University Press, 1990.

Giddens, Anthony. *A Contemporary Critique of Historical Materialism*, vol. 2: *The Nation-State and Violence*. Berkeley and Los Angeles, CA: University of California Press, 1985.

Glete, Jan (ed.). *Naval History 1500–1680*. Aldershot: Ashgate, 2005.

Glüsing, Jens, Udo Ludwig and Wieland Wagner. 'Regelrecht abgeschlachtet', *Der Spiegel* 34, 20 August 2001, 68–74.

Gordon, Stewart. *The Marathas 1600–1818*. (The New Cambridge History of India, vol. 2/4). Cambridge: Cambridge University Press, 1993.

Gosse, Philip. *The Pirates' Who's Who: Giving Particulars of the Lives & Deaths of the Pirates & Buccaneers*. New York: Burt Franklin, 1924; online at http://www.gutenberg.org/files/19564/19564-h/19564-h.htm (accessed 2 December 2018).

— *The History of Piracy*. New York: Tudor Publishing Company, 1932.

Gould, Harry D. 'Cicero's Ghost: Rethinking the Social Construction of Piracy', in Michael J. Struett, John D. Carlson and Mark T. Nance (eds): *Maritime Piracy and the Construction of Global Governance*, 23–46. London and New York: Routledge, 2013.

Griggs, Mary Beth. 'Robot Ships and Pepper Spray: The Latest in Pirate-Fighting Tech'. *Smithsonian.com SmartNews*, 13 October 2014; online at https://www.smithsonianmag.com/smart-news/robot-ships-and-pepper-spray-latest-pirate-fighting-tech-180953000 (accessed 2 December 2018).

Guilmartin Jr, John F. *Galleons and Galleys*. London: Cassell & Co., 2002.

Hajari, Nisid. 'Bungles in the Jungle'. *Time*, 11 September 2000. http://content.time.com/time/world/article/0,8599,2039805,00.html (accessed 2 December 2018).

Hakluyt, Richard. *The Principal Navigations, Voyages, Traffiques & Discoveries of the English Nation, made by Sea or Over Land*. London: George Bishop and Ralph Newberie, 1589 (e-book).

Halsall, Paul. 'Abbo's Wars of Count Odo with the Northmen in the Reign of Charles the Fat'. Medieval Sourcebook. New York: Fordham University, 2011; online at http://www.fordham.edu/halsall/source/843bertin.asp#abbo (accessed 2 December 2018).

Hamilton, Donny. 'Pirates and Merchants: Port Royal, Jamaica', in Russell K. Skowronek and Charles R. Ewen (eds): *X Marks the Spot: The Archaeology of Piracy*, 13–30. Gainesville, FL: University Press of Florida, 2006.

Hampden, John (ed.). *Francis Drake, Privateer: Contemporary Narratives and Documents*. London: Eyre Methuen, 1972.

Hansen, Magnus Boding. 'The Somali Pirates are Back (SPOILER ALERT: They Never Really Left)'. *IRIN News*, 19 July 2017; online at http://www.irinnews.org/feature/2017/07/19/somali-pirates-are-back-spoiler-alert-they-never-really-left (accessed 2 December 2018).

Hastings, Justin V. 'Geographies of State Failure and Sophistication in Maritime Piracy Hijackings'. *Political Geography*, vol. 28, issue 4 (2009), 213–23.

Hawkins, Richard. *The observations of Sir Richard Havvkins Knight, in his voyage into the South Sea. Anno Domini 1593* [electronic book]. London: Printed by I[ohn] D[awson] for Iohn Iaggard, and are to be sold at his shop at the Hand and the Starre in Fleete-streete, neere the Temple Gate, 1622.

Haywood, Robert and Roberta Spivak. *Maritime Piracy*. London and New York: Routledge, 2012.

Hebb, David D. *Piracy and the English Government, 1616–1642*. Aldershot: Scolar Press, 1994.

Hedeager, Lotte. 'From Warrior to Trade Economy', in William W. Fitzhugh and Elisabeth I. Ward (eds): *Vikings: The North Atlantic Saga*, 84–5. Washington, DC and London: Smithsonian Institution Press in association with National Museum of Natural History, 2000.

Heers, Jacques. *The Barbary Corsairs: Warfare in the Mediterranean, 1480–1580*. London: Greenhill Books, 2003.

Heinsius, Paul. *Das Schiff der Hansischen Frühzeit*. Weimar: Verlag Hermann Böhlaus Nachfolger, 1956.

Heinze, Eric H. 'A "Global War on Piracy"? International Law and the Use of Force against Sea Pirates', in Michael J. Struett, John D. Carlson and Mark T. Nance (eds): *Maritime Piracy and the Construction of Global Governance*, 47–70. London and New York: Routledge, 2013.

Hellyer, Robert. 'Poor but Not Pirates: The Tsushima Domain and Foreign Relations in Early Modern Japan', in Robert J. Antony (ed): *Elusive Pirates, Pervasive Smugglers. Violence and Clandestine Trade in the Greater China Seas*, 115–26. Hong Kong: Hong Kong University Press, 2010.

Herbert-Burns, Rupert. 'Compound Piracy at Sea in the Early Twenty-First Century: A Tactical to Operational-Level Perspective on Contemporary, Multiphase Piratical Methodology', in Peter Lehr (ed.): *Violence at Sea. Piracy in the Age of Global Terrorism*, 95–120. London and New York: Routledge, 2011 (paperback edition).

Higgins, Roland L. 'Pirates in Gowns and Caps: Gentry Law-Breaking in the Mid-Ming'. *Ming Studies*, vol. 1980, no. 1 (1980), 30–7.

Hill, John E. *Through the Jade Gate to Rome: A Study of the Silk Routes during the Later Han Dynasty, 1st to 2nd Centuries CE*. Charleston, SC: Book Surge Publishing, 2009.

Hobsbawm, Eric. *Bandits*. London: Abacus, 2012 (reprint).

Hollander, Lee. *Heimskringla: History of the Kings of Norway*. Austin, TX: University of Texas Press, 2009 (7th edition).

Hourani, George F. *Arab Seafaring in the Indian Ocean in Ancient and Early Medieval Times*. Princeton, NJ: Princeton University Press, 1995.

Hreinsson Viðar et al. (eds). *The Complete Sagas of Icelanders: Including 49 Tales*. Reykjavík: Leifur Eiríksson, 1997.

Hucker, Charles O. 'Hu Tsung-hien's Campaign against Hsu Hai', in Frank A. Kiernan Jr and John K. Fairbank (eds): *Chinese Ways in Warfare*, 273–311. Cambridge: Cambridge University Press, 1974.

Hunter, Robyn. 'Somali Pirates Living the High Life'. BBC, 28 October 2008; online at http://news.bbc.co.uk/1/hi/world/africa/7650415.stm (accessed 2 December 2018).

Huntingford, George W.B (trans. and ed.). *The Periplus of the Erythraean Sea, by an Unknown Author, with Some Extracts from Agatharkhides 'On the Erythraean Sea'*. London: Hakluyt Society, 1980.

Hympendahl, Klaus. *Pirates Aboard! 40 Cases of Piracy Today and what Bluewater Cruisers Can Do About It*. Dobbs Ferry, NY: Sheridan House, 2003.

IMO. *Djibouti Code of Conduct. Project Implementation Unit*. Maritime Safety Division, June 2011–January 2012; online at http://www.imo.org/en/OurWork/Security/PIU/Documents/PIU_Brochure_1st_edition.pdf (accessed 2 December 2018).

— *Somali Piracy Warning for Yachts*, 2013; online at http://www.imo.org/en/OurWork/Security/PiracyArmedRobbery/Guidance/NonIMO%20Oiracy%20Guidance/Yachting%20Piracy%20Bulletin%20Final%20Version.pdf (accessed 2 December 2018).

Isenberg, David. 'The Rise of Private Maritime Security Companies'. *Huffpost Business*, 29 July 2012; online at http://www.huffingtonpost.com/david-isenberg/private-military-contractors_b_1548523.html (accessed 2 December 2018).

iWitness News. 'Murder of German Sailor "Another Nail" in St. Vincent's "Economic Coffin" '. 7 March 2016. https://www.iwnsvg.com/2016/03/07/murder-of-german-sailor-another-nail-in-st-vincents-economic-coffin/ (accessed 2 December 2018).

Jameson, John Franklin. *Privateering and Piracy in the Colonial Period*. New York: August M. Kelly Publishers, 1970 (reprint of the 1923 edition; e-book).

Jamieson, Alan G. *Lords of the Sea: A History of the Barbary Corsairs*. London: Reaktion Books, 2012.

Jensen, Richard Bach (2001): 'The United States, International Policing and the War against Anarchist Terrorism, 1900–1914', *Terrorism and Political Violence*, vol. 13, no. 1 (Spring 2001), 15–46.

Jimoh, Akinsola. 'Maritime Piracy and Lethal Violence Offshore in Nigeria'. IFRA-Nigeria Working Papers Series, no. 51, 30 June 2015; online at http://www.nigeriawatch.org/media/html/WP2Jimoh.pdf (accessed 2 December 2018).

Johnson, Charles. *A General History of the Pyrates*. Edited and with a new postscript by Manuel Schonhorn. Mineola, NY: Dover Publications, 1999 (original manuscript 1724).

Kaiser, Wolfgang and Guillaume Calafat. 'Violence, Protection and Commerce: Corsairing and *Ars Piratica* in the Early Modern Mediterranean', in Stefan Eklöf Amirell and Leos Müller (eds): *Persistent Piracy: Maritime Violence and State-Formation in Global Historical Perspective*, 69–92. London: Palgrave Macmillan, 2014.

Kamal-Deen, Ali. 'The Anatomy of Gulf of Guinea Piracy'. *Naval War College Review*, vol. 68, no. 1 (Winter 2015).

Karraker, Cyrus H. *Piracy Was a Business*. Rindge, NH: Richard R. Smith, 1953.

Kashubsky, Mikhail. 'Offshore Energy Force Majeure: Nigeria's Local Problem with Global Consequences'. *Maritime Studies*, issue 160 (2008), 20–6.

Keay, John. *The Honourable Company: A History of the English East India Company*. London: HarperCollins, 1993.

Keen, Maurice. *The Outlaws of Medieval Legend*. London: Routledge & Kegan Paul, 1987.

Kelly, Thomas E. 'Eustache the Monk', in Thomas H. Ohlgren (ed.): *Medieval Outlaws*, 61–98. Phoenix Mill: Sutton Publishers, 1998.

Kelsey, Harry. *Sir Francis Drake. The Queen's Pirate*. New Haven and London: Yale University Press, 2000.

Kennedy, Hugh. *Mongols, Huns and Vikings: Nomads at War*. London: Cassell, 2002.

Keppel, Henry. *The Expedition to Borneo of H.M.S. Dido: The Royal Navy, Rajah Brooke and the Malay Pirates & Dyak Head-Hunters, 1843 – Two Volumes in 1 Special Edition*. Driffield: Leonaur, 2010 (original manuscript 1843).

Klausmann, Ulrike, Marion Meinzerin and Gabriel Kuhn. *Women Pirates and the Politics of the Jolly Roger*. Montreal, New York and London: Black Rose Books, 1997.

Koburger, Charles W. 'Selamat Datang, Kapitan: Post-World War II Piracy in the South China Sea', in Bruce A. Elleman, Andrew Forbes and David Rosenberg (eds): *Piracy and Maritime Crime: Historical and Modern Case Studies*, 65–77. Newport, RI: Naval War College Press, 2010.

Koester, Thomas. 'Human Error in the Maritime Working Domain'. Danish Maritime Institute, undated.

Koh, Jeremy. 'Drop in piracy in regional waters'. *The Straits Times*, 20 September 2016. https://www.straitstimes.com/singapore/drop-in-piracy-in-regional-waters (accessed 2 December 2018).

Konrad, John. 'The Protector: Anti Piracy Robot'. *gCaptain*, 10 December 2007; online at http://gcaptain.com/the-protector-anti-piracy-robot/ (accessed 2 December 2018).

Konstam, Angus. *The History of Pirates*. Guilford, CO: Lyons Press, 2002.

— *Blackbeard: America's Most Notorious Pirate*. Hoboken, NJ: John Wiley & Sons, 2006.

Kontorovich, Eugene. ' "A Guantanamo on the Sea": The Difficulty of Prosecuting Pirates and Terrorists'. *California Law Review*, issue 98 (2010), 243–76.

Kotiuk, Krzysztof. *'Frohe Ostern Hansa Stavanger': 121 Tage in der Hand von Piraten*. Hamburg: Delius Klasing, 2010.

Kraska, James. *Contemporary Maritime Piracy: International Law, Strategy, and Diplomacy at Sea*. Santa Barbara, CA, Denver, CO and Oxford: Praeger, 2011.

Kuhlmann, Jeffrey. 'Piracy: Understanding the Real Threat'. *Counterterrorism: Journal of Counterterrorism and Homeland Security International*, vol. 15, no. 4 (Winter 2009/2010): 36.

Lambert, Andrew. 'The Limits of Naval Power: The Merchant Brigg *Three Sisters*, Riff Pirates, and British Battleships', in Bruce A. Elleman, Andrew Forbes and David Rosenberg (eds): *Piracy and Maritime Crime: Historical and Modern Case Studies*, 173–90. Naval War College Newport Papers 35. Newport, RI: Naval War College Press, 2010.

Lambert, Frank. *The Barbary Wars: American Independence in the Atlantic World*. New York: Hill and Wang, 2005.

Lane, Frederic C. 'Venetian Merchant Galleys, 1300–1334: Private and Communal Operation'. *Speculum: A Journal of Medieval Studies*, vol. 38, no. 2 (April 1963), 179–205.

Lane, Kris E. *Blood and Silver: A History of Piracy in the Caribbean and Central America*. Oxford: Signal Books, 1999.

Lane-Poole, Stanley. *The Story of the Barbary Corsairs*. General Books, 2009 (originally published 1891).

Leeson, Peter T. *The Invisible Hook. The Hidden Economics of Pirates*. Princeton, NJ and Oxford: Princeton University Press, 2009.

Le Golif, Louis Adhemar Timotheé. *The Memoirs of a Buccaneer; Being the Wondrous and Unrepentant Account of the Prodigious Adventures and Amours of King Louis XVI's Loyal Servant Louis Adhemar Timotheé Le Golif, Told by Himself*. London: Allen & Unwin, 1954.

Lehr, Peter. 'Maritime Piracy as a US Foreign Policy Problem', in Ralph G. Carter (ed.): *Contemporary Cases in US Foreign Policy: From Terrorism to Trade*, 200–28. Washington, DC: CQ Press, 2011 (4th edition).

—'Somali Piracy and International Crime', in Emma Leonard and Gilbert Ramsay (eds): *Globalizing Somalia: Multilateral, International, and Transnational Repercussions of Conflict*, 116–37. London and New York: Bloomsbury, 2013.

Lehr, Peter and Hendrick Lehmann. 'Somalia: Pirates' New Paradise', in Peter Lehr (ed.): *Violence at Sea: Piracy in the Age of Global Terrorism*, 1–22. London and New York: Routledge, 2011.

Leur, Jacob Cornelis van. 'On Early Asian Trade', in Jacob C. van Leur: *Indonesian Trade and Society: Essays in Asian Social and Economic History*, 1–144. The Hague and Bandung: W. van Hove Publishers, 1955.

Levander, Oskar. 'Forget Autonomous Cars: Autonomous Ships Are Almost Here'. *IEEE Spectrum*, 28 January 2017; online at https://spectrum.ieee.org/transportation/marine/forget-autonomous-cars-autonomous-ships-are-almost-here (accessed 2 December 2018).

Levathes, Louise. *When China Ruled the Seas: The Treasure Fleet of the Dragon Throne, 1405–1433*. Oxford: Oxford University Press, 1996.

Lewis, Diane. 'The Growth of the Country Trade to the Straits of Malacca 1760–1777'. *Journal of the Malayan Branch of the Royal Asiatic Society (JMBRAS)*, vol. 43 (1970), 115–18.

Lilius, Aleko E. *I Sailed with Chinese Pirates*. Hong Kong: Earnshaw Books, 1930 (reprinted 2009).

Lim, Ivy M. 'From *Haijin* to *Kaihai:* The Jiajing Court's Search for a *Modus Operandi* along the South-Eastern Coast (1522–1567)'. *Journal of the British Association for Chinese Studies*, vol. 2 (July 2013), 1–26.

Liss, Carolin. 'Maritime Piracy in Southeast Asia'. *Southeast Asian Affairs* (2003), 52–68.

— 'The Challenges of Piracy in Southeast Asia and the Role of Australia'. *APSNet Policy Forum*, 25 October 2007; online at www.nautilus.org/apsnet/the-challenges-of-piracy-in-southeast-asia-and-the-role-of-australia/#axzz35qy1AaU9 (accessed 2 December 2018).

Little, Benerson. *The Sea Rover's Practice: Pirate Tactics and Techniques, 1630–1730*. Washington, DC: Potomac Books, 2007.

— *Pirate Hunting: The Fight Against Pirates, Privateers, and Sea Raiders from Antiquity to the Present*. Washington, DC: Potomac Books, 2010.

Lizé, Patrick. 'Piracy in the Indian Ocean: Mauritius and the Pirate Ship *Speaker*', in Russell K. Skowronek and Charles R. Ewen (eds): *X Marks the Spot: The Archaeology of Piracy*, 81–99. Gainesville, FL: University Press of Florida, 2006.

Lloyd, Christopher. *English Corsairs on the Barbary Coast*. London: Collins, 1981.

Loades, David. *England's Maritime Empire: Seapower, Commerce and Policy 1490–1690*. Harlow: Pearson Education, 2000.

Lunsford-Poe, Virginia West. *Piracy and Privateering in the Golden Age Netherlands*. New York and Basingstoke: Palgrave Macmillan, 2005.

Lupsha, Peter. 'Transnational Organized Crime versus the Nation-State'. *Transnational Organized Crime*, vol. 2, no. 1 (Spring 1996), 21–48.

Luttrell, Anthony. 'The Hospitallers at Rhodes, 1306–1421', in Harry W. Hazard (ed.): *A History of the Crusades*, vol. 3: *The Fourteenth and Fifteenth Centuries*, 278–313. Madison, WI: University of Madison Press, 1975.

Mabee, Brian. 'Pirates, Privateers and the Political Economy of Private Violence'. *Global Change, Peace & Security*, vol. 21, no. 2 (June 2009), 139–52.

Magnusson, Magnus. *Vikings!* London, Sydney and Toronto: The Bodley Head, 1980.

Mainwaring, Sir Henry. 'Of the Beginnings, Practices, and Suppression of Pirates', in G.E. Manwaring and W.G. Perrin: *The Life and Works of Sir Henry Mainwaring*, vol. 2, 3–52. London: Navy Records Society, 1922 (original manuscript 1617).

Mann, Michael. *The Sources of Social Power*, vol. 1: *A History of Power from the Beginning to AD 1760*. Cambridge, MA: Cambridge University Press, 2012 (new edition).

Manwaring, George E. (ed.). *The Life and Works of Sir Henry Mainwaring*, Volume I. London: Navy Records Society, 1920.

MAREX. 'Chinese Navy Hands Pirates Over to Somali Authorities'. *The Maritime Executive*, 8 May 2017. https://www.maritime-executive.com/article/chinese-navy-hands-pirates-over-to-somali-authorities (accessed 2 December 2018).

Maritime Foundation. 'Tackling piracy in the Gulf of Aden'. 28 October 2009. https://www.maritimefoundation.uk/2009/tackling-piracy-in-the-gulf-of-aden/ (accessed 2 December 2018).

Maritime Herald. 'Sinking of Very Large Ore Carrier *Stellar Daily* in South Atlantic Was Confirmed', 1 April 2017; online at http://www.maritimeherald.com/2017/sinking-of-very-large-ore-carrier-stellar-daily-in-south-atlantic-was-confirmed/ (accessed 2 December 2018).

Marley, David F. *Modern Piracy: A Reference Handbook*. Santa Barbara, CA: ABC-CLIO, 2011.

Marsden, John. *The Fury of the Northmen: Saints, Shrines and Sea-Raiders in the Viking Age, AD 793–878*. London: Kyle Cathie Ltd, 1996.

Marshall, Adrian G. *Nemesis: The First Iron Warship and Her World*. Singapore: Ridge Books, 2016.

Marx, Jenifer G. 'Brethren of the Coast', in David Cordingly (ed.): *Pirates. Terror on the High Seas – From the Caribbean to the South China Sea*, 36–57. East Bridgewater, MA: World Publications Group, 2007.

Marx, Robert F. *Port Royal: The Sunken City*. Southend-on-Sea: Aqua Press, 2003 (2nd edition).

Masefield, John. *On the Spanish Main. Or, Some English Forays on the Isthmus of Darien, with a Description of the Buccaneers and a Short Account of Old-Time Ships and Sailors*. London: Methuen & Co., 1906.

Matthew Paris, *Matthew Paris's English History from the Year 1235 to 1273*. Translated by J.A. Giles. London: Henry G. Bohn, 1852–4 (3 vols).

McDermott, James (ed.). *The Third Voyage of Martin Frobisher to Baffin Island, 1578*. London: Hakluyt Society, 2001.

MEBA. 'Don't Give Up the Ship! Quick Thinking and a Boatload of Know-How Saves the *Maersk Alabama*'. *MEBA Marine Officers Magazine* (Summer 2009); online at http://www.mebaunion.org/assets/1/6/The_Story_of_the_MAERSK_ALABAMA.PDF (accessed 2 December 2018).

Meier, Dirk. *Seafarers, Merchants and Pirates in the Middle Ages*. Woodbridge: The Boydell Press, 2006.

Miller, Harry. *Pirates of the Far East*. London: Robert Hale and Co., 1970.

Ministry of Foreign Affairs (Japan). *Regional Cooperation Agreement on Combating Piracy and Armed Robbery against Ships in Asia*. Tokyo: Ministry of Foreign Affairs, undated; online at http://www.mofa.go.jp/mofaj/gaiko/kaiyo/pdfs/kyotei_s.pdf (accessed 2 December 2018).

Mitchell, David. *Pirates*. London: Thames and Hudson, 1976.

Morris, Christopher. 'The Viking Age in Europe', in William W. Fitzhugh and Elisabeth I. Ward (eds): *Vikings: The North Atlantic Saga*, 99–102. Washington, DC and London: Smithsonian Institution Press in association with National Museum of Natural History, 2000.

MSC–HOA. 'The Maritime Security Centre – Horn of Africa (MSCHOA): Safeguarding trade through the High Risk Area'. *MSC HOA* 2018. https://on-shore.mschoa.org/about-mschoa/ (accessed 2 December 2018).

— *BMP 4: Best Management Practices for Protection against Somalia Based Piracy – Version 4 – August 2011*. Edinburgh: Witherby Publishing Group, 2011; online at http://eunavfor.eu/wp-content/uploads/2013/01/bmp4-low-res_sept_5_20111.pdf (accessed 2 December 2018).

Mueller, Gerhard O. W. and Freda Adler. *Outlaws of the Ocean: The Complete Book of Contemporary Crime on the High Seas*. New York: Hearst Marine Books, 1985.

MUNIN. 'MUNIN Results'. *Maritime Unmanned Navigation through Intelligence in Networks* (MUNIN). 2016. http://www.unmanned-ship.org/munin/about/munin-results-2/ (accessed 2 December 2018).

Murphy, Martin. 'The Troubled Waters of Africa: Piracy in the African Littoral'. *Journal of the Middle East and Africa*, vol. 2, no. 1 (2011), 65–83.

Murray, Dian. 'Cheng I Sao in Fact and Fiction', in C.R. Pennell (ed.): *Bandits at Sea: A Pirates Reader*, 253–82. New York and London: New York University Press, 2001.

Mwangura, Andrew. 'Somalia: Pirates or Protectors?' *AllAfrica.com*, 20 May 2010; online at http://allafrica.com/stories/201005200856.html (accessed 2 December 2018).

Nagourney, Adam and Jeffrey Gettleman. 'Pirates Brutally End Yachting Dream'. *New York Times*, 22 February 2011; online at http://www.nytimes.com/2011/02/23/world/africa/23pirates.html (accessed 2 December 2018).

NATO. 'Operation Ocean Shield'. November 2014. https://www.nato.int/nato_static_fl2014/assets/pdf/pdf_topics/141202a-Factsheet-OceanShield-en.pdf (accessed 2 December 2018).

NBC News. 'Four American Hostages Killed by Somali Pirates'. 22 February 2011; online at http://www.nbcnews.com/id/41715530/ns/world_news-africa/t/four-american-hostages-killed-somali-pirates/#.WgNOEq10d24 (accessed 26 September 2018).

Needham, Joseph. *Science and Civilisation in China*, vol. 4: *Physics and Physical Technology*, part 3: *Civil Engineering and Nautics*. Cambridge: Cambridge University Press, 1971.

NZ Herald. 'Sir Peter Blake Killed in Amazon Pirate Attack'. 7 December 2001; online at http://www.nzherald.co.nz/peter-blake–1948–2001/news/article.cfm?c_id=320&objectid=232024 (accessed 26 September 2018).

Oceans Beyond Piracy. 'Definition/classification of piracy'. Undated. http://oceansbeyondpiracy.org/sites/default/files/attachments/Piracy%20definition%20table.pdf (accessed 2 December 2018).

O'Kane, John (trans.). *The Ship of Sulaimān*. London: Routledge, 2008.

Ong-Webb, Gerard (ed.). *Piracy, Maritime Terrorism and Securing the Malacca Straits*. Singapore: ISEAS, 2006.

Oppenheim, M. *Naval Tracts of Sir William Monson in Six Books*. London: Navy Records Society, 1902–1914.

Ormerod, Henry A. *Piracy in the Ancient World: An Essay in Mediterranean History*. Baltimore, MD: The Johns Hopkins University Press, 1997 (originally published 1924).

Osinowo, Adeniyi A. 'Combating Piracy in the Gulf of Guinea'. *Africa Security Brief*, no. 30 (February 2015).

Padfield, Peter. *Guns at Sea*. London: Hugh Evelyn, 1973.

Palmer, Andrews. *The New Pirates: Modern Global Piracy from Somalia to the South China Sea*. London and New York: I.B. Tauris, 2014.

Pálsson, Hermann and Paul Edwards (trans.). *Orkneyinga Saga: The History of the Earls of Orkney*. London: Penguin Books, 1978.

Pandey, Sanjay. 'Pirates of the Bay of Bengal'. *Al Jazeera*, 16 September 2015; online at http://www.aljazeera.com/indepth/features/2015/09/pirates-bay-bengal–150914123258304.html (accessed 2 December 2018).

Panikkar, K.M. *Asia and Western Dominance: A Survey of the Vasco da Gama Epoch of Asian History, 1498–1945*. London: Allen & Unwin, 1953.

Parkinson, Cyril Northcote. *Britannia Rules: The Classic Age of Naval History, 1793–1815*. London: Weidenfeld & Nicolson, 1977.

Parthesius, Robert. *Dutch Ships in Tropical Waters: The Development of the Dutch East India Company (VOC) Shipping Network in Asia 1595–1660*. Amsterdam: Amsterdam University Press, 2010.

Pawson, Michael and David Buisseret. *Port Royal, Jamaica*. Oxford: Clarendon Press, 1975.

Pearlman, Jonathan. 'Cruise passengers Ordered to Switch off Lights and Music at Night to "Be Prepared for Pirate Attack" '. *Telegraph*, 8 August 2017; online at http://www.telegraph.co.uk/news/2017/08/08/cruise-passengers-ordered-switch-lights-music-night-prepared (accessed 2 December 2018).

Pennell, C.R. (ed.). *Bandits at Sea: A Pirates Reader*. New York and London: New York University Press, 2001.

Pérotin-Dumon, Anne. 'The Pirate and the Emperor: Power and the Law on the Seas, 1450–1850', in C.R. Pennell (ed.): *Bandits at Sea: A Pirates Reader*, 25–54. New York and London: New York University Press, 2001.

Pérouse de Montclos, Marc-Antoine. 'Maritime Piracy in Nigeria: Old Wine in New Bottles?' *Studies in Conflict & Terrorism*, vol. 35 (2012), 531–41.

Petrucci, Maria Grazia. 'Pirates, Gunpowder, and Christianity in Late Sixteenth-Century Japan', in Robert J. Antony (ed.): *Elusive Pirates, Pervasive Smugglers: Violence and Clandestine Trade in the Greater China Seas*, 59–71. Hong Kong: Hong Kong University Press, 2010.

Pflanz, Mike and Thomas Harding. 'Europe's Mainland Piracy Attack Will Escalate Conflict'. *Telegraph*, 15 May 2012; online at http://www.telegraph.co.uk/news/worldnews/piracy/9267522/Europes-mainland-piracy-attack-will-escalate-conflict.html (accessed 2 December 2018).

Phillips, Don, Damien Gayle and Nicola Slawson. ' "I Will Have My Boat Stolen": Final Days of British Kayaker killed in Brazil'. *Guardian*, 20 September 2017; online at https://www.theguardian.com/world/2017/sep/20/emma-kelty-british-kayaker-brazil (accessed 2 December 2018).

Phillips, Richard and Stephen Talty. *A Captain's Duty: Somali Pirates, Navy SEALs, and Dangerous Days at Sea*. New York: Hyperion Books, 2010.

Pires, Tomé. *The Suma Oriental of Tomé Pire. An Account of the East, From the Red Sea to Japan, Written in Malacca and India in 1512–1515*. London: Hakluyt Society, 1944 (2 vols).

Polo, Marco. *The Travels of Marco Polo*. Translated and with an introduction by Ronald Latham. London: Penguin Books, 1958.

Porter, Jonathan. *Macau, the Imaginary City: Culture and Society, 1557 to the Present*. Boulder, CO: Westview Press, 1999.

Preston, Diana and Michael Preston. *A Pirate of Exquisite Mind: The Life of William Dampier – Explorer, Naturalist and Buccaneer*. London: Corgi Books, 2005.

Pretty, Francis. 'The Admirable and Prosperous Voyage of the Worshipful Master Thomas Cavendish', in Edward John Payne (ed.): *Voyages of Elizabethan Seaman*, 343–404. Oxford: Clarendon Press, 1907.

Price, Neil. ' "Laid Waste, Plundered, and Burned" ', in William W. Fitzhugh and Elisabeth I. Ward (eds): *Vikings: The North Atlantic Saga*, 116–26. Washington, DC and London: Smithsonian Institution Press in association with National Museum of Natural History, 2000.

— 'Ship-Men and Slaughter-Wolves: Pirate Polities in the Viking Age', in Stefan Eklöf Amirell and Leos Müller (eds): *Persistent Piracy: Maritime Violence and State-Formation in Global Historical Perspective*, 51–68. London: Palgrave Macmillan, 2014.

Pryor, John H. *Geography, Technology, and War: Studies in the Maritime History of the Mediterranean, 649–1571*. Cambridge: Cambridge University Press, 1988.

Puhle, Matthias. *Die Vitalienbrüder. Klaus Störtebeker und die Seeräuber der Hansezeit*. Frankfurt and New York: Campus Verlag, 2012.

Rau, Reinhold (ed.). *Quellen zur karolingischen Reichsgeschichte. Regino Chronik*. Darmstadt: Wissenschaftliche Buchgesellschaft, 1960.

Raveneau de Lussan, Sieur. *A Journal of a Voyage Made into the South Sea, by the Bucaniers of Freebooters of America, from the Year 1684 to 1689*. London: Tho. Newborough, John Nicholson, and Benj. Tooke 1698 (e-book).

Rediker, Marcus. *Between the Devil and the Deep Blue Sea: Merchant Seamen, Pirates, and the Anglo-American Maritime World, 1700–1750*. Cambridge and New York: Cambridge University Press/Canto, 1993.

— 'Liberty beneath the Jolly Roger: The Lives of Anne Bonny and Mary Read, Pirates', in C.R. Pennell (ed.): *Bandits at Sea: A Pirates Reader*, 299–320. New York and London: New York University Press, 2001.

— *Villains of All Nations. Atlantic Piracy in the Golden Age*. London and New York: Verso, 2004.

— 'Libertalia: The Pirate's Utopia', in David Cordingly (ed.): *Pirates. Terror on the High Seas – From the Caribbean to the South China Sea*, 124–39. East Bridgewater, MA: World Publications Group, 2007 (reprint).

Reid, Antony. 'Violence at Sea: Unpacking "Piracy" in the Claims of States over Asian Seas', in Robert J. Antony (ed.): *Elusive Pirates, Pervasive Smugglers: Violence and Clandestine Trade in the Greater China Seas*, 15–26. Hong Kong: Hong Kong University Press, 2010.

Rider, David. 'NATO ends Ocean Shield'. *Maritime Security Review*, 15 December 2016; online at http://www.marsecreview.com/2016/12/nato-ends-ocean-shield/ (accessed 2 December 2018).

Riley-Smith, Jonathan. *Hospitallers: The History of the Order of St John*. London and Rio Grande: The Hambledon Press, 1999.

— *The Knights Hospitaller in the Levant*, c. *1070–1309*. London: Palgrave Macmillan, 2012.

Ringrose, Basil. *Bucaniers of America*, vol. 2. London: William Crooke, 1685.

Risso, Patricia. 'Cross-Cultural Perceptions of Piracy: Maritime Violence in the Western Indian Ocean and Persian Gulf Region during a Long Eighteenth Century'. *Journal of World History*, vol. 12, no. 2 (2001), 293–319.

Ritchie, Robert C. *Captain Kidd and the War against the Pirates*. New York: Barnes & Noble, 1989.

— 'Living with Pirates'. *Rethinking History*, vol. 13, no. 3 (2009), 411–18.

Roach, J. Ashley. 'Enhancing Maritime Security in the Straits of Malacca and Singapore', *Journal of International Affairs*, vol. 59, no. 1 (Fall/Winter 2005), 97–116.

Rogers, Woodes. *Life Aboard a British Privateer in the Times of Queen Anne: Being the Journal of Captain Woodes Rogers, Master Mariner – With Notes and Illustrations by Robert C. Leslie.* Honolulu, HI: University Press of the Pacific, 2004 (reprint of the 1889 edition).

Rogoziński, Jan. *Honor Among Thieves: Captain Kidd, Henry Every, and the Pirate Democracy in the Indian Ocean.* Mechanicsburg, PA: Stackpole Books, 2000.

Ronald, Susan. *The Pirate Queen: Queen Elizabeth I, Her Pirate Adventurers, and the Dawn of Empire.* New York: HarperCollins, 2008.

Ronzitti, Natalino. *The Law of Naval Warfare: A Collection of Agreements and Documents with Commentaries.* The Hague: Martinus Nijhoff, 1988.

Rossi, Ettore. 'The Hospitallers at Rhodes, 1421–1523', in Harry W. Hazard (ed.): *A History of the Crusades*, vol. 3, *The Fourteenth and Fifteenth Centuries*, 314–39. Madison, WI: University of Madison Press, 1975.

Rowse, Alfred Leslie. *Eminent Elizabethans.* Athens, GA: University of Georgia Press, 1983.

Rusby, Kevin. *Hunting Pirate Heaven: A Voyage in Search of the Lost Pirate Settlements of the Indian Ocean.* London: Constable, 2001.

Rutter, Owen. *The Pirate Wind: Tales of the Sea-Robbers of Malaya.* Oxford: Oxford University Press, 1986 (originally published 1930).

Sandars, N.K. *The Sea Peoples: Warriors of the Ancient Mediterranean 1250–1150 BC.* London: Thames and Hudson, 1978.

Sawyer, P.H. *Kings and Vikings.* London and New York: Routledge, 1996.

Saxo Grammaticus. *Gesta Danorum: The History of the Danes.* Edited by Karsten Friis-Jensen, translated by Peter Fisher. Oxford: Clarendon Press, 2015 (original manuscript *c.* 1218).

Sazvar, Nastaran. 'Zheng Chenggong (1624–1662): Ein Held im Wandel der Zeit. Die Verzerrung einer historischen Figur durch mythische Verklärung und politische Instrumentalisierung'. *Monumenta Serica*, vol. 58 (2010), 153–247.

Scammell, G.V. *The World Encompassed: The First European Maritime Empires c. 800–1650.* London and New York: Methuen, 1981.

Schuler, Mike. 'US to Drop Charges Against *CEC Future* Pirate Negotiator'. *gCaptain*, 10 February 2014; online at http://gcaptain.com/u-s-to-drop-charges-against-cec-future-pirate-negotiator (accessed 2 December 2018).

— 'Hong Kong-Flagged Bulk Carrier Attacked by Pirates Off Somalia'. *gCaptain*, 19 October 2018. https://gcaptain.com/hong-kong-flagged-bulk-carrier-attacked-by-pirates-off-somalia/ (accessed 2 December 2018).

Schuman, Michael. 'How to Defeat Pirates: Success in the Strait'. *Time*, 22 April 2009; online at http://content.time.com/time/world/article/0,8599,1893032,00.html (accessed 2 December 2018).

Schurz, William Lytle. *The Manila Galleon.* Manila: Historical Conservation Society, 1985.

Sellin, Paul R. *Treasure, Treason and the Tower: El Dorado and the Murder of Sir Walter Raleigh.* Farnham and Burlington, VT: Ashgate, 2011.

Senior, Clive. *A Nation of Pirates: English Piracy in its Heyday.* Newton Abbot: David & Charles, 1976.

Setton, Kenneth M. 'The Catalans in Greece, 1380–1462', in Harry W. Hazard (ed.): *A History of the Crusades*, vol. 3: *The Fourteenth and Fifteenth Centuries*, 167–224. Madison, WI: University of Madison Press, 1975.

Seward, Desmond. *The Monks of War.* London: Eyre Methuen, 1972.

Shapinsky, Peter D. 'Japanese Pirates and Sea Tenure in the Sixteenth Century Seto Inland Sea: A Case Study of the Murakami *Kaizoku*'. Paper presented at *Seascapes Conference Proceedings*, American Historical Association, 2003; online at http://webdoc.sub.gwdg.de/ebook/p/2005/history_cooperative/www.historycooperative.org/proceedings/seascapes/shapinsky.html (accessed 2 December 2018).

— 'From Sea Bandits to Sea Lords: Nonstate Violence and Pirate Identities in Fifteenth- and Sixteenth-Century Japan', in Robert J. Antony (ed.): *Elusive Pirates, Pervasive Smugglers: Violence and Clandestine Trade in the Greater China Seas*, 27–41. Hong Kong: Hong Kong University Press, 2010.

— *Lords of the Sea: Pirates, Violence, and Commerce in Late Medieval Japan* (Michigan Monograph Series in Japanese Studies Book 76). Ann Arbor, MI: Center for Japanese Studies, University of Michigan, 2014.

Shipping Position Online. 'SP Brussels Attack: Ship Owner Says No Crew Was Killed By Pirates'. 25 May 2014; online at http://shippingposition.com.ng/content/sp-brussels-attack-ship-owner-says-no-crew-was-killed-pirates (accessed 2 December 2018).

Sim, Y.H. Teddy. 'Studying Piracy and Surreptitious Activities in Southeast Asia in the Early Modern Period', in Y.H. Teddy Sim (ed.): *Piracy and Surreptitious Activities in the Malay Archipelago and Adjacent Seas, 1600–1840*, 1–17. Singapore: Springer, 2014.

Simeon of Durham. *A History of the Church of Durham*. Translated by Joseph Stephenson. Lampeter: Llanerch Enterprises, 1988 (facsimile reprint).

Simon, Sheldon W. 'Safety and Security in the Malacca Straits: The Limits of Collaboration'. *Asian Security*, vol. 7, issue 1 (2011), 27–43.

Sjoberg, Laura and Caron E. Gentry. *Mothers, Monsters, Whores: Women's Violence in Global Politics*. London: Zed, 2007.

Skowronek, Russell K. and Charles R. Ewen (eds). *X Marks the Spot. The Archaeology of Piracy*. Gainesville, FL: University Press of Florida, 2006.

Smith, John. *An Accidence for the Sea*. London: Benjamin Fisher, 1636 (e-book).

Smyth, Alfred P. 'The Effect of Scandinavian Raiders on the English and Irish Churches: A Preliminary Assessment', in Brendan Smith (ed.): *Britain and Ireland 900–1300: Insular Responses to Medieval European Change*, 1–38. Cambridge: Cambridge University Press, 1999.

Snelders, Stephen. *The Devil's Anarchy: The Sea Robberies of the Most Famous Pirate Claes G. Compaen – The Very Remarkable Travels of Jan Erasmus Reyning, Buccaneer*. Brooklyn, NY: Autonomedia, 2005.

Sofge, Erik. 'Robot Boats Hunt High-Tech Pirates on the High-Speed Seas'. *Popular Mechanics*, 30 October 2007; online at http://www.popularmechanics.com/military/navy-ships/a2234/4229443 (accessed 2 December 2018).

Somerville, Angus A. and R. Andrew McDonald (eds). *The Viking Age: A Reader*. Toronto: University of Toronto Press, 2010.

de Souza, Philip. *Piracy in the Graeco-Roman World*. Cambridge: Cambridge University Press, 1999.

— 'Piracy in Classical Antiquity: The Origins and Evolution of the Concept', in Stefan Eklöf Amirell and Leos Müller (eds): *Persistent Piracy: Maritime Violence and State-Formation in Global Historical Perspective*, 24–50. London: Palgrave Macmillan, 2014.

Spence, Richard T. *The Privateering Earl*. Stroud: Alan Sutton Publishing, 1995.

Spiegel Online. 'Mission Impossible: German Elite Troop Abandons Plan to Free Pirate Hostages'. 4 May 2009; online at http://www.spiegel.de/international/germany/mission-impossible-german-elite-troop-abandons-plan-to-free-pirate-hostages-a-622766.html (accessed 2 December 2018).

Stanton, Charles D. *Norman Naval Operations in the Mediterranean*. Woodbridge: The Boydell Press, 2011.

Starkey, David J. 'Voluntaries and Sea Robbers: A Review of the Academic Literature on Privateering, Corsairing, Buccaneering and Piracy'. *The Mariner's Mirror*, vol. 97, no. 1 (2011), 127–47.

Steensgaard, Niels. *The Asian Trade Revolution of the Seventeenth Century: The East India Companies and the Decline of the Caravan Trade*. Chicago, IL: University of Chicago Press, 1974.

Stewart, Douglas. *The Brutal Seas: Organised Crime at Work*. Bloomington, IN: AuthorHouse, 2006.

Strayer, Joseph R. *On the Medieval Origins of the Modern State*. Princeton, NJ: Princeton University Press, 1970.

Struett, Michel J., John D. Carlson and Mark T. Nance (eds). *Maritime Piracy and the Construction of Global Governance.* London and New York: Routledge, 2013.

Struys, Jan Janszoon. *The Voyages and Travels of John Struys through Italy, Greece, Muscovy, Tartary, Media, Persia, East-India, Japan, and other Countries in Europe, Africa and Asia.* London: Abel Swalle and Sam. Crowch, 1684 (e-book).

Subrahmanyam, Sanjay. *The Career and Legend of Vasco da Gama.* Cambridge: Cambridge University Press, 1997.

Sutton, Jean. *Lords of the East: The East India Company and its Ships (1600–1874).* London: Conway Maritime Press, 2000.

Taleb, Nassim Nicholas. *The Black Swan: The Impact of the Highly Improbable.* London: Penguin, 2010 (2nd edition).

Talty, Stephen. *Empire of Blue Water: Henry Morgan and the Pirates Who Ruled the Caribbean Waters.* London: Pocket Books, 2007.

Tarkawi, Barak. 'State and Armed Force in International Conflict', in Alejandro Colás and Bryan Mabee (eds): *Mercenaries, Pirates, Bandits and Empires: Private Violence in Historical Context,* 33–53. London: Hurst & Company, 2010.

Tarling, Nicholas. *Piracy and Politics in the Malay World: A Study of British Imperialism in Nineteenth-Century Southeast Asia.* Melbourne: F.W. Cheshire, 1963.

Teichmann, Fritz. *Die Stellung und Politik der hansischen Seestädte gegenüber den Vitalienbrüdern in den nordischen Thronwirren 1389–1400* (Inaugural Dissertation). Halle: Vereinigte Universität Halle-Wittenberg, 1931.

Telegraph. 'Russia Releases Pirates Because They "Too Expensive to Feed" '. 7 May 2010; online at http://www.telegraph.co.uk/news/worldnews/europe/russia/7690960/Russia-releases-pirates-because-they-too-expensive-to-feed.html (accessed 2 December 2018).

Tenenti, Alberto. *Piracy and the Decline of Venice, 1580–1615.* London: Longmans, Green and Co., 1967.

Thomson, Janice E. *Mercenaries, Pirates, and Sovereigns: State-Building and Extraterritorial Violence in Early Modern Europe.* Princeton, NJ: Princeton University Press, 1994.

Thorup, Mikkel. 'Enemy of Humanity: The Anti-Piracy Discourse in Present-Day Anti-Terrorism'. *Terrorism and Political Violence,* vol. 21, no. 3 (July–September 2011), 401–11.

Tiele, P.A. (ed.). *De Opkomst van het Nederlandsch gezag in Oost-Indië,* s'Gravenhage: Martinus Nijhoff, 1890; online at http://www.archive.org/stream/deopkomstvanhet06devegoog/deopkomstvanhet06devegoog_djvu.txt (accessed 2 December 2018).

Tinniswood, Adrian. *Pirates of Barbary.* London: Vintage Books, 2011.

Toussaint, Auguste. *Les Frères Surcouf.* Paris: Flammarion, 1919.

Tracy, Larissa. *Torture and Brutality in Medieval Literature: Negotiations of National Identity.* Cambridge: D.S. Brewer, 2012.

Triandafyllidou, Anna and Thanos Maroukis. *Migrant Smuggling: Irregular Migration from Asia and Africa to Europe.* London: Palgrave Macmillan.

Trocki, Carl A. *Prince of Pirates: The Temenggongs and the Development of Johor and Singapore 1784–1885.* Singapore: National University of Singapore Press, 2007 (2nd edition).

Turnbull, Stephen. *Fighting Ships of the Far East,* vol. 1: *China and Southeast Asia 202 BC–AD 1419* (New Vanguard Series 61). Oxford: Osprey Publishing, 2002.

— *Fighting Ships of the Far East,* vol. 2: *Japan and Korea AD 612–1639* (New Vanguard Series 63). Oxford: Osprey Publishing, 2003.

— *Pirate of the Far East, 811–1639.* (Warrior Series 125). Oxford: Osprey Publishing, 2007.

United Nations Division for Ocean Affairs and the Law of the Sea, 'Piracy Under International Law'. *Oceans & Law of the Sea.* New York: United Nations, 4 April 2012; online at http://www.un.org/depts/los/piracy/piracy.htm (accessed 2 December 2018).

United Nations Monitoring Group on Somalia and Eritrea. *Report of the Monitoring Group on Somalia and Eritrea.* New York: United Nations, 18 July 2011; online at http://www.un.org/ga/search/view_doc.asp?symbol=S/2011/433 (accessed 2 December 2018).

Unwin, Rayner. *The Defeat of John Hawkins: A Biography of His Third Slaving Voyage.* London: Allen & Unwin, 1960.

Van der Cruysse, Dirk. *Siam & the West, 1500–1700.* Chiang Mai: Silkworm Books, 2002.

Visiak, E.H. *Buccaneer Ballads.* London: Elkin Mathews, 1910.

Vitkus, Daniel J. (ed.). *Piracy, Slavery, and Redemption: Barbary Captivity Narratives from Early Modern England.* New York: Columbia University Press, 2001.

Wadhams, Nick. 'American Hostage Deaths: A Case of Pirate Anxiety'. *Time,* 23 February 2011; online at http://content.time.com/time/world/article/0,8599,2053344,00.html (accessed 2 December 2018).

Wang, Wensheng. *White Lotus Rebels and South China Pirates: Crisis and Reform in the Qing Empire.* Cambridge, MA and London: Cambridge University Press, 2014.

Ward, Edward. *A Trip to Jamaica: With a True Character of the People and Island – By the Author of Sot's Paradise.* London: J. How, 1700.

Warren, James Francis. 'The Sulu Zone: The World Capitalist Economy and the Historical Imagination'. *Comparative Asian Studies,* vol. 20 (1998).

— *Iranun and Balangingi. Globalization, Maritime Raiding and the Birth of Ethnicity.* Singapore: Singapore University Press, 2002.

—'A Tale of Two Centuries: The Globalisation of Maritime Raiding and Piracy in Southeast Asia at the End of the Eighteenth and Twentieth Centuries'. Asia Research Institute Working Paper Series no. 2 (June). Singapore: NUS, 2003.

— *The Sulu Zone 1768–1898: The Dynamics of External Trade, Slavery, and Ethnicity in the Transformation of a Southeast Asian Maritime State.* Singapore: NUS Press, 2007 (2nd edition).

Washington Times. 'Arming Sailors: Gun-Free Zones are Dangerous at Sea'. 11 May 2009; online at http://www.washingtontimes.com/news/2009/may/11/arming-sailors/ (accessed 2 December 2018).

Weber, Jacques. 'The Successor States (1739–61)', in Claude Markovits (ed.): *A History of Modern India, 1480–1950,* 187–207. London: Anthem Press, 2004.

Weber, Max. *The Theory of Social and Economic Organization.* Translated by A.M. Henderson and Talcott Parsons. Edited with an introduction by T. Parsons. New York: The Free Press, 1964.

Wees, Hans van. *Status Warriors: War, Violence and Society in Homer and History.* Amsterdam: J.C. Gieben, 1992.

Westberg, Andreas Bruvik. 'Bloodshed and Breaking Wave: The First Outbreak of Somali Piracy'. *Scientia Militaria, South African Journal of Military Studies,* vol. 43, no. 2 (2015) 1–38.

— 'Anti-Piracy in a Sea of Predation: The Interaction of Navies, Fishermen and Pirates off the Coast of Somalia'. *Journal of the Indian Ocean Region,* vol. 12, no. 2 (2016), 209–26.

Wheatley, Paul. *The Golden Khersonese: Studies in the Historical Geography of the Malay Peninsula before AD 1500.* Kuala Lumpur: University of Malaya Press, 1966.

Wheelan, Joseph. *Jefferson's War: America's First War on Terror 1801–1805.* New York: Carroll & Graf, 2003.

White, George. *Reflections on a Scandalous Paper, Entituled, The Answer of the East-India-Company to Two Printed Papers of Mr. Samuel White . . .* London: publisher not identified, 1689 (e-book).

Williams, Norman Lloyd. *Sir Walter Raleigh.* London: Eyre & Spottiswoode, 1962.

Willson, David Harris. *King James VI and I.* London: Jonathan Cape, 1956.

Wilson, Ben. *Empire of the Deep: The Rise and Fall of the British Navy.* London: Weidenfeld & Nicolson, 2013.

Wilson, Peter Lamborn. *Pirate Utopias: Moorish Corsairs & European Renegadoes.* Brooklyn, NY: Autonomedia, 2003 (2nd revised edition).

Wintergerst, Martin. *Der durch Europam lauffende, durch Asiam fahrende, und in Ostindien lange Zeit gebliebene Schwabe: oder Reissbeschreibung, welche in 22 Jahren an bemeldt Oerther verrichtet.* Memmingen: Johann Wilhelm Müllers, Buchbinder daselbst, 1712 (e-book).

Wolters, O.W. *The Fall of Srivijaya in Malay History.* London: Lund Humphries, 1970.

Woodard, Colin. *The Republic of Pirates: Being the True and Surprising Story of the Caribbean Pirates and the Man Who Brought Them Down.* Orlando, FL: Houghton Mifflin, 2007.

Woodbury, George. *The Great Days of Piracy.* London and New York: Elek, 1954.

Woolsey, Matt. 'Top-Earning Pirates'. *Forbes,* 19 September 2008; online at https://financesonline.com/top–10-richest-pirates-in-history-blackbeard-drake-others-worth-millions/ (accessed 2 December 2018).

Young, Adam J. *Contemporary Maritime Piracy in Southeast Asia: History, Causes and Remedies.* Singapore: ISEAS Publishing, 2007.

Zack, Richard. *The Pirate Hunter: The True Story of Captain Kidd.* London: Headline Book Publishing, 2002.

Zahedieh, Nuala. 'Trade, Plunder, and Economic Development in Early English Jamaica, 1655–89'. *Economic History Review,* vol. 39, no. 2 (1986), 205–22.

Zaman, Fahim and Naziha Syed Ali. 'Dockyard attackers planned to hijack Navy frigate'. *The Dawn,* 13 September 2014. https://www.dawn.com/news/1131654 (accessed 2 December 2018).

Zimmerling, Dieter. *Störtebeker & Co. Die Blütezeit der Seeräuber in Nord- und Ostsee.* Hamburg: Verlag Die Hanse, 2000.

Index